THE FIVE RIGHTS OF THE INDIVIDUAL

PHILIP SCHUYLER

iUniverse, Inc.
Bloomington

The Five Rights of the Individual

iUniverse books may be ordered through booksellers or by contacting:

iUniverse
1663 Liberty Drive
Bloomington, IN 47403
www.iuniverse.com
1-800-Authors (1-800-288-4677)

Because of the dynamic nature of the Internet, any web addresses or links contained in this book may have changed since publication and may no longer be valid. The views expressed in this work are solely those of the author and do not necessarily reflect the views of the publisher, and the publisher hereby disclaims any responsibility for them.

Any people depicted in stock imagery provided by Thinkstock are models, and such images are being used for illustrative purposes only.

Certain stock imagery © Thinkstock.

ISBN: 978-1-4697-8201-0 (sc)
ISBN: 978-1-4697-8203-4 (e)
ISBN: 978-1-4697-8202-7 (hc)

Library of Congress Control Number: 2012903393

Printed in the United States of America

iUniverse rev. date: 6/5/2012

For Becky Schuyler
1959–2010

CONTENTS

INTRODUCTION

Each day, the US government makes more laws than any one person can read. The volume and triviality of regulation can make life in America seem like a never-ending series of inconveniences, distractions, and new restraints on personal liberties and traditions. Excessive regulation often forces the individual to choose between compliance and his pursuit of happiness. Of those who break the law, many are arrested, charged, convicted, and imprisoned. The result is an American gulag system. Over the past forty years, while the US population has increased 50 percent, its prison population has increased 1,000 percent.

Government was instituted to protect rights, which requires it to be able to detain people, question them, and invade their privacy on occasion. Otherwise the system cannot work because rights become a shield for the guilty as well as the innocent. But when the State exceeds its authority, it can violate some rights, trying to protect others. It can also violate rights by passing laws that protect no one, laws that penalize individuals in deference to a presumed greater good for society. Since the 1930s, when government arrogated to itself the means to create such laws, it has made a countless number of them, of which drug prohibition laws have had the greatest impact. Millions of Americans have been arrested on minor drug charges and almost a million people that didn't harm anyone are currently incarcerated.

Chapter 1 of *The Five Rights of the Individual* introduces the Five Rights and reveals how our quest for happiness leads us to prize justice and morality, giving rise to a right to life, the source of the other four rights. Chapter 2 covers how and where in the US Constitution the Five Rights are guaranteed. Chapter 3 pertains to the Great Depression and the New Deal and the changes they engendered in our form of government. Chapter 4 is about how the changes subjected personal exercises of the Five Rights to majority rule. Chapter 5 covers the resulting boom in regulation during the second half of the twentieth century and how it contributed to the US prison population. Chapters 6 through 10 each deal solely with one of the Five Rights. Chapter 6 pertains to the right to life, which protects individuals from harm. Chapter 7 covers the right to liberty, which entitles the individual to all freedoms guaranteed under the umbrellas of privacy and free speech. Chapter 8 is about the right to property, how it relates to liberty, and the ways in which government can violate property rights. Chapter 9 covers the right to pursue happiness, Prohibition, and current antidrug laws. Chapter 10 pertains to the right to equality before the law and the rights of African Americans in the United States since the passage of the Fourteenth Amendment. Chapter 11 is about the opponents of liberty—the two groups of individuals with the least regard for the Five Rights. And chapter 12 lists some bogus rights and gives a quick review of the Five Rights.

CHAPTER 1
The Source of Rights

Nature gave us life and, through our ability to choose and act, liberty, but nature cannot give a right to life or liberty because a right requires the compliance of others. It has meaning only if people are obliged to honor it. If there is to be a right to life, then each person must be obliged not to kill. If there is to be a right to liberty, then no one can enslave or command anyone else. Nature cannot imbue us with self-interest *and* guarantee that each of us will honor others' rights. It determines how things are, not how they ought to be.[1] What is natural is not necessarily moral. Male aggression, for example, is natural, but that doesn't mean it's morally right.

The supreme law of morality is that all of our actions must be derived from universal principles. In other words, how would it be if everyone did it? Would it square with all others' rights and be workable within the order? What if someone did it to you? If an action cannot be supported by a universal principle, it's not proper conduct. Kant's categorical imperative is, *act only according to a maxim that you would like to see made into a general law.*[2] If you cannot reasonably will this, you must refrain, because the action violates objective morality. When enraged, you might be tempted to burn someone's house down, but that couldn't be willed as a generally accepted practice. Throwing garbage out of your car window does not directly violate anyone's rights, but what if everyone did it? Since that's not a viable alternative, it's better if no one does it, including you. This is how morality works: recognizing the need to act in certain manners because acting otherwise is unworkable or undesirable on a large scale. Take the example of charity. Say you choose not to give at

1

all. A society could exist without any charitable actions, but it would not be possible to wish for it because you or your family could find yourselves in need of aid. Since you can't reasonably will a world in which no one helps anyone else, charity is moral.

It's impossible to will a world of universal license, one in which thievery, assault, and murder are commonplace. It's impossible to will a world in which individuals *don't* have a just claim to a minimal level of consideration from others. Since this is the definition of a right, it's impossible to will a world in which individuals *don't* have rights. Thus, rights are moral.

The Five Rights

1. The Right to Life

Life is thrust on us unannounced. By the time we realize we are alive, we are alive. We did not choose it, but life is self-sustaining and self-replicating. If we did not choose to live but are driven to continue living, then we are motivated by circumstances not of our making. Who would choose to trade their energy, sexuality, and teeth for anxiety, pain, and eventual death? Yet this is the choice life is, and something tells us to take the trade. Perhaps life is precious because we are born so late in the day. Goethe was wrong when he said that life is the childhood of our immortality.[3] The opposite is true. Life is the tail end of a very long existence: the last one fifty-millionth of it (the last eighty years of matter that has been replicating for four billion years). When we die, we are not leaving home, but going home, and when we get there, requirements end. Death needs nothing to continue. Life has needs, making things matter. Since things have no meaning on their own, yet they have importance, it must stem from our desire for them. So if anything at all matters, we must matter, since we are the absolute giver of value to other things. If anything is worth protecting, the individual is.[4]

Human beings, realizing this, established a right to life. What is its basis? If a chimpanzee does not have a right to life and a human being does, what gives us one? Does it have to do with the complexity of our brains? Does any organism that can represent its long-term duty to itself and its species and choose it over immediate wants have a right to life? Does knowledge of our mortality make us more worthy of existence than lesser-understanding animals? These claims are insufficient. Nature gave us life and the capacities to sustain it, but nature offers no *right* to life—any of us can die at any time. The right to life comes from utility. People created a right to life for the same reason they created language: it served their needs. They concluded that a human life, being short and finite, was precious and that for each person to live in peace required a fundamental construct: no one may intentionally harm anyone. The right to life protects each person from bodily injury, restraint, or compulsion; it requires that coercion be banned among individuals and used sparingly by government.

The right to life generates laws against murder, kidnapping, physical attack, harassment, arson, blackmail, libel, nuisance, and racial and sexual discrimination. Because the right to life obliges each person to respect the next as a rational being, honoring his means and ends, it is also irreconcilable with fraud. As Friedrich Hayek observed, when you deceive someone, you do not treat him as a rational being with aims of his own but as a stepping-stone to achieve your aims.[5] The difference between coercion and deception is that the victim is aware of coercion.

The right to life is not a right to any job or standard of living. It guarantees the individual access to the free market; it allows him to compete and to have all of the conveniences of modern life—but not at the expense of anyone else. If a person may not intimidate or deceive others, he can only interact with them by their consent. When anyone can decline any offer, only a reasonable proposal and a sound argument can influence him. Thanks to the right to life, rationality triumphs. Negotiation, compromise, and contracts, rather than threats and weapons, are the usual tools of interaction.

2. The Right to Liberty

The right to life complementarily implies the right to liberty because, when you let people be (honor their right to life), they do as they like (exercise their right to liberty). Liberty is unfettered choice of thought or action. It's the absence of man-made impediments, allowing the

3

individual to pick from a menu untrimmed by authority, permitting him to pursue his aims, making each an end in himself.

The right to liberty encompasses everything that takes place within the skin—all reactions and all thinking—and it permits us to feel as we will. It includes the freedom to have spiritual beliefs or not. It includes freedom of opinion and speech, freedom of association and assembly, and freedom to make contracts with whom one chooses. It includes the freedom to travel, to choose a mate or an occupation (by mutual consent), and to plan and shape one's life according to his priorities. Liberty allows the individual to criticize government, to publish unpopular opinions, or to make films that offend.

Liberty seems a comfortable old friend because it is embedded so deeply in us. No one has to tell us that freedom is *right*. After Jefferson left Washington, DC, and the trappings of the presidency and retired to Virginia, he wrote, "My health is perfect and my strength considerably reinforced by the activities of the course I pursue. I talk of plows and harrows, of seeding and harvesting with my neighbors, and of politics if they choose, with as little reserve as the rest of my fellow citizens, and feel at length the blessing of being free to say and do as I please without being responsible to any mortal."[6] This is liberty.

Liberty requires mutual forbearance. People must be permitted to respond to their appetites, which can mean having to endure drivel, contradiction, and bad taste. Though the other guy's choices may be foolish and irritating, his right to liberty obliges you and all others to let him act on them. Your freedom is likewise predicated on others' tolerance, on their ability to refrain from making laws. If the right to liberty is not given enough import, it gets pecked to death by regulation because there is always political pressure to act and the advantages of regulating always seem apparent.

A law that violates the right to liberty is usually an attempt to prohibit an act that breaches no one's rights but is widely found intolerable (physician-assisted suicide, for example). Condemnation of an act, though, is no reason to prohibit it. The freedom to do something has nothing to do with the number of people who favor or oppose it. Rather, it's government's job to *protect* unpopular exercises of liberty. We all have preferences in which we are in the minority.

If liberty were subject to a vote, each of these could be banned, but as with all of the Five Rights, the right to liberty supersedes majority rule. If it were any other way, people we never meet would determine what we could and couldn't do, even within our four walls.

Having liberty allows us to incorporate morality into our decisions. Remove free choice, and the consideration of right or wrong drops from the equation. If a man shoves someone who falls into a third person and injures him, the shoved person has committed no wrong—he had no choice in the matter. If one person blackmails another into giving a million dollars to diabetes research, the giver is not acting out of a sense of generosity. Only when a person has the opportunity to choose among unadulterated alternatives can a choice be moral or immoral. If coerced, he is not acting morally but rationally, relative to the circumstances.

Self-improvement too requires liberty. Free action yields firsthand experience and instructive screw-ups. Wrong choices lead to internal governors on actions. The individual learns to voluntarily refrain; he gains a strength born of resisting; he acquires a habit of making right choices, learning and growing. If he is the sum of his conduct, then the fewer opportunities to conduct himself, the less he can become. Recall Plato's warning that it is possible to "have so little justice in one's self that one must get it from others, who thus become masters and judges over one."[7] Liberty, though, forces accountability on the individual. He can't have freedom of choice *and* the right to sidestep the consequences of bad ones.

For the right to liberty to be meaningful, the individual must have a location to exercise it where he can't be overruled by the State in the name of the general welfare, a free space where he may act as he pleases, provided he does not violate common law. Private property is that place.

3. The Right to Property

Nature made us separate beings, each with our own brain, mouth, and stomach. For this reason, at some point, we must separate the things we need to sustain us. Property marks this separation. A person's property is his and his alone. Ownership includes the right to set boundaries and to exclude others, establishing a protected sphere within which the owner's rights take precedence, where he is theoretically autonomous. It affords privacy and allows the individual to shape his surroundings to himself.

We warm to our belongings. Some things, we feel, are *ours*. Empathizing, we feel that some things belong to others and that it's right to let each person keep the proceeds of his labor. It is just to give each his due, and private property is the means. The right to property lets the individual earn and spend money, and in allowing him to sustain himself, it transforms liberty from a concept into real options. Liberty permits freedom of choice regarding present action; property permits freedom of choice regarding the fruits of past action—savings. Money is stored-up work. Deserving of the same respect as work, capital to be deployed is productivity-in-waiting. It's a block of freedom of choice. Without the right to allocate his earnings, the individual can be forced to serve interests other than his own. If his earnings can be taken and used for things he doesn't support, he's not an end in himself. If his house or bank accounts can be confiscated, he can be reduced to dependence at any time.

By letting an individual store his labor as an asset, property rights create an incentive to produce a surplus. There is a story about a man from the Dutch East India Company suggesting to the sultan of Java that he encourage his people to work harder, produce surpluses, trade, live better, and create tax revenue. The sultan replied that his people had no reason to do those things because they owned nothing. Everything in their lives belonged to the sultan. Property rights encourage initiative, promoting people to use their abilities to their fullest, thereby maximizing a nation's productivity.

4. The Right to Pursue Happiness

The right to pursue happiness permits us to define it as we like at any given moment. We do not have to stick to our ideals on every occasion or explain our actions. It includes the right to do "wrong" things—to dress wrong, to eat the wrong foods, drink alcohol, smoke, take drugs, have the wrong interests or relationships, espouse the wrong political views, believe in the wrong religion, harm one's self, or commit suicide. It can mean seeking sanctuary from boredom, pain, anxiety, or depression. We try to escape the awful feelings of heartache, homesickness, loneliness, or grief, and as new concerns replace old ones, we do.

The right to pursue happiness is personal. One person's passion is another's tedium. One prefers tales, another reality. One person cannot see a proposal without its drawbacks and will always be skeptical. Another embraces ideas wholly. Some pursue happiness through the intentional dimming of consciousness. We seek happiness, but we don't get to pick what constitutes it. And if we can't choose what makes *us* happy, we certainly can't do it for others. Happiness only has meaning in the context of each person's definition.

A government that can use its lawmaking power to prohibit unhealthy personal behavior can ban any action for the ostensible good of the individual. A personal choice may be unwise, but to force individuals to act "rightly" is a greater evil than allowing them to act self-destructively, because it violates their right to pursue happiness, however damaging the pursuit might be for some.

5. The Right to Equality before the Law

Serving one's self is a rightful end, but since everyone else may do the same, one person's rights must stop where another's begin. Without recognition of the other guy's equal rights, any action can be ascribed to the actor's pursuit of happiness and defended as his right.

Equality requires that all individuals be subject to the same laws. Laws must be clear with predictable consequences when broken. Laws must be general and abstract, referring to unknown future cases involving unknown parties. Each dispute must be decided according to its merits impartially, and being equal before the law, individuals found guilty of the same crime should receive the same punishment. (Since each person must submit to any rule we collectively impose on anyone, equality preserves freedom by engaging self-interest: the laws we wish to live by limit how much we can restrain others.)

Equality before the law does not omit the possibility of vast differences in status, responsibility, or wealth. It does not exclude the prospect of one person having to take commands from another, assuming he has agreed to, as an employee or a soldier, for example. Equality has nothing to do with trying to make people the same. That requires coercion. Equality refers to the equal protection of the

7

laws, to government not sacrificing one person's rights for another in a misguided attempt to achieve "equality." When government must include every citizen in its plans, regardless of sex, race, religion, age, or income, its preferential motivations are thwarted, reducing its ability to take sides for political gain.

Equality has another, separate meaning that is often overlooked: the people and the government are equal in that each must answer to the other. The people agree to abide by government's laws, provided that the lawmakers abide by the Constitution.

The Five Rights are not separate entities, but five facets of one right: the right to life. That's why most actions can be defended by more than one of the Five Rights. The right to contract, for example, can be seen as a right associated with liberty or with property. The right to choose an occupation can be categorized as a right of liberty or as part of a pursuit of happiness. The right of gays to marry is supported by three of the Five Rights: to liberty, to pursue happiness, and to equality before the law.

The Source of Rights

To achieve our goals, we compile, process, and organize information, reconciling new knowledge with old, and we envision chains of cause and effect, choosing the path of least resistance. Several steps may be involved, each a means to another means, leading to some end. The one general end, the thing we desire for its own sake rather than as a means of achieving something else, is happiness. It begets all other desires. We do not exist just to survive (if we did, there would be no suicides). We don't choose what gives us pleasure; we discover it. We use reason to resolve conflicting interests in trying to achieve our ends, but passions determine those ends. Want is a feeling, and we live to dispatch wants.

Physically, we seek fresh air. The feelings of hunger and thirst cause us to eat and drink. Hot and cold drive us to clothe and shelter ourselves. Fatigue puts us to sleep. We seek freedom of movement, comfort, health, human contact, smoothness, softness, and pleasant sights, sounds, smells, and tastes. And we seek sexual release, upon which the species propagates itself.

Psychologically, human happiness has four main components:

The first is self-image. Our ever-changing estimation of self-worth generates uneasiness or pleasure. We seek self-pride through beauty, purpose, fitness, and recognition. When we experience validation, accomplishment, or victory, our spirits are high and our sense of well-being swells.

How others see us affects our spirits. The more recognized, liked, and wanted we seem to be, the better we feel. We long for acceptance, respect, fame—whatever reinforces the notion that we are needed and special. Youth craves glory; age craves repute. Camaraderie bolsters self-pride. When people make friends and exchange goodwill, becoming more open and honest with one another, it fuels the self-esteem of each. When the bond is accompanied by an attraction to beauty that releases a flood of brain chemicals inspiring affection and concern and cheerful, oblivious self-possession, love is born. Because nothing reinforces self-image like the feeling of indispensability implicit in love, romantic acceptance (or rejection) can be especially gratifying (or injurious) to self-worth.

Self-esteem can induce people to sacrifice their health or safety. A person's honor is the image he holds of himself, and many would give their life for their honor. That a person would trade his life for what he thinks of himself attests to the potency of pride. Another example, this with regard to sexual self-esteem: it's not uncommon for an individual to work half a lifetime to build a home and family and then risk it for smiling eyes and the hope of pleasant friction.

Pride underlies art, knowledge, and wealth. It leads us to conceive, invent, build, and compete. Consider our infatuation with contests and gambling—with winning for the ego boost, for the feel of being right—and consider the gloom we experience when we lose or get passed over. Many of our sorrows stem from pride-related mistakes. Such is our self-love that esteem from two people delights us, since our vanity quickly inflates it to long-deserved recognition, and such is the fragility of ego that any criticism with merit, no matter how softly put or gracefully received, leaves a mark.

The second component of happiness is diversion. Whether in the form of novelty or some agreeable pursuit or competition, there is pleasure in being mentally engaged. Television, movies, music, reading, writing, and painting are diversions. Friends and family provide diversion, as do sports, politics, philosophy, museums, and comic books: anything that captures interest. Alcohol and drugs can provide diversion in the form of escape. A common happy diversion is the contemplation of past or future gratifications, since neither fond recollection nor anticipation of pleasure disappoints.

Our greatest diversion is a sense of purpose. We need something to do with our lives. We all want to matter, and yet to the solar system, the galaxy, the universe, none of us does. Mattering requires a smaller scale, a more close-fitting purpose that we must supply ourselves. There is satisfaction in pursuing a goal, and without one, nothing yields that joy. Having an aim promotes us to mix and match what we know to discover things we didn't know. Purpose produces happiness along the way in the pleasure we take from mental accidents that work and in the completion of productive work. Happy are those who discover what they want most of all, because at any time they need only ask themselves, what can I do right now toward that end, even remotely? Possibly the best moments in a person's life are when he realizes that he is actively achieving his greatest potential—when he knows he's doing the right thing for the right reasons and feels that he's good at it.

Where there is insufficient diversion, clouds gather. Emptiness gains a foothold. Working toward a goal restores focus, concern, and sometimes passion. Happiness is absorption, losing self-consciousness, becoming unaware of the passage of time. The chase, the contest, the stir—it's the amusement that matters, not the prize, and it's the lack of diversion that makes depression or imprisonment punitive.

We spend most of our time involved with the first two components of happiness: self-image and diversion. But it's the next two—reciprocity and sympathy—that give rise, respectively, to our institutions of justice and morality.

The third component of happiness is reciprocity. Whether reacting to disrespect, indifference, or hospitality, we are given to respond in kind. Gratitude and devotion exist because nature has inclined us to have regard for people who have treated us well, but our desire to reciprocate can also make us vengeful. When infuriated, the first questions to spring to mind are, what can I do to him, and what might he do to me? The benevolent billionaire and the mass-murdering terrorist are motivated by reciprocity. We sometimes commit to reciprocity against our interests, as when we refuse to forgive someone though it's the only reasonable course. We want to return injury for injury. Whether a military invasion or deciding whose turn it is to buy dinner, we are driven toward what's fair and right, what will make things *equal*. Even our superstitions and afterlife myths are based on tit-for-tat.

For an animal to reciprocate, it must be able to recognize other individuals and remember past favors and affronts. Most primates can do this, as can elephants and dolphins. Vampire bats share meals of blood with one another and repay debts. Bonobos and chimpanzees repay aid and insults, remembering who groomed them or intervened on their behalf and which individuals withheld favors. Chimpanzees form alliances and play politics. Many apes practice revenge, and macaques have been known to practice indirect revenge, injuring the offspring of enemies.[8] Why did nature ingrain the feeling that turnabout is fair play? There can only be one reason: a sense of reciprocity bestowed an evolutionary advantage.

Humans are particularly adept at assessing each other's favors, services, and slights and keeping score. We are sensitive to being used for another person's ends too frequently. We live long lives and encounter many of the same people repeatedly, recognize them, recall how things went, and forecast who is likely to cooperate honestly in the future and who's likely to cheat if given an opportunity—and we talk to one another about our findings. We cooperate with some individuals to prevent being exploited by others. Collaboration begets trade, and reciprocity begets fair dealing: what you don't want done to you, don't do to others. We feel deceit as an injustice. Square dealing feels right and leads to more trade.

What is there to prevent individuals from shirking their end or otherwise seeking a free ride? Animals that cannot solve the "free-rider" problem cannot live in social groups, for if the free-riders took advantage, multiplied, and were evolutionarily successful, they would come to outnumber the individuals who can be trusted to keep their side in a bargain. But the free-riders could not maintain a group because it would lack cohesiveness—no one could trust anyone else.

If, on the other hand, most individuals honored their obligations, and also took steps to identify and exclude the free-riders, cooperation could last.

In the West, humans responded to the free-rider problem by instituting a system of justice based on respect for property rights, the keeping of promises, and equality before the law, each of which depends on reciprocation.

Property rights. Since justice is giving a person his due, each person must be permitted the exclusive right to his earnings and possessions. Justice obliges all others to respect his property.

The keeping of promises. In any agreement, each party commits to do something. Justice is following through on that word. Where there are no promises, there are none to keep. Honoring agreements is the beginning of civilization.

Equality before the law. Justice requires that the rules are the same for everyone, for if the law treats two people differently, then whoever has the advantage can exploit the difference to contravene the first two tenets of justice.

Our drive to reciprocate inspired our canons of justice.

The fourth component of happiness is mutual sympathy. We have the ability to empathize—to project ourselves into the circumstances and mind-set of another person, allowing us to feel, to a degree, what he feels. His happiness affects ours, as does his discomfort. We share emotional pain most. We don't share the soreness of a friend's sprained ankle as we do his embarrassment or sorrow.[9]

It's fortunate that empathy is a component of our happiness, because it is the basis of morality. Adopting the perspective of others permits us to see ourselves through their eyes and to judge our actions as they would. Viewing our choices and actions from their station, with their concerns, creates distance and gives us an impartial sense of how things *ought* to be. It provides a basis for approval or disapproval from which we determine objective right and wrong.

What is, is based on our sensory input. What ought to be, is a residual feeling. Actions that please us upon reflection, we consider virtuous. Those that make us uneasy, we consider wrong. And no vote or enactment can change it. Legalizing assault would not make it okay—it would still offend our sense of what constitutes equitable and acceptable behavior. Not wanting to be attacked, we empathize and conclude that one person should not injure another. We like being left in quiet possession of our belongings, and we don't like being lied to or cheated. Because we empathize, we respect privacy and honesty. For the same reason, we admire these virtues:

Generosity. Whether one is gracious with words, time, or money, magnanimity is appreciated.

Selflessness. Say a child is drowning in rapids. A man tries to dive into the water to save the child. Seeing that it's hopeless, others try to stop him. He gets free and dives in, but the others are right. The man cannot rescue the child and both drown. The man's action could be called futile, even foolish, but not immoral. Why do we readily recognize this as an act of goodness? Because moral good or ill is founded on how we feel about an act at a gut level, on whether the traits being exhibited are generally commendable or harmful. Our sentiments, not our reason, distinguish moral good, and selfless sacrifice in the service of another, though not always rational, is always laudable.

Patience. It's a virtue because it gives wisdom time to grow.

Kindness. Counseled basketball coach John Wooden, "Consider the rights of others before your own feelings, and the feelings of others before your own rights."[10] Kindness is key. A bright person matures when he stops ridiculing and starts listening carefully enough to respond kindly.

Perseverance. Perhaps nothing is more advantageous than the ability to stay with a job. Perseverance is the closest thing there is to magic.

Self-sufficiency. Useful to mankind is the individual who is self-sufficient, for if he serves himself, no one need be forced to serve him. Any surplus, whether he stores it in a bank, spends it, or leaves it behind after death, becomes useful to others.

Consistency. Plain talk and predictable behavior put people at ease. Keeping a regular course implies dependability.

Temperance. It is the ability to resist overindulgence, to see when a pleasure is becoming injurious and withdraw, to employ prudence when needed.

Duty. An act of duty is the performance of a promise. It is doing something because you have beforehand contracted with yourself, or others, to do it.

Courage. Whereas temperance is the ability to walk away from the pleasurable, courage is the ability to face something potentially painful. It is less a matter of bravado than of resolve and resilience. It is energy born of hope, creating guts, and freedom requires it. Observed Churchill, "Courage is rightly esteemed the first of human qualities ... because it is the quality which guarantees all others."[11]

Character. The person of character rises above life's trials, sees what must be done, returns to himself, and does it. Character is philosophical tranquility, which is helpful in enduring misfortune and adapting.

Morality requires each of us to reconcile our actions with the rights of others. Its mechanism is anxiety, which protects others' rights by notifying us when we are about to do something that would shame us if it were discovered. Our moral sense manages our passions and afterwards judges its own performance, rewarding us with self-satisfaction or penalizing us with self-condemnation.

Our desire to reciprocate begets our sense of justice, and empathy produces our sense of morality. Our regard for justice and morality led us to create the right of each individual to life, whose premise is that no one may harm another. Liberty's premise is that each person can do as he chooses. Thus, a free civilization's premise is, *each person can do as he chooses provided he does not harm another.* This is the point at which the subjective choices of each person can be reconciled with objective universal law.

The Five Rights are supreme. Put the individual first and no individual can be sacrificed. Put something else first, like "the good of the whole" or "society" or "national security," and individuals can be sacrificed to that end. It does not matter if the purpose is called law and order, safety, or the general welfare. The State can impose restrictions, rescind options, and assign duties as it sees fit: practices that are incompatible with a system in which all individuals are permitted to use "their knowledge for their purposes," the time-honored definition of liberty.[12] In an open order, government honestly informs; it influences the choices of individuals by appealing to their reason and sense of right and wrong and otherwise lets them be. But all governments try to go further, leaving the designers of a government with the problem of how to sufficiently empower it while simultaneously limiting it. Optimally, government would be able to make and enforce needed laws but unable to make laws that breach the Five Rights. This is attempted in practice by delegating to government legislative power limited by constitutional principles.

CHAPTER 2
Constitutional Guarantees

When the Declaration of Independence was signed, each state had its own laws and legislature. Each had been created under a different philosophy, but it was clear to all that the coming war for independence would require their union, so in June 1776, delegates representing the states at the Continental Congress met to form a "firm league of friendship," resulting in the Articles of Confederation. Under the Articles, ratified the following year, the national government passed legislation but had no power to enforce it and, without the power to tax, no way to fund its plans. After the war, with the nation buried in debt, Congress twice proposed amendments to the Articles of Confederation to allow it to raise revenue by collecting duties on imports, but since the proposals had to be ratified by all thirteen states, they failed. Wrote Rufus King to Elbridge Gerry in 1786, "The treasury now is literally without a penny."[13]

Each state cared little about the problems of others. They acted like private fiefdoms, disregarding Congress's demands and passing laws contrary to national law. They would not contribute to the national treasury when requested, violated treaties that had been established by the national government, passed laws that forced creditors to accept worthless or severely depreciated paper money, and passed laws violating the rights of minorities within their borders. A stronger national government was needed, and whatever other powers it was to have, it had to be able to curb unjust legislation by the states, the source of the greatest rights violations at the time. It had to be dominant and truly national, which meant that it had to have the ability to tax the people directly rather than through the states. Without enough power, a new national government would be no better than under the Articles of Confederation.

In Philadelphia, during the sweltering summer of 1787, the attendees of the Constitutional Convention sought to create a stronger government—but not *too* strong, Their greatest concern was the same as Locke's had been: how do you give government the means to make and enforce necessary laws and to administrate, but prevent it from using those means to interfere with traditional personal liberties? The founders wanted a government in which, through frequent elections and the amendment process, the people would never become extraneous. Washington and Hamilton favored a robust central authority—they feared uprisings more than the rest. Hamilton had been Washington's aide-de-camp during the war, and both had seen firsthand the futility trying to manage a large, complex organization with insufficient powers. Wrote Hamilton, "If individuals are to have liberty, then their government must have a proper degree of authority to make and execute the laws with vigor."[14] Madison and Jefferson (who was in France at the time) feared the other extreme: government using its lawmaking ability to increase its role at will, eventually transforming itself from the representative of the people into their manager. Madison wanted a strong central government, but one in which powers were separated so that they acted like a brake on one another. Madison distrusted human nature, noting that people were "generally governed by rather base and selfish motives, by suspicion, jealousy, and desire for self-aggrandizement."[15] He found the power to make laws and to tax in opposition to freedom and perhaps impossible to contain. Jefferson concurred, noting, "The natural progress of things is for liberty to yield and government to gain ground."[16] In the context of centuries, they feared that limited government might be as ephemeral and fleeting as a dream after waking up.

The US Constitution does not grant rights. It creates the federal government, gives it certain powers, restricts it to those, and reserves to the states or the people all others. It establishes the fundamental organs of government, their organization, purpose, and jurisdiction, and standards upon which lawmaking is to be based. A constitution is to ordinary laws as laws are to a particular case. The first sets general principles within which the second must be adjudicated.[17] A person acts illegally when he breaks a law. A government acts illegally when it violates a constitutional principle. As a judge may not ignore the law to apply his own view to a case, government may not set aside constitutionality to pursue its aims of the moment. The system subordinates strong but transitory sentiments to democratically pre-established principles. It places the Five Rights beyond the reach of majority rule (except through changes to the Constitution). Eighteenth-century Americans distrusted authority; that's why no strong central government had been formed in the years since the end of the Revolutionary War and the reason that after the new Constitution emerged, the states proposed *eighty* amendments, later reduced to nineteen, then twelve, ten of which were ratified and became the Bill of Rights in December 1791.

The new Constitution limited both federal and state government by dividing power between them. Congress could "lay and collect taxes," "regulate commerce with foreign nations," "raise and support armies," and some other things, and make laws "necessary and proper" to carry out these duties. All remaining lawmaking powers, unspecified, belonged to the states, giving each government practical veto power over the other. When the expansion of one domain must come at the expense of the other, political territoriality often results in a standoff.

Within the federal and state governments, the founders further divided power among legislative, executive, and judicial branches. Since passions cannot be reasoned away, ambitions stemming from them, wrote Hamilton in *The Federalist,* No. 51, must be set against other ambitions, thwarting both; otherwise, there is nothing to prevent every infatuation from ruling the day. Government lurches from one crisis to the next, making new laws to appease the populace. The separation of powers helps prevent government from overreacting. As intended by the founders, each branch, in striving for its own solution to be the one used, restrains the others, stifling or muting government action, making it difficult to pass and keep new laws, yet government can respond to the deeper, more long-lived sentiments of the people through its democratic and constitutional elements: the rights of assembly and petition, frequent elections, and the ability to make amendments to the Constitution.

The United States Constitution is about 7,300 words; among the state constitutions, only Vermont's is shorter. And yet, what emerged from Philadelphia was a stronger government than anyone (except perhaps Washington and Hamilton) had wanted. Section eight of the new Constitution enumerated government's specific powers—eighteen of them, seven of which had existed under the Articles of Confederation. Of the eleven new powers, three were of particular importance in view of subsequent interpretation. They are contained in the first, third, and eighteenth clauses.

Clause one gave government the power to tax "to pay the Debts and provide for the common Defense and general Welfare of the United States." The wording came from the Articles of Confederation, where it had been taken to mean that taxation for specific projects like a dam or road was not permissible because it would benefit particular states or areas rather than the "general welfare."

The final clause, Clause eighteen, gave Congress the ability "to make all Laws which shall be necessary and proper for carrying into execution" its enumerated powers. Congress could not make any laws it chose, only those necessary to implement its seventeen preceding powers. In 1790, Alexander Hamilton proposed that government establish a national bank. Opponents said that the Constitution gave government no such power. Hamilton responded that it depended on the way you defined the word "necessary." Hamilton chose to define it as "conducive to" or "appropriate to" rather than "essential to," as Madison and most of the founders seemingly intended. Chief Justice John Marshall sanctioned Hamilton's looser interpretation of the word "necessary" in 1819 in *McCulloch v. Maryland*, expanding government's realm, but even Hamilton would be surprised at the laxness of today's interpretation. In a letter to a US senator, Hamilton suggested an amendment to the Constitution to allow the federal government to build interstate canals to stitch the nation together. It is noteworthy that Hamilton assumed an amendment was needed because he did not think that the "necessary and proper" clause permitted it.[18]

Broadly interpreting the power to tax for the general welfare enables government to fund its plans, and the "necessary and proper" clause permits it to make laws needed to execute its enumerated powers. But what lets it make laws that have nothing to do with its listed powers? It has regulated entire industries and markets and made countless laws regarding construction, workplace safety, banking, insurance, pollution, drugs, air travel, space, and so on. Where did it get these powers?

From one word. Clause three gave government the power to control "commerce," specifically, "to regulate commerce with foreign nations, and among the several states, and with Indian tribes." That's all of it. The intent was to prevent the states from erecting trade barriers with one another, and it worked. The lack of state-to-state duties made the United States internally the largest free trade area on earth. But the commerce clause was eventually used to regulate nearly all forms of transportation and communication including shipping, harbors, canals, rivers, lakes, railroads, highways, bus lines, airlines, telegraphs and telephones, radio, television, and the Internet. The Supreme Court ruled that the commerce clause was a positive grant of power to make economic regulations, making it the constitutional basis for rent control, price floors and ceilings, subsidies, and laws against white-collar crime including fraud, embezzlement, stock market manipulation, insider trading, and money laundering.[19]

In the 1930s, the Supreme Court ruled that an activity need not actually affect commerce for it to be regulated, only that there is a "rational basis" for assuming it *could* harm commerce. Because any action or thing that has value can be exchanged for something else, which is commerce, that commodity—food, products, labor—was subject to federal regulation. Under this interpretation, government could regulate the working hours of assembly line workers (and the assembly processes itself) because the finished product could be transported to another state. It could regulate a business that operated wholly within one state but ordered *any* of its supplies from out of state or had a single employee that had to cross state lines to get to work.[20]

The commerce clause was used to regulate corporations, shopkeepers, wages, markets, terms, and quantities farmers could grow. In 1941, a Midwest farmer named Roscoe Filburn grew twelve acres of wheat more than the government allowed. Though Filburn showed that the surplus was for personal use, the Supreme Court upheld the government's case, ruling that the growing of extra wheat affected supply, which could affect prices and thus interstate commerce.[21] The could-possibly-affect-commerce reasoning underlies most federal laws today. In *Gonzales v. Raich* (2005), the Supreme Court ruled that under its power to regulate commerce, the federal government could ban growing marijuana even in states that had approved its medicinal use. As with the growing of wheat in *Filburn*, the Court ruled that the government "could have rationally concluded" that individuals growing marijuana for personal use could affect the market price, which could affect commerce.[22]

Government's self-serving reading of the commerce clause has given it many powers that the founders clearly did not intend, but it has had positive aspects too. A stricter interpretation would likely have prevented the federal government from enacting pollution laws, desegregating, outlawing racial discrimination, prosecuting organized crime, and funding research and universities. On the downside, government's interpretation of taxing for the "general welfare" to make laws that are "necessary and proper" to regulate "commerce" permits it to make nearly any law that can be made politically palatable. It is only a slight exaggeration to say that all three branches of government now interpret Section eight of the Constitution to read, "Make whatever laws you think are needed." As the founders feared, the federal government has been able to increase its arena almost at will.

The Bill of Rights has held up better. Of the fifty-five delegates at the convention, only two—George Mason and Elbridge Gerry—favored a Bill of Rights, and the state delegations voted unanimously against including one, so when the Constitution emerged in 1789, it had no Bill of Rights. Many southerners did not want one because, as Charles Pinckney put it, "Such bills generally begin by declaring that all men are by nature born free. Now, we should make that declaration with very bad grace when a large part of our property consists in men who are actually born slaves."[23] In addition, the state constitutions already had their own bills of rights.

Opposition also came from delegates who feared that listing

particular rights in a compilation might render any unlisted rights nonexistent. No document could possibly name all particular applications of the Five Rights. Should there be a right to have children? To climb trees? To keep goldfish? To eat meat, wear a hat, or learn to swim? And if those rights are not listed, does that mean the people do not have them? In *The Federalist*, Alexander Hamilton asked, why spell out things the government is restrained from doing when it has no power to do them?[24] If we do, any restraints not specifically spelled out will be lost by default. Why, for example, state that government may not abridge freedom of speech when it has been granted no power to do so? Hamilton's concerns were well founded. On several occasions, it has been argued that since a right of the people (e.g., privacy of mail, choice of what goes into one's body) was not included in the Bill of Rights, it did not exist.

The argument for including a bill of rights was stronger, however. When the states had established their own constitutions, each had taken it for granted that a bill of rights should be included because they knew that governments routinely overstepped themselves. A bill of rights might help safeguard the Five Rights. Madison, though initially against one, knew that government was left a lot of leeway by the Constitution's "necessary and proper" clause, and he had to admit that a bill of rights was one way of limiting this discretion. Jefferson was wholly in favor of including one, writing from Paris, "A bill of rights is what the people are entitled to against every government on earth, general or particular, and what no just government should refuse, or rest on inferences."[25] And most Americans wanted one. They felt that they had "natural rights," as Locke had claimed, and wanted them declared. They were especially concerned about having their homes searched without warrants, being summarily arrested, and being tried in admiralty courts without juries.

A Bill of Rights was added to the Constitution. To deal with the problem of unlisted rights being presumed nonexistent, the founders created the Ninth Amendment, which said, in effect, just because a right isn't listed in the Bill of Rights doesn't mean it doesn't exist. The Ninth Amendment established a presumption of liberty. It made the Bill of Rights open-ended.

The Amendments

Today, the Bill of Rights and the Fourteenth Amendment are the greatest protectors of the Five Rights. Some amendments set election procedures or specify terms of office. Others apply to specific liberties: the Second Amendment guarantees the right to bear arms. The Sixth Amendment guarantees trial by jury in criminal cases. The Thirteenth banished slavery. The Fifteenth gave African Americans the right to vote; the Nineteenth did the same for women; the Twenty-Sixth extended it to eighteen-year-olds. Regarding rights in general—the Five Rights—they rest on five amendments:

First Amendment

The First Amendment guarantees to the people freedom of speech, the press, and religion; the right of peaceful assembly; and the right to petition government for a redress of grievances. It permits individuals to take in whatever ideas they choose and to associate with whom they please, privately if they like. Government cannot compel individuals to participate in ceremonies that violate their religious beliefs. States and localities may not require prayers or other religious exercises in public schools.

Freedom of speech permits provocative language. In protest of the Vietnam War, Paul Cohen went into a Los Angeles courthouse wearing a jacket inscribed, "Fuck the Draft." He was arrested under a state law that made "offensive conduct" a crime. The Supreme Court ruled that the expletive was protected under the First Amendment. Writing for the majority in *Cohen v. California*, Justice John Marshall Harlan noted, if the State had the power to outlaw public use of one word, it could outlaw others and, by censoring particular words, prohibit the expression of unpopular views.[26]

The First Amendment allows individuals to hold, teach, or encourage any idea that does not directly oppose vital national interests. It protects actions that outrage, like flag burning. Noted the Supreme Court, "If there is a bedrock principle underlying the First Amendment, it is that the government may not prohibit the expression of an idea simply because society finds the idea offensive or disagreeable. We have not recognized an exception to this principle

23

even where our flag has been involved."[27] The right to free speech has exceptions, including defamation, obscenity, and speech that is intended and likely to incite violence. The Court has ruled that government may abridge freedoms of speech and of the press when they present a "clear and present danger" to the community or advocate overthrow of the government.

Most Supreme Court decisions have upheld First Amendment rights. In *New York Times Co. v. Sullivan* (1964), a police commissioner in Alabama sued the newspaper for defamation for its allegations of police brutality in Montgomery. Though the *Times* article did contain errors, the Court ruled that the *Times* was protected under the First Amendment, noting that "debate on public issues should be uninhibited, robust, and wide open and that it may well include vehement, caustic, and sometimes unpleasantly sharp attacks on government and public officials." The *Times* statements were not made out of "actual malice."[28]

Fourth Amendment

The Fourth Amendment guarantees "the right of the people to be secure in their persons, houses, papers, and effects, against unreasonable searches and seizures." Unless there is an emergency, government may not perform a search without a warrant. A proper search requires (1) prior judicial approval (2) to search a specific place (3) for particularly described items (4) with probable cause that the search will uncover evidence of a crime under investigation.

A search is defined as an intrusion by government on an individual's "reasonable expectation of privacy," which covers mail, papers in desk drawers, medical information, and telephone conversations, but not e-mails, bank statements, or telephone bills, since those can be seen by others. The "open fields" doctrine holds that the government does not require a warrant to search pastures, open water, woods, and other such areas since people in outdoor, unprotected places have no expectation of privacy.

The Fourth Amendment does not prohibit all searches, only "unreasonable" ones. A search requires probable cause, which is more than simple suspicion. There must be reliable information that a crime has been or is being committed and the facts must objectively support a belief that evidence of wrongdoing is to be found. A general justification for a search—that the search would be good for public safety, for example—is insufficient.

The instrument for enforcing Fourth Amendment rights is the exclusionary rule. When police find evidence of guilt through an illegal search, the rule prohibits that evidence from being used in court. According to the Supreme Court, the exclusionary rule "gives to the individual no more than that which the Constitution guarantees him."[29] Efforts to bring the guilty to justice do not justify the sacrifice of privacy rights.

Some prosecutors and police view the Fourth Amendment as impeding effective law enforcement, and the judiciary has at times been sympathetic to this view. It has created exceptions according to a "special needs doctrine," under which the court applies a balancing test to see if the needs of law enforcement outweigh the privacy interests of the person claiming Fourth Amendment protection. If they do, no warrant is required.

Fifth Amendment

The Fifth Amendment has four parts, the first three of which name particular rights of the accused: the right to a grand jury, freedom from double jeopardy, and the right to refuse to testify on grounds of self-incrimination.

The final part of the Fifth Amendment is much more extensive. It is an explicit guarantee of three of the Five Rights: no person shall "be deprived of life, liberty, or property without due process of law; nor shall private property be taken for public use without just compensation." Government cannot confine a person or confiscate his money, house, car, or business unless he is legally found guilty of a crime and the action is part of the decreed sentence. Whether the State seeks to put someone to death or take his children away, it can never do so arbitrarily. It must follow set ethical procedures—due process—and prove that the defendant is guilty beyond a reasonable doubt.

The Fifth Amendment's guarantee of life includes protection from intentional injury. Its guarantee of liberty permits the individual to adopt beliefs as he chooses, move freely, and pursue his interests.

The Fifth Amendment's clause, "nor shall private property be taken for public use without just compensation," limits government's power of eminent domain.

Ninth Amendment

To alleviate the fear that nonenumerated rights might be considered nonexistent, Madison proposed the Ninth Amendment: "The enumeration in the Constitution of certain rights shall not be construed to deny or disparage others retained by the people." The people had unnamed rights that cannot be rescinded by government because they were never granted by government. They preceded it—customary self-evident rights.

The Ninth Amendment subordinated government to the traditional rights of individuals rather than the reverse. The founders recognized that in the future, unmentioned rights might be specified, and the Ninth Amendment provided a way for that to happen without having to alter the Constitution. Section eight of the Constitution enumerated government's powers and no more. The Bill of Rights listed some of the rights of individuals and said they had many more. The Ninth Amendment was how the founders said, the Bill of Rights is a *sample* of the particular rights each person has, not a manifest.

Fourteenth Amendment

Lincoln's Emancipation Proclamation of 1863 freed the slaves in the Confederate states. Two years later, after the North had won the war, the passage of the Thirteenth Amendment freed all slaves in all US states and territories. But the abolition of slavery did not prevent the defeated South from trying to preserve as much of the prewar order as possible by passing laws known as black codes, which denied ex-slaves the same rights as whites, especially pertaining to voting and ownership of property. The codes required blacks to sign long labor contracts and forbade them from serving on juries or testifying against whites. They allowed police to restrict the right of African Americans to carry firearms or knives or to move freely.

The Fourteenth Amendment banned black codes. It overturned the prewar *Dred Scott* ruling. It granted all newly freed slaves full citizenship. And for *all* individuals, it reaffirmed four of the Five Rights. Its second sentence reads, "No state shall make or enforce any law which shall abridge the privileges or immunities of citizens of the United States, *nor shall any state* [italics added] deprive any person of life, liberty, or property, without due process of law, nor deny to any person within its jurisdiction the equal protection of the laws." Before the ratification of the Fourteenth Amendment in 1868, the Bill of Rights applied only to the federal government. The Fifth Amendment's guarantees of life, liberty, and property were not binding on the states, which should have respected the rights on the basis of the Constitution as it was, but since they had not, went the postwar reasoning, a new amendment was needed to ensure compliance. The Fourteenth Amendment required the states to respect the same "privileges and immunities" as guaranteed by the federal government by refraining from making laws that breached the Five Rights.

But just five years later the Supreme Court made its first and most detrimental ruling on the Fourteenth Amendment in the *Slaughterhouse Cases* (1873), in which the Court defined "privileges and immunities" very narrowly, ruling that the phrase did not refer to the Five Rights but only to particular rights that came with US citizenship like habeas corpus, voting, access to navigable waters, and equal treatment in court and in sentencing. In recognizing so few Fourteenth Amendment rights, the Court gutted the amendment, ruling in effect that it did *not* extend the protections of the Bill of Rights to the states. In dissent, Justice Stephen Field wrote that the majority's reading of the Fourteenth Amendment made it into a "vain and idle enactment, which accomplished nothing."[30] It was indeed a huge setback. It took a century for an accumulation of Supreme Court decisions to undo the damage. A second blow to equal rights came in *Plessy v. Ferguson* (1896), when the Supreme Court ruled that states could legally impose segregation by race as long as they provided "separate but equal" facilities. Though the Court acknowledged that the segregated facilities were almost never equal, the position stood for fifty-eight years before the Court finally reversed itself in *Brown v. Board of Education* (1954), in which it ruled that segregation was a denial of rights under the equal protection clause, that the separation itself was wrong.[31]

Because the Fourteenth Amendment guarantees the equal protection of the laws, it underpins civil rights and discrimination law. Under the equal protection clause, the Supreme Court overturned laws barring African Americans from juries and laws discriminating against Chinese Americans in the regulation of laundry businesses. It prohibited racial discrimination in marriage laws, voting, hiring, and housing. It prohibited sexual harassment. The Court has relied on the Fourteenth Amendment to defend the equal rights of women, the disabled, and illegitimate children.

The Fourteenth Amendment is arguably the single best protector of the Five Rights, yet its originators—John Bingham, Thaddeus Stevens, and Charles Sumner—are virtually unknown except to historians.

CHAPTER 3
Metamorphosis

Government once managed defense, the courts, national monuments, and not much else. Lincoln was the first president to suggest that it should also take any obviously required action that market forces could not produce, and he set the first example with the Emancipation Proclamation. The first major federal regulatory agency, the Interstate Commerce Commission, was created in 1887. At about the same time, President Grover Cleveland married a girl named Frances in the White House, who, at twenty-one and just out of college, became by far the youngest first lady. Cleveland was otherwise a typical nineteenth-century laissez-faire president. He opposed taxes, subsidies, and proactive government. He thought government should stay out of the way and let people fend for themselves. During the depression of the 1890s, the most severe to that date, he did almost nothing, which aggravated the people—most wanted government to intervene.

In the twentieth century, President Theodore Roosevelt did intercede. He created the Meat Inspection Act and the Pure Food and Drug Administration. He split up monopolies and participated in disputes on behalf of labor. During his second term, railroad regulation depressed stock prices, which led to a run on banks in 1907 and caused the third largest bank in New York City, the Knickerbocker Trust Company, to close. In response, government created the Federal Reserve System in 1913 to back up individual banks with credit. Though the United States had resisted establishing a central bank for more than a century, it finally acknowledged that without a source of credit at the worst of times, markets broke down,

29

causing periodic panics. The Federal Reserve System could create deposits at the Federal Reserve Banks through bookkeeping entries. With its power to create money as needed, it allowed banks to make loans beyond their gold reserves. This is cheap monetary policy, in which low interest rates penalize saving and reward borrowing and speculation and promote rapid economic expansion. If you think of the flow of money like the flow of electric current, to use Alan Greenspan's metaphor, "the government, through the Federal Reserve System, put a penny in the fuse-box."[32] Cheap money creates financial bubbles that must eventually burst, as this one did in late 1929.

The lesson about cheap money—the 1920s boom and crash—was perhaps inevitable. The Federal Reserve System had no blueprint to go by; creating assets with a stroke of a pen was new, and no one knew how far it could be taken. But the Federal Reserve's conduct from 1930 to 1932 is less pardonable. As output fell and banks closed in late 1930, it was well known that the proper response for the Federal Reserve was to make large-scale open market purchases of government bonds, which would provide the banks with the additional cash necessary to meet the needs of skittish depositors. The Federal Reserve had used this technique successfully before, but it did not act. In the month of December 1930, 352 banks failed. In the spring of 1931, a second bank run developed; again the Federal Reserve did not act. In September, it acted, but wrongly. Great Britain abandoned the gold standard that month. The Federal Reserve feared that gold buyers shut out in Britain would jump across the Atlantic and create a run on US gold reserves, so the Fed *raised* interest rates more sharply than it ever had in the past. The sharp interest rate hike, after two years of depression, was highly deflationary. Prices collapsed, fear spread, people held their remaining dollars tight, and the depression became the Great Depression. Unemployment exceeded 15 percent. Forty percent of all the banks in America disappeared. "For every three dollars of deposits and currency in the hands of the public in 1929, less than two dollars remained in 1933—a monetary collapse without precedent."[33] When asset values in a prominent nation collapse, deflation spreads; the United States exported the Great Depression to the world.

The Federal Reserve System had a legislative mandate to prevent the monetary collapse, and it had the knowledge and means to prevent it. From 1931 to 1933, the New York Federal Reserve Bank repeatedly urged it to engage in large-scale open market purchases. Secretary of the Treasury Ogden L. Mills pleaded with the Federal Reserve to intervene. Mills later stated, "For a great central banking system to stand by with a 70 percent gold reserve without taking active steps in such a situation was inconceivable and almost unforgivable."[34] The Federal Reserve System, set up as the lender of last resort, instead acted like a novice investor, paralyzed by indecision into hoarding cash when it should most have used it.

Another action contributed to the collapse. President Hoover signed the Smoot-Hawley tariff, which raised import duties an average of 59 percent on more than 25,000 commodities and goods.[35] By increasing prices of foreign products in the US market, went the thinking, the tariffs would induce Americans to buy American, and the surge in demand would restart the economy, but it backfired badly. US trading partners retaliated with their own import duties. Britain placed a 100 percent tariff on goods from the United States.[36] Spain increased tariffs on American cars by 150 percent. Sales of US cars in Italy dropped 90 percent.[37] As prices rose while people were already cash-starved, the Depression deepened, especially in the United States. Farmers, the biggest proponents of Smoot-Hawley, saw their exports fall from $1.8 billion in 1929 to $590 million in 1933.[38]

In March 1929, the United States accounted for 44 percent of the gross national product of the world, more than that of the countries of Western Europe combined.[39] Seven months later, the stock market crashed, and for the next ten years Americans wondered where it all went, fearing each new week. When Franklin D. Roosevelt was elected president in November 1932, more than fifteen million Americans were unemployed—there was, of course, no unemployment insurance—and for those with jobs the average income was half what it had been three years earlier.[40] In March 1933, on the day President Roosevelt was inaugurated, the New York Stock Exchange had closed its doors.

The last crisis in memory was World War I, during which government had taken control of much of industrial production. That again became the inclination. It had seemed to work during war, so why not in a war against falling prices and rising unemployment? President Roosevelt, an experimenter and an optimist, held to no philosophical dogmas and had no fear of the untried—and there was overwhelming pressure for him to do *something*, so the president used emergency powers. Two days after taking office, Roosevelt closed the nation's banks and appointed a receiver to reorganize them. Congress affirmed his Emergency Banking Act. Roosevelt gave a fireside chat explaining what he had done, and on the following day, March 13, the banks reopened. Roosevelt used authority a president was only supposed to have during wartime, but the action reinforced the banks as intended and in just eight days. It also led to the creation of the Federal Deposit Insurance Corporation, through which government insured people's savings, creating confidence, and bank runs became rare events.

One of FDR's influences was Professor Charles G. Haines, a progressive leader who believed that government should have powers not granted in the Constitution, which he found outmoded and confining, a fusty relic from horse-and-buggy times. Rather than a government with strictly defined powers, wrote Haines, "[T]he American people should establish governments on a theory of trust in men in public affairs."[41] Haines and a number of other intellectuals felt that government could do a better job for individuals than they themselves could and therefore should. This contradicted the philosophy of Jefferson and Madison, who feared the tendency of government to overreach, to sacrifice a known principle to an immediate motive. They had tried to restrain lawmakers. Where power is concerned, wrote Jefferson, "let no more be heard of confidence in man, but bind him from mischief by the chains of the Constitution."[42]

But President Roosevelt couldn't be chained. During his first fifteen months in office, he signed 674 executive orders, an average of 2 per business day—more than any one person could read.[43] During the first month of his administration, Roosevelt and Congress created the Civilian Conservation Corps, a popular program that employed over three million men to provide flood relief and fight forest fires, build roads and fences, and provide pest control. The Corps planted three billion trees, constructed 46,000 bridges, installed telephoned lines, and provided relief in disasters and emergencies. The Works Progress Administration spent $5 billion on public needs including highways, conservation, irrigation, housing, hospitals, schools, playgrounds, and airports. It also subsidized artists, writers, and actors.[44]

The Social Security Act created the nation's first system of old-age pensions and unemployment insurance including grants for the blind, the handicapped, and dependent children. It was eventually a godsend for many, but not during the 1930s. It took money *out* of the system during the Depression; it did not start sending out monthly payments until January 1, 1940, when Ida May Fuller of Ludlow, Vermont, became the first recipient.[45] (Social Security is often compared to insurance, but most insurance is voluntary and Social Security is not. Also, insurance yields positive cash flow. Premiums are invested to fund the claims to be made later. Social Security is pay-as-you-go. There is no pool of appreciating assets being shepherded by wise ombudsmen. Money is taken from young and given to old.)

The New Deal involved a lot more: the Securities and Exchange Commission regulated new stock issues, required accurate company information, and enforced laws against insider trading and market manipulation. The Reconstruction Finance Corporation became the nation's largest bank; it spawned the Farm Credit Corporation, which spent over a billion dollars to save millions of rural families from foreclosure. The Fair Labor Standards Act and the Wagner Act established minimum working conditions. Government-backed mortgage insurance, through the Federal Housing Administration, made home loans available. The National Youth Administration set up apprenticeship training for 2.7 million jobless and made grants to students. The Public Works Administration built 17,000 buildings.[46] New Deal funding created massive dams at Bonneville on the Columbia River and at Grand Coulee, then the greatest concrete structure in the world. New Deal programs built canals, harbors, shelters, and zoos. They created national parks including Big Bend, Olympic National Park, Cape Hatteras National Seashore, and the Everglades. The Tennessee Valley Authority and the Rural

Electrification Administration brought electricity to millions, including over 12,000 rural schools. Before it, only one farm in nine had electricity. People hauled water in pails, used outdoor latrines, and got their only indoor light from smoky kerosene lamps.

Some New Deal programs were of questionable constitutionality, however. The rights to liberty and property permitted an individual to compete in any industry he selected, run his business as he liked, and offer goods at prices of his choosing, but New Deal regulations often disregarded these rights. Some programs were challenged on the basis that they violated the equal protection clause of the Fourteenth Amendment. Programs that took from some to give to others, or benefited employees at the direct expense of employers, or subsidized farmers at the expense of consumers, or established cartels could hardly be called equitable. New Deal statutes were also challenged on the basis that the Constitution did not empower any president to enact them. Wrote William Howard Taft, "The president can exercise no power which cannot be fairly and reasonably traced to some specific grant of power in the Federal Constitution. There is no undefined residuum of power which he can exercise because it seems to him to be in the public interest."[47] Concurring, the Supreme Court struck down a dozen New Deal programs.

Two of the most criticized programs were the National Industrial Recovery Act (NIRA) and the Agricultural Adjustment Act. The first was emblematic of the New Deal. It empowered government to set prices and restrict output and determined who could enter what businesses. The NIRA imposed more than seven hundred industrial codes to protect established companies from new competitors. Joseph Schechter, a man who operated slaughterhouses and sold chickens in New York City, charged that the NIRA was unconstitutional because it regulated his business and set his prices though his business operated wholly in New York State, beyond the reach of the national government, empowered only to regulate interstate commerce. The Court unanimously agreed with Schechter, finding that the NIRA codes involved "an unconstitutional delegation of legislative power,"[48] and struck down the National Industrial Recovery Act in 1935. The Guffey Act, a mini-NIRA that applied to mining and the bituminous coal industry, was also declared unconstitutional.[49]

Food prices were abysmal. Fifteen years earlier, World War I had caused a huge shortage in grain supplies from Russia and Europe, leaving Canada and the United States to make up the difference. In response, American agriculture burgeoned during the war and created overcapacity afterward. Falling food prices drove farmers into bankruptcy. President Roosevelt created the Agricultural Adjustment Administration (AAA) to help increase commodities prices by destroying supplies. To try to raise the income of hog farmers, it slaughtered millions of piglets. The AAA paid cotton growers to destroy their planted crops. Killing cotton while people needed clothes and destroying food while they were hungry made the AAA a target of ridicule. The Supreme Court ruled that the Agricultural Adjustment Administration, in trying to raise prices for farmers, violated the equal protection clause of the Fourteenth Amendment since it was not for the welfare of the general public but for that of farmers. Noted Justice Roberts in the majority opinion, the general welfare "has never been thought to connote the expropriation of money from one group for the benefit of another."[50] The Court ruled that the federal government did not have the power to establish cartels or set prices in agriculture, mining, or manufacturing.

The invalidation of the NIRA and the AAA jeopardized pending New Deal legislation. It was feared that Social Security would be found unconstitutional too. But President Roosevelt knew he had time on his side. When a program gets killed, the people who would have gained from it get angry. From their point of view, government told them that they were entitled to funds and then broke that promise, cheating them. President Roosevelt created entitlements and then waited while ire grew over the Court's refusal to provide the masses with "economic justice."

People need someone to blame. Wall Street, wild speculators, corrupt bankers, corporations, and the rich—who are accused of both hoarding and spending frivolously—all make good, politically acceptable targets. The rich are never popular, but they are hated most in a depression, and in 1936 rich and poor were as polarized as ever. President Roosevelt, as politically astute as any American since Benjamin Franklin, frequently communicated his distaste for big business and the wealthy. In speeches he referred to them as "privileged princes," "economic royalists," and "money changers."[51] He often used "investor" and "employer" as epithets. FDR's castigations of the rich made him hugely popular. He delighted in the political capital he gained when newspapers accused him of being a traitor to his class.

Roosevelt won a second term by the widest margin since James Monroe, but the Supreme Court remained an obstacle. FDR was annoyed that although he had the people and Congress solidly behind him, nine old men still stood in the way of his reforms. On February 5, 1937, three months after his reelection, he sent a special message to Congress, proposing to reorganize the judiciary altogether. Frustrated by the Court defeats and emboldened by his landslide reelection, Roosevelt proposed to appoint a new Supreme Court justice for each sitting justice over the age of seventy who refused to retire, meaning six new justices immediately appointed by him, allowing him to remake the Court in his image. What came to be called the Court-packing bill effectively placed the judiciary under FDR, erasing the main check on the legality of government action.

Though President Roosevelt presented the Court-packing plan as judicial reform required to get rid of "aged or infirm" justices, claiming that "younger blood will revitalize the courts," it was clear that FDR and his supporters wanted to change the Court because they wanted to reinterpret the Constitution.[52] As Roosevelt supporter Senator Robert J. Bulkley of Ohio put it, "A constitution is not an idol to be worshipped; it is an instrument of government to be worked."[53] Most, though, saw the plan as an audacious power grab. Many of Roosevelt's former backers opposed him. Some who were over seventy themselves took exception to FDR's implication that the justices were flummoxed, overworked men gone dim with the years. Others resented his lack of regard for the Supreme Court as an institution simply because it kept telling him that the federal government's power was limited by the Constitution. Roosevelt himself acknowledged that if successful he might well forge new executive "power which in some hands would be dangerous."[54]

Seven weeks after Roosevelt's threat to remake it, the Supreme Court relented. It was widely conceded that as a tradeoff for the certain defeat of the Court-packing bill in Congress, the Supreme

Court allowed pending New Deal legislation to stand, though it meant reversing itself on recent rulings. The Court had previously struck down laws that imposed limits on wages or hours worked, seeing them as class legislation favoring unions and employees at the expense of proprietors and the public, but in March 1937 it upheld a minimum wage law identical to one it had struck down ten months earlier in *Tipaldo*. Then in *West Coast Hotel Co. v. Parrish*, the Court upheld a Washington State minimum wage law as a legitimate measure to protect health, safety, and welfare. The reversals demonstrated the Court's new view. It upheld the National Labor Relations Act and validated Social Security. It upheld the Fair Labor Standards Act. And although the Agricultural Adjustment Act had been struck down, it was replaced by a new act with the same name and similar mandate to fix quotas, destroy surpluses, and fine any farmer who produced or sold more than his allotment—and was upheld. The Supreme Court rulings granted the federal government powers it had never had before.

Though President Roosevelt was succeeding, he continued to promote his Court-packing plan even after Justice Van Devanter announced his resignation, giving FDR another appointment. The Court-packing bill was defeated in the Senate. The report of the Senate Judiciary Committee stated that the preservation of the constitutional system was "immeasurably more important ... than the immediate adoption of any legislation however beneficial."[55] It supported "the continuation and perpetuation of government and rule by law, as distinguished from government and rule by men, and in this we are but reasserting the principles basic to the Constitution of the United States." The committee added, "If the Court of last resort is to be made to respond to a prevalent sentiment of a current hour, politically imposed, that Court must ultimately become subservient to the pressure of public opinion of the hour, which might embrace mob passion abhorrent to a more calm, lasting consideration."[56] In the end, the Court-packing plan was harshly rebuked by the Senate Judiciary Committee as "a vicious precedent" and "an invasion of judicial power which has never before been attempted in this country."[57]

But it didn't matter. As it turned out, within two and a half years of the failure of the plan, Roosevelt was able to appoint five of the nine justices. (By the time of his death, FDR had filled eight vacancies, one fewer than George Washington.) "The Court is now his," wrote Wendell Willkie. "Mr. Roosevelt has accomplished exactly what he would have accomplished if he had won the court fight."[58] He added, "During the past three years, the American people have had a series of majority opinions that substantially change their form of government. [The Court] has wiped out state and local lines, and has relentlessly extended Federal authority to every farm, every hamlet, every business firm and manufacturing plant in the country."[59] Willkie wasn't exaggerating. As President Roosevelt observed, he lost the battle but won the war. Admirers compared him to Augustus, detractors to Lenin. The Roosevelt Court, as it was called, never again struck down a New Deal law, multiplying, permanently it seems, the role of the State. The Supreme Court has since not invalidated a single major statute regulating the economy or business and has routinely upheld social legislation.

The issue is not whether New Deal programs were desirable or successful—some were both. The issue is John Selden's "gap at which each man's liberty may in time go out,"[60] the gap between what government can and cannot do. New Deal legislation included the kind of positivist actions that Alexander Hamilton, the most management-minded of the founders, had stressed that government was not empowered to take. Hamilton might have asked, for example, how can it influence prices? Where in the Constitution is that power granted? Regardless, the National Recovery Administration was chartered to "stabilize production, raise prices, and protect labour and consumers."

Formerly, the federal government could only regulate businesses that were involved in interstate commerce, but the requirement was dropped, leaving no distinction between interstate and local commerce or between commerce and production. Under the new definition, nearly anything could be said to affect commerce: driving, smoking, planting carrots, rafting on a river, divorce, death. All could be regulated. Night watchmen, janitors, elevator operators, and window washers too. The regulatory power granted to lawmakers during the 1930s turned constitutionalism on its head. Instead of being free people due to a government of limited powers, Americans became people with vacuous rights due to government's unlimited power to legislate. Ours was no longer a constitutional republic, but one in which rights could be sacrificed to a government aim, vigorous group, or affecting cause.

This was especially true of property rights. After the 1930s, what a person earned was no longer his except to the extent that others permitted him to keep it. The general welfare had never been interpreted to include the power of government to transfer wealth, but it was so interpreted, and government has since treated individuals' assets as objects of potential administration.

Congress and the state governments could regulate economic concerns with impunity. In *Carolene Products*, Justice Stone wrote that legislation that breached property rights was entitled to a presumption of necessity.[61] In other words, if government made the law, they must have had a good reason. Oklahoma passed a law forbidding opticians from making glasses without a prescription from a licensed ophthalmologist. The law was passed to protect eye doctors' profits and to impede the company that would become LensCrafters, but the Supreme Court upheld the law on the reasoning that although it was not essential, neither was it irrational. The message: laws would get the benefit of the doubt. Protectionist legislation was doable. Businesses refocused. Hate a competitor? Declare his product harmful and try to get it banned. Getting undersold? Demand price controls. Want out of a contract? Get it declared void. Want to be subsidized? Petition for it. It was time and effort well spent now that the Supreme Court no longer distinguished between economic legislation that served a valid public purpose and class legislation intended to advance one group's interests.

In his State of the Union Address of January 1944, President Roosevelt unveiled a "second Bill of Rights," but whereas the original Bill of Rights protected the Five Rights by restraining government, FDR's bill sought to make the State each person's economic manager. FDR declared, "Necessitous men are not free men," which is true.[62] There are some things we *must* do to live, so we can never be truly free of our nature, but before the 1930s that truism had never been taken to mean that whatever people find necessary, others should be forced to supply. Roosevelt listed a number of things as needing to be guaranteed by government that clearly did not need to be guaranteed since they had never been guaranteed before, and the nation had been advancing nicely for a century and a half. FDR's list of new rights included "the right to a useful and remunerative job," to adequate pay, food, clothing, and recreation, "the right to a good education," "a decent home," "medical care," and freedom from "the economic fears of old age, sickness, accident, and unemployment." He added that every farmer had a right to profitable prices at which to sell products and to "freedom from unfair competition."[63]

It's impossible to guarantee these things. Government cannot guarantee someone a job unless it forces someone else to provide one. Houses and medical care are not found lying about in nature; carpenters, doctors, and nurses must be paid a mutually agreed-upon wage. If they don't agree to what is being offered, how can government guarantee their services without compelling them? How can it increase commodities prices without imposing price controls and quotas, or destroying surpluses? How can it prevent people in other nations from accepting jobs there to build products at lower prices, creating "unfair competition"? The original Bill of Rights was negative in the sense that it named things government could *not* do, complementarily permitting freedom. FDR's second bill of rights was redistributive: it named things that earners and savers henceforth *must* do for nonearners and nonsavers.

By reinterpreting the Constitution, the federal government shifted its role from the protection of each person's rights to its current one, which is, in Mill's words, "to compel people to conform to its notions of personal, as well as social excellence."[64] Government tries to make things better—healthier, fairer. That may sound noble, but no government can bring about fairness because it isn't within the power of government to change people's inborn abilities and shortcomings, undo their poor decisions, manage fate, or even to satisfactorily define fairness. Government can only make and enforce rules, which it can use to protect the rights of all individuals equally or to force some to benefit others. No longer a detached referee, it openly takes sides, and a group can use a politically favored status to gain at the expense of the rest.

The federal income tax began in 1913. The top rate first skyrocketed during World War I, hitting 77 percent. In 1922, it was lowered to 58 percent and then slashed three years later to 25 percent, back almost to prewar levels. It remained low for the rest of the 1920s. As the Depression deepened during the 1930s, government more than doubled the top rate to 63 percent, and then raised it steadily to pay for New Deal undertakings and for WWII, until it reached an all-time high of 94 percent in 1945. *The top rate stayed at or near 90 percent for the next two decades.* It was lowered to 70 percent in 1964, then to 50 percent in 1982, then to a modern low of 28 percent in 1988. (It is currently 35 percent.)[65]

Before the 1930s, federal government activity was minimal and cheap: it used about 3 percent of the gross domestic product; after the 1930s, it required 20 percent or more.[66] From the formation of the republic in 1787 until 1929, spending by government at all levels combined never exceeded 12 percent of income (except during times of major war). Since 1933, it has never been under 20 percent, and in recent decades about forty cents of each dollar earned by a person has been taken and used for purposes other than his. And there is evidently no limit to the taxation possibilities. When the top tax rate was at its highest—over 90 percent—one would think government couldn't take any more, but on April 22, 1942, FDR issued a message to Congress in which he declared, "No American citizen ought to have a net income, after he has paid his taxes, of more than $25,000 a year."[67] The Treasury Department submitted to the House Ways and Means Committee a proposal calling for a 100 percent tax on all income over $25,000. It failed, but the fact that it was considered demonstrates how fully a person's efforts could be expropriated now that property rights and the right to equality before the law provided no defense against confiscatory taxes.

A temporary welfare state emerged and became permanent. President Truman's Fair Deal extended Roosevelt's New Deal. When the Department of Health, Education, and Welfare was established in 1953, its budget was $2 billion, less than 5 percent of expenditures on national defense. A quarter-century later, in 1978, the HEW budget was $160 billion, one and a half times as much as the total spending on defense. At the end of the Eisenhower years, in 1960, there were about a hundred federal programs. By 1976, there were more than one thousand.[68] Under Lyndon Johnson's War on Poverty and Great Society initiatives, programs were expanded, payments were increased, Medicare and Medicaid were established, welfare was increased, and public housing and urban renewal programs were added or enlarged. From 1949 to 1965, welfare spending increased slowly, taking sixteen years to double from $20 billion to $40 billion annually (in constant dollars), and during the same period the US poverty rate decreased from 34 to 14 percent.[69] After 1965, spending on welfare programs multiplied many times while the poverty rate remained unchanged. Whereas spending to help people survive can be defended on humanitarian grounds, spending to reduce poverty failed and can possibly be counterproductive. It has been argued that as public support increases, private effort decreases.

Formerly, government had no choice but to let the individual take care of himself, which induced self-sufficiency. When he knew no one was going to rescue him from bad decisions or bad luck, he was left with personal commitment alone, creating a reservoir of ingenuity. As the State took a greater role, it gradually replaced the notion of self-reliance as a means to happiness with the idea that government "owes" those with less, fostering dependence and whetting appetites for wants. Each benefit granted increases the resolve of the beneficiary to try for more. When something works, you do it again, better.

Today, proponents of New Deal policies correctly note that millions of people were better off after President Roosevelt than before him and that the beneficiaries were generally people who needed the help. They usually neglect to mention, however, that for the majority, people who worked before, during, and after the Depression, taxes tripled. And the New Deal failed to reduce unemployment. While federal government outlays doubled, the median annual unemployment rate remained above 17 percent, and at no point during the 1930s did it drop below 14 percent.[70] It did not drop substantially until after the war.

The New Deal did initiate Social Security, unemployment insurance, and several other things few people would want to do without. Most importantly, in subsequent decades, changes that occurred in the 1930s allowed government to recognize and better defend rights that had never been sufficiently protected. A federal government held strictly to its enumerated constitutional powers would not have had the means to outlaw school segregation in the 1950s; it could not have banned racial discrimination in places that served the public during the 1960s; it would not have had the means to create a potent Environmental Protection Agency; nor would it have been able to mandate ramps and parking for the handicapped. The downside of proactive government is that it can't say no. It is forever under pressure to pass laws that are popular but violate rights. The Constitution prevented it for over 140 years, but once government crossed the line, it exposed itself (and as their protector, the Five Rights) to the vicissitudes of public opinion and to organized interests.[71]

CHAPTER 4
Despotic Democracy

Majority rule is a rational way to decide an issue, but there are situations in which it's clearly inapplicable. First, any circumstance not within the control of human beings: majority rule can't change weather or the length of a day or the rate of acceleration due to gravity. It can't make a fish from scratch, resurrect the dead, or make truths untrue or fantasies real. Second, majority rule does not apply when rules have been predetermined by man. It does not apply in any organized command structure—military, corporate, or bureaucratic. Majority rule does not apply in a jury trial; preset rules require a unanimous decision. When there is a close call in a football game, the crowd does not get a vote. Officials decide according to preset rules. Your neighbors cannot come to your house and take your favorite chair because they outnumber you three to one; preset rules, property rights in this case, take precedence. Third, majority rule does not apply to personal choices. The person you marry, how you spend your money, the clothes you pick to wear, and your choice of breakfast cereal are not determined by majority rule because they fall within the protected sphere of the individual.

The Constitution formally subordinated majority rule to set principles and, in doing so, shielded lawmakers politically. When a majority tried to push through a law that violated the rights of some, lawmakers could point to the Constitution and refuse and it could not be held against them, but once lawmakers showed that they would slip around the Constitution given sufficient reason, political action committees (PACs) formed to provide it. There are over 4,000 registered PACs in Washington. Each promotes legislation according it its cause (e.g., farm subsidies, trade barriers, obscenity laws). Each PAC claims that's its desires are in the public interest, which is impossible since the costs in liberty and in dollars are borne by individuals, who *are* the public, and if all requests were approved liberty would be smothered and individuals bankrupt. Because each PAC cares more about what it wants than about what other PACs get, they team up, create coalitions, and form temporary majorities. Individually, the initiatives would fail, but so aligned, they become law. Each group gets what it wanted most along with things it didn't want or finds irrelevant, and the political objectives of a few are imposed on all as the proper course.

The power to coerce is irresistible to exploitation. Imagine being able to *make* everyone act the way you prefer, to do the thing you think is most important, to fund your causes. When lawmakers pulled free of their constitutional shackles, they stripped themselves of the ability to protect the Five Rights, leaving no issue off limits to legislative consideration and majority rule.

Some might ask, is majority rule superseding constitutional principles such a bad thing? If most people are in favor of a law, why not pass it? Aren't the people supposed to rule in a democracy? Not as a despot. "Rule by the will of the people" means that the citizens of the nation elect their government and agree to abide by its laws, provided it respects the rights of every individual to life, liberty, property, the pursuit of happiness, and equality under the law. In a principled democracy, the majority rule, but not across all boundaries. Many in the late eighteenth century, including Alexander Hamilton and John Adams, wrongly thought that representative democracy would automatically protect individuals' rights. They reasoned, if the people could replace any representative who didn't carry out their wishes, they would always be in control of their government. But electing government is not the same thing as controlling it. After witnessing Hitler's rise firsthand, Hayek wrote, "Perhaps the fact that we have seen millions voting themselves into complete dependence on a tyrant has made our generation understand that to choose one's government is not necessarily to secure freedom."[72] Jefferson too saw that government had to be restrained by more than the inertia of majority rule; otherwise, as he warned while advocating additional restraints on the Virginia legislature, "One hundred seventy-three despots would surely be as oppressive as one."[73] Cicero concurred: "The rabble is just as tyrannical as one man."[74] And the French Revolution confirmed it. A system that allows injustice provided a majority approves it—democracy without principles—is as bankrupt as any other system without principles. Some acts are wrong regardless of how many people support them. Lincoln insisted that Kansas could not, even by majority rule, choose to have slavery.

Democracy without principles is nine people voting to execute a tenth though he has committed no crime. It is a jury convicting a defendant based on rage rather than on the facts of the case. Democracy without principles is a vote that makes it illegal for some groups to assemble in private; it is the majority party in Congress passing a law that prohibits the other party from advertising on television. Rights prevent these things. Majority rule alone does not. In a democracy, there is no need for rights when the majority is with you, only when it's against you. The Five Rights protect all minorities, including the smallest minority, the individual. In a highly publicized murder case, no matter how many people think a defendant is guilty, he has the right to a fair trial and all other rights of the accused. If the accused retain their rights against majority opinion, shouldn't the unaccused?

The Constitution was based on classical liberalism: the principle that every individual has the right to use his knowledge for his aims provided he doesn't harm, coerce, or defraud another person. Aside from that doctrine and secondary to it, democracy was to be the procedural form of government. Constitutionality would determine what legislative options were available; majority rule would be the method for deciding among them. But after the metamorphosis, majority rule was left to choose among *all* options, allowing government to rule on any issue, to be dictatorial within proper democratic procedures. If lawmakers are unbounded, and the majority controls lawmakers, then the majority is unbounded. Over the past eighty years, the US form of government has moved steadily from a constitutional republic administered through democracy toward a *despotic democracy*—democratic in structure with open forums, elections, and consensus decision-making, but with uncontained lawmaking powers. Despotic democracy is unlimited government of all individuals by the majority on each issue. In a despotic democracy, people are not mutually free but mutually controlled. They don't live comfortably within their rights, but neurotically, fearing which pleasure might be voted away next for being out of favor. "The people" revoke one another's liberties rather than a central authority, but since the State is the enforcer of the democratically produced laws, the result to the individual is oppression by the State. By providing the legal means for some to dominate others, despotic democracy makes government, which was formed to protect individuals from one another's injustice, the tool of it.

In a lucid exposition of the rule of law in Cicero's *The Republic,* Scipio concludes that freedom requires "an equal partnership in justice," in which no person or group has legal power to veto another's actions.[75] Without this equality, the majority can ban the actions of the minority, interfering with every individual's choices at some point because no person is in the majority on every issue. In transforming political sentiment into lawmaking power, despotic democracy invites the prohibition of any practice thought unsafe, unhealthy, unfair, or unwholesome—so long as people can be persuaded to vote against it. This is not difficult since those whom it does not concern—the majority—are inclined to take the safe route and legislate against a questionable practice of just a few individuals. When a 98 percent majority violates the rights of the other 2 percent, the protests of the 2 percent go unheard, but it's unjustifiable coercion. If it were acceptable, a 94 percent majority could coerce the other 6 percent. Eighty and 70 percent majorities could do the same, and so on. A big group violating the rights of a small one is a greater evil than readily apparent; it's the moral equivalent of a husband hitting his wife because he is larger, or a country using military might to suppress a small neighbor. It's might over right; force over reason; barbarism that wouldn't be tolerated physically or any way other than despotic democracy because it would be seen for what it is.

When minority actions can be outlawed, millions of individuals' personal choices can be banned though many may still perceive the nation as free. It only seems pernicious to those affected, each of whom feels that if is he is not harming another, and if he is not negatively affecting his neighborhood, he should not have to answer to others—it's a gut feel that that's how things should be. Lincoln once expressed it, "I am for the people of the whole nation doing just as they please in all matters which concern the whole nation; for those of each part doing just as they choose in all matters which concern no other part; and for each doing just as he chooses in all matters which concern nobody else."[76]

Since each choice is up to each individual and him alone, it is irrelevant if others find his actions foolhardy, depraved, or self-destructive: their findings are not silage for legislation. The area between actions that harm others and those that merely offend forever requires defense, however, because individuals have a double standard regarding rights that reduces to, what I do is my business; what you do is your business unless I have a real problem with it. When people find something thoroughly objectionable, they have trouble sitting still. Other times, they don't staunchly oppose an act but wouldn't mind a ban out of a general sense of propriety. Though people balk at having their actions ruled on by indifferent strangers, they perfunctorily do it to others, concluding, if choice A is obviously correct, then the holdout should have to comply for everyone's good including his own. It's difficult to accept that free individuals have the right to think and act *wrongly*, to choose unworkable means, or to act selfishly, oddly, or to their own detriment, but being correct does not permit one to impose correctness.

The rights double standard lets people take irreconcilable positions on issues of the day. For example, a person employs a rights double standard who favors freedom of religion but not when it involves animal sacrifice; who favors legal alcohol, tobacco, and antidepressants but not marijuana; who passionately avows his First Amendment right to free speech while denying another person's Second Amendment right to possess firearms; who favors legalized prostitution on the basis that each person's life is his own business but sees nothing wrong with a military draft; who swears by his property rights while being subsidized; who favors free market competition but supports legislation to foil competitors; who demands the right to raise children without State interference but seeks to deny the same right to parents he finds wanting; who supports the right of his little girl to compete in "boys'" sports on the basis of equal rights but disapproves of gay marriage; who values his privacy and that of his family but favors surveillance of others; who practices personal rites or beliefs regarding his mortality but seeks to block that same right of others.

Despotic democracy allows the leading edge of the rights double standard—the overlap of actual rights—to be made into law. From the perspective of individuals whose liberties are restricted, this is not self-government but interference. They employ the same means in retaliation, seeking to legislate invalid assertions of their rights. Competing rights double standards become an arms race, but instead of outspending one another to build more bombs, squandering productivity, groups outvote one another to make more rules, squandering freedom. In a despotic democracy, "government by the will of the people" becomes the coercion of all by all, leaving all of us the victims of our hypocrisy.

If individuals had no rights double standard, there would be no reason for competitive lawmaking. Each would observe that by *not* usurping others' rights he insured his own. Mutual restraint is not within human capability, however, because it's not our nature to trust strangers as friends or to accept their traditions without judgment. Evolution makes us responsible to ourselves and close family, and our *Homo sapiens* heritage induces loyalty to a group and wariness of other groups. We defend those closest to us, serve them voluntarily without remuneration, and take them into our confidence. We can share so many experiences that we continue to love a person beyond his existence. In contrast, there are billions of people we will never encounter and whose happiness has no bearing on ours. Ignoring, criticizing, or accusing them comes easier to us. We are subjective too in that each of us has his own experiences, beliefs, priorities, and misconceptions. We are alike, though, in that we promote our views, confident that we are doing right, fearing the imagined extremes of adversaries, and petitioning government to make our concerns into laws. By our nature, we support rules that help us to attain our goals and hinder rivals from attaining theirs, rules calculated to treat different people differently.

Understanding that groups would try to use government to impose their will on all, the founders intentionally authorized no power for Congress to violate the Five Rights, save taxation, thereby making rights preeminent, but the twentieth century relegated constitutional principles to guidelines and subordinated lawmakers to politics. Forced to satisfy many different concerns, some of which are contradictory, lawmakers cannot uphold the Five Rights or even be consistent. How is it possible to keep government from sacrificing the principles on which it is founded—the Five Rights of the individual—to political utility when the people comprising government must serve political utility to survive in their positions?

CHAPTER 5
Leviathan

All regulations having general applicability and legal effect are published daily in the *Federal Register*. Between 1970 and 1979, the *Federal Register* tripled in size from 17,660 pages to over 40,000 pages annually—that's over eleven feet of shelf space for each new year's worth of rules.[77] Spending on government agencies quintupled during the 1970s from $1 billion to over $5 billion.[78] Typical of the decade were President Nixon's wage and price controls and President Carter's twenty-thousand-person Department of Energy—two attempts to control free markets that did more harm than good. Milton Friedman showed that the Department of Energy's attempt to hold down domestic oil prices in 1979 *caused* gas station lines that year by interfering with the distribution of supply, while the agency's cost added nine cents to the price of each gallon of gas.[79]

The election of Ronald Reagan in 1980 was billed as a return to traditional values, and in some ways it was. Reagan recognized the potential of free-market capitalism and how to realize it. He cut domestic spending, cut taxes (the top rate was lowered from 70 percent to 38 percent and then 28 percent), and deregulated industries, starting with airlines and trucking. Freeing up business and leaving more money in the pockets of individuals worked. Inflation dropped from 13 percent to under 6 percent, interest rates and unemployment fell by half, and the economy took off.[80]

But President Reagan also ushered in a moralism that recognized no personal sphere of liberty within which individuals were free to disagree and act as they please. Dogmatic views toward lifestyle, reproductive rights, drug use, and religion, and an authoritarian interpretation of rules, impelled people to comply with accepted and sometimes stilted norms. Whereas Roosevelt repealed Prohibition and regulated business and the economy, Reagan went the opposite way, deregulating the economy but encouraging a narrowly defined "correctness" in personal life that sometimes chafed. When Congress passed a resolution requesting that Reagan declare 1983 the "Year of the Bible," stating that "the Bible, the Word of God, has made a unique contribution in shaping the United States as a distinctive and blessed nation and people,"[81] Reagan signed it, to the chagrin of religious minorities, nonreligious people, and everyone who believed in the separation of Church and State. Following Reagan, Presidents Bush and Clinton continued to expand government in the areas that most concerned them, respectively, illegal drugs and family values, and health care, education, and cigarette smoking.

Public officials nurture government growth by defining health and safety a bit more stringently all the time. Initially, regulations were meant to protect the individual from epidemics, from tainted food, and in public places, but the category has grown to include financial health, psychological well-being, and safety with hot coffee or near a swimming pool. Public places once meant buildings or common areas administered by government, but it now refers to anywhere that people gather in numbers: baseball stadiums, factories, parking lots, malls, and so on.[82] This distinction scarcely matters though, since government has gone beyond public places of any kind, regulating individuals' actions within their four walls and mandating "correct" personal choices regarding their bodies, time, and money.

Good intentions pave the way. The State provides a service, say, useful information about major health risks. The service eventually grows into an institution that dispenses advice and promotes health-oriented rules. Legislators make laws and government imposes them either directly or by compelling corporations to force their employees to comply. Fixated on making things "better" to the exclusion of the Five Rights, congressmen, agency heads, and some CEOs ultimately seek to restrict personal actions, even on private property, citing health, safety, or cost cutting. It's how we went from a Surgeon General's warning on a pack of cigarettes (a valid attempt to inform) to companies banning employees from smoking in their own homes (a violation of all of the Five Rights).

Government seldom gets smaller. In the private sector, what works survives and what doesn't fades, but government lacks this evolutionary efficiency. It has no self-pruning mechanism to expunge dysfunctional or wasteful mutations. Whereas a business must provide a wanted product or service, the survival of a government agency depends on data shaped by people whose careers are linked to what it suggests. Government employees, like all of us, act in their interests. They see themselves as working for the side that gets paid less and tries to help people rather than sell them something. Both the administrators of a program and the winners in the distribution of dollars see it as a right, and they fight for it with the zeal of true believers, so that once established, a program can be politically impossible to terminate, prompting President Reagan to once comment, "A government bureau is the nearest thing to eternal life we'll ever see on this earth."[83]

Events too fuel legislation. When something newsworthy happens, television and the Internet, due to their market-driven tendency to exploit sensational anomalies, overstate the case for more rules. "Live and let live" makes a less engaging story than "There ought to be a law!" Overreaction and anxiety grow government. For confident, forward-thinking people, more rules are irrelevant, inconvenient, or worse.

Leaders grow government by creating in the mind of the individual something for which he should sacrifice—a purpose to outshine his self-interest. Socialist or communist orders have done it by casting self-interest as shameful and directing the individual to serve the public good, which it defines. American politicians often use nationalism to accomplish the same end. President Kennedy's famous line from his inaugural address, "Ask not what your country can do for you; ask what you can do for your country," was in direct contradiction to Jefferson's ideal of a "wise and frugal government, which shall restrain men from injuring one another, which shall otherwise leave them free to regulate their own pursuits of industry and improvement."[84] Kennedy asked Americans to subordinate their interests to their nation's "long twilight struggle," though it was peacetime. That his plea was immortalized attests to our transformation from a country founded on individual liberty to one in which the people are expected to sacrifice for goals set by each new administration. If President Kennedy had wanted to express the American ideal of the 1776–1930 era, he would have said, "Ask not what your country can do for you; ask what you can do for yourself."

Wearing different hats contributes to government's tendency to tread heavily. Hayek observed that government has two separate tasks. When administering law, it acts as a judge—an impartial body that decides disputes within established rules. It seeks to resolve conflicts *apart* from its goals, and its rulings apply to everyone. In its directorial role, it acts like a CEO of a corporation with tasks to accomplish and underlings to supervise, and it assigns tasks to its operatives *based on* its goals. Its role as a judge does not involve commands. As a CEO, it issues commands to its employees, but it pays them and they are free to leave and take a job elsewhere, so they are not coerced. But blending its two roles allows government to make rules and impose them on all, creating a directed organization. When a government body sees itself as managing the nation, as one runs a company rather than as individuals who get paid to provide services to a freely functioning order, it takes on the responsibilities of a manager, enacting legislation that compels all individuals to conform to its plan for the firm.

Late each January, the president of the United States makes his State of the Union address. The speech rarely includes references to the Five Rights because it is not about Americans but America. It's like a corporate mission statement: what we accomplished last year, our goals for the new year, long-term goals. The trouble is, America is not a corporation. A corporation is a group of specifically chosen people and resources brought together and managed for a particular purpose. The only way America can be run like one big company, organized to achieve specific goals with the president and Congress acting as CEO and board of directors, is if government treats individuals as corporations treat employees: issuing orders as a boss does, establishing a culture, rewarding conformity and penalizing dissent, judging performance, managing personnel and assets, sharing only the information that it chooses to share, and expecting individuals to give their all for the corporation. The private company offers a salary and benefits; an individual may accept the terms or decline and seek a better offer; the employer/employee relationship is voluntary on both sides. Government too attempts to organize and motivate, but it uses laws instead, making crimes of opposed activities and criminals of people who engage in them. An individual can choose to ignore a corporation he doesn't like, but with a government agency, he must obey or risk penalty.

Congress creates each federal agency, but an accurate organizational chart of the relationship between Congress and its agencies would not show each reporting to Congress at the top, as one might expect. It would show some as separate balloons floating above Congress, tethered to it by a thin strand. Though technically beholden to Congress, each acts as an independent entity; some can do things that Congress can't. Obviously one lawmaking body cannot bestow on another powers it does not itself possess, but that's the result when Congress grants an agency indistinct authority or a combination of legislative, executive, and judicial powers. An agency that can make, enforce, and interpret laws is a small government unto itself, operating according to *its* charter and concerns, the first of which is its own survival and expansion. Some agencies have authority undreamt of by the founders.

New rules are now written faster than ever. Three hundred fifty pages per business day are added to the *Federal Register*—over 70,000 pages per year.[85] People don't read 350 pages per day, including your Congressman, which means that he can create more laws than he or anyone else can know. Congress keeps up the pace of legislation through the use of 26,000 aides and assistants who handle the details and the devils in them.[86] Unelected government employees determine precisely what laws get passed. Agency heads and experienced, high-level administrators are adept at getting their preferences in legislation through subtleties and stonewalling. Bureaucrats have personal, professional, and ideological motives to expand their domains, much as their counterparts in private enterprise try to grow their businesses, but while business growth creates wealth for owners, and jobs, and provides the tax revenues that pay for government's activities, the same incentives in government employees bring higher taxes and more rules.

With innumerable laws and potent government agencies to enforce them, the United States has the highest incarceration rate of any populous country. There are currently 2 million individuals in America's prisons and jails, and 1.1 million of them are incarcerated for nonviolent crimes.[87] Several hundred thousand individuals who have not hurt anyone else are being forced to live in cages. The total number—two million—is more than triple the number of prisoners held twenty years ago and *ten times* as many as forty years ago.[88] Today's incarceration is four times the average rate for the first three quarters of the twentieth century.[89] If the US prison population were a city, it would rank as the fourth largest in the nation, between Chicago and Houston.[90] Over two decades, the state of California built one college campus and twenty-one prisons.[91] The combined prison populations of France, Great Britain, Germany, Japan, Singapore, and the Netherlands could fit inside California's penal institutions, with room to spare. According to the Bureau of Justice Statistics, if current incarceration trends continue, the chance that an American child born this year will go to jail in his life are one in twenty.[92]

If overregulation is not the cause of America's high incarceration rate and the rate is appropriate, it must be concluded that two million Americans belong in jail because Americans are bad, significantly more villainous than people in other countries, and four times as criminal as past Americans, but there is no evidence to support this claim. The simpler explanation is that in making so many rules, government has created more rule breakers and, with ever-improving methods of catching them, more prisoners.

CHAPTER 6
The Right to Life

Spontaneous Order and Common Law

Life exists because substances combine. Atoms combine to form molecules. Some of the more complex molecules, amino acids, combine in long chains to form proteins. Proteins bind tightly to form living organisms called cells, the smallest unit that is considered a life form because cells can make copies of themselves by dividing. Some living organisms, like bacteria, consist of only one cell. A person has one hundred trillion cells. The combining and separating—life—happens spontaneously. Human beings exist because in nature, tiny elements interact to form complex systems so well designed that they seem to have been created by an intelligence with a purpose in mind, but of course that's an illusion. Every plant and animal, including us, is a unit of spontaneous order.

The phrase "spontaneous order," coined by Michael Polyani and popularized by Hayek, describes a system that is self-managing because each of its many separate elements is self-managing.[93] In a human body, each cell is an individual living entity that works for itself but weighs the influences acting on it and responds to its neighbors, and as it does, it performs a small fraction of the adaptation of the overall organism.[94] When the separate actions of the cells are viewed together, the predictable manner in which they react is spontaneous order, the whole of which seems to be self-correcting. Though a spontaneous order is always in transition, its elements' regular cooperation and competition yield general rules of interaction. Because order results from concordance, from relationships between elements rather than the elements themselves, elements can change, but the relationships remain and order persists.[95] Spontaneous order is called different things by different branches of science—cybernetics, homeostasis, self-organization, synergetics, complexity, polycentrics, adaptive systems theory—but all refer to the same process of naturally occurring order.

As living cells are the elements of a human being, humans themselves can be the elements of a spontaneous order. It arises whenever a large number of people interact. Every community, city, and nation is a spontaneous order of individuals, within which customs form, and some of them become rules of behavior. Though the rules are not formally imposed, everyone knows them and most people follow them. For example, no central authority imposes manners, yet they exist. Who makes rules of civility? We all do, unconsciously, with our judgments and commentary. Manners accommodate us because we are self-conscious and have weaknesses that need indulging, and manners help shield our easily bruised psyches. We prize patience, affability, warmth, good humor, and charm. We try to avoid causing anxiety. We learn to self-edit, to show interest, to display the sentiment proper to the situation: it's wrong to act giddy at a funeral or sour at a celebration. Excessive self-love makes an unseemly exposure. Inappropriate silence reads as dismay. Gratitude costs nothing to give and means much to its recipient, and ingratitude is repellent. We learn not to rave about our happiness to someone in distress. We indulge friends' beliefs and foibles and learn to treat them in accordance with how they see themselves. We learn to avoid the temptation to make the quick but unkind remark. "One of the very best rules of conversation," wrote Swift, "is to never say anything which any of the company wish had been left unsaid."[96]

Along with manners, other products of spontaneous order include language, writing, and money.[97] Each of these came about on its own. No person or group invented or decreed English, Spanish, or any other widely used language. Traditions were learned and adapted by each successive generation, producing rules of pronunciation, syntax, and grammar. New inventions and circumstances gave rise to new words.[98] Language is "the result of human action but not of human design."[99]

A system designed to accomplish a goal is different: it's directed from the top down. A spontaneous order is undirected; it's an unconscious *result*, a holistic view of the actions of the member elements (e.g., people). A managed organization requires a manager who can overrule the decisions of individuals. A spontaneous order *is* the decisions of individuals. Unlike a directed system, which costs money to establish and maintain, spontaneous order is self-organizing and free. Managed order substitutes laws for liberty; it seeks a goal not of every individual's choosing and forces compliance. To achieve a single deliberate end, like winning a war, requires a command structure and a sacrifice of individuals' rights to that end. Spontaneous order serves individuals' multiple and varied ends, some of which are irreconcilable.

As the self-interested actions of individuals writ large, spontaneous order is the only system consistent with liberty. Being the comprehensive result of free choice, there is no way to reconstitute spontaneous order without inhibiting free choice. It cannot be consciously managed toward a goal because it is by definition order without commands. Any attempt to manage it changes the behavior of the elements. Spontaneous order is like quantum mechanics. It is not empirical, not the sum of its parts: it's the actions of its parts. If you try to take it apart to see how it works, it doesn't.

A spontaneous order can be widely dispersed and enormously complex, far exceeding human capacity to design, manage, or fully comprehend. It employs individual bits of knowledge that are in each person's head, not accessible to anyone else, and exist nowhere as a whole. It utilizes these disparate bits of information more efficiently than authority can, because government can only draw on the information, skills, and energy individuals choose to offer in pursuit of interests other than their own. When a person acts in his interests, he uses all the information he can access, so the greatest possible portion of all the knowledge possessed by an order is utilized. The exchange of ideas that would otherwise remain abstract and unconnected leads individuals and their nations to prosper in loose proportion to the degree of liberty they are allowed.

In addition to ideas, people exchange goods and services. Individuals trade their labor for money, which they trade for services and finished products. They trade based on their desires, and on availability and prices, each always adapting to perpetually changing circumstances. Each person weighs the cost of a product against its value to him and uses his dollars like votes. Separately, each has freedom of choice; collectively, they determine which products and services survive, forming another spontaneous order: the free market.

Market forces—self-interested individuals forming a self-correcting body of knowledge—also play a part in science, technology, communications, and medicine. In each, a useful heritage exists, information is shared, discoveries are made, innovations crop up, and the most fitting of them become part of the body of knowledge for the next generation.[100] An element of self-interest—recognition—entices competing scientists to publish their discoveries, parts of which are used by others to make other discoveries. Each compares his work to the known body of work, feeling his way along, working on a different part of the same jigsaw puzzle.[101] Clutter is minimized because they don't share work in progress, just results.[102] Each researcher acts independently and for himself, but because they communicate and share a common underlying purpose—a quest for comprehension and efficiency—understanding evolves.

Culture and common law are also forms of spontaneous order. Man did not preconceive and then intentionally construct our customs and rules any more than he premeditated and managed his biological development. The sifting was not done by natural selection but by survival of the fittest *traditions*. Cultural evolution takes far less time than biological evolution because gradations of change take place all through life rather than once per generation, but both are undirected processes of continual adaption, and the result of each is, what works survives and what doesn't doesn't. We have the customs and laws of interaction that we do because they served our predecessors well.

Practices spring up; if they work, they spread, creating customs, some of which generate rules. Rules evolved hand-in-hand with civilization long before governments existed. Much later, lawmakers discerned the rules by observing people in their unsupervised dealings with one another. Wide consistencies were noted and shaped into legal concepts and finally written law. Common law is the articulation of naturally occurring rules of interaction. It does not come from outside or above the existing order, but from what has seemed equitable and workable in the past.

Whereas *statutes* are enacted by legislatures and *regulations* are made by executive branch agencies pursuant to a grant of authority by a legislature, *common law* arises from court decisions. It is made by judges in their resolution of disputes, a by-product of their quest for equivalence. A court decision not only resolves a particular conflict, but many others because it informs, allowing individuals to consider the consequences of their actions beforehand. For a judge to create law, a case must come before him, and the only way a case gets to court is if there is a disagreement, so common law cannot spring from what an individual does within his four walls nor from any situation in which all participation is voluntary and there is no dispute. Before ruling, a judge considers traditions of right and wrong, constitutional principles, pertinent laws, and what experience tells him are the reasonable expectations of individuals.[103] Any new ruling must fill a gap in the body of existing law while remaining consistent with it. Proper common law must fit like a missing strut in the structure of existing rules. Scandium, gallium, germanium, and hafnium are chemical elements whose existence was predicted by the periodic table before they were discovered. This process—intuiting that something should exist in a currently empty spot within a known structure—suggests how judges "find" common law. It is not so much invented as discovered.[104]

Common law is unrelated to particular aims of government. It commands nothing; it referees. It is objective and abstract. Common law has no means to discriminate because it makes no references to any particular groups.[105] It is passive, constant, and lasting. It embodies long experience and rests on widely diffuse but altogether overwhelming opinion; few dispute its rationale or necessity.

Nature gave each individual a life and made each an end in himself. If coerced, he is reduced to a component in someone else's plan. In providing for the punishment of individuals who harm, coerce, or defraud, common law secures each person's right to life.

("Harm" includes harassment, defamation, and discrimination, but not competition, criticism, or rudeness.) *Spontaneous order yields common law, which secures the right to life, which is the source of the other four rights.*

Violations of the Right to Life

The right to life has generally been well protected by government. Crime is taken seriously, especially violent crime. Laws are enforced against assault, battery, armed robbery, rape, and murder, and against property crimes like fraud and vandalism. Regarding *government* violations of the individual's right to life, two are noteworthy, one of which is now defunct: a military draft.

Conscription was practiced in ancient Greece and Rome. France restarted the draft in 1789 and created the greatest army in Europe, first under the Assembly and then under Napoleon. During the nineteenth century, every major nation followed France's example, including the United States during the Civil War, both North and South. In the North, the first US draft provoked major riots in which thirty-eight conscription officials were murdered.[106]

The most recent reincarnation of the US draft lasted for thirty years, from 1940 to 1970, the latter being a bad year to be a young man in America. In 1970, the US government drafted 162,746 men to fight in an extremely unpopular war, generally men who didn't have the connections to get a deferment.[107] Though no one was conscripted to fight in the recent Iraq war, tens of thousands of reservists were called up, and many of those who served felt like they had been drafted when Uncle Sam used "stop loss" orders to prevent them from leaving the military when their service contracts were completed, forcing them to serve against their will from that point.

After the Vietnam War, Congress replaced the draft with an all-volunteer army. Other nations with all-volunteer armies include Australia, Canada, Japan, and the United Kingdom, but here in the United States, a draft is always within months of resurrection if needed. The Supreme Court has consistently upheld government's right to compel military service, and by law men must register with the Selective Service System within thirty days of their eighteenth birthday. Those who refuse face denial of financial aid for college and denial of government employment, and some states are considering withholding diplomas and driver's licenses. During the Vietnam years, more than fifty thousand Americans fled the draft to Canada. President Carter pardoned them in 1977, but half stayed there. Laws have changed since then. Should a draft ever be reinstated, Canada would no longer be a viable option for most draft-age men. Nor is the National Guard a way to avoid active combat anymore. It was heavily called on to fight in Iraq; in 2005, National Guard soldiers comprised 45 percent of all troops in Iraq, a far greater percentage than in any previous war. Another consideration: any reinstitution of the draft could include women.[108]

A military draft is the surest way to build a fighting force, but it has a big disadvantage. Because people fear for their loved ones and every family has someone who could be affected, drafting young people creates mass dissent for whatever action is being considered. It precipitates protest, which helps to unify opposition to the administration and can undermine foreign policy. Conscription also enables military adventurism. Volunteers, being able to say no, prod a nation to use its military might more judiciously, making it harder to wage wars of opportunity. People are quicker to enlist when the cause is truly that of defense.

A military draft is wrong. It is forced servitude. It is confiscation of a person's time and labor, the severest of government intrusions into the life of the individual, antithetical to a government formed to protect rights. The person unlucky enough to be drafted faces three dreadful choices. He can go to war and kill people or possibly be maimed or killed himself. He can choose to accept the consequences of refusing and face a prison sentence. Or he can seek a way of avoiding or evading the draft, which is dishonorable and often dishonest. A military draft violates the individual's right to life by forcing him to serve the State.

Today, with no military draft, government violations of an individual's right to life usually involve police or prosecutors abusing their authority. When a suspect does not have the mental capacity or strength of will to avoid manipulation, police can extract false confessions that lead to wrongful imprisonments. In Broward County, Florida, police extracted a false confession from Anthony Caravella.

He was convicted on charges of rape and murder, imprisoned as a fifteen-year-old mentally challenged boy, and after being exonerated by DNA evidence, released from prison as a forty-one-year-old man with no marketable skills. Also in Broward County, another mentally challenged man, Jerry Frank Townsend, served twenty-two years for a crime he didn't commit before being released on DNA evidence.[109] In Douglas County, Colorado, police searching for a sexual predator reported as being over forty and stocky arrested a man named Tyler Sanchez, though he was nineteen and thin. Two sets of male DNA were found on the victim's underwear, and neither of them matched Sanchez, but the prosecution went forward anyway because Sanchez, who was mentally disabled and hearing impaired, had confessed to the crime after thirty-eight hours of interrogation, repeating to detectives the details of the case that they had endlessly repeated to him.[110]

After seventeen hours of being held in custody and questioned in New York City, Ozem Goldwire, an autistic man, confessed to killing his sister although he didn't commit the crime. He spent a year in Rikers Island before being released.[111] In North Carolina, Greg Taylor spent seventeen years in prison for a murder he didn't commit because a crime lab analyst led jurors to believe that a substance found in Taylor's truck was human blood, though the analyst had done tests that showed otherwise.[112] Curtis McGhee and Terry Harrington were found guilty in the murder of a retired police officer in Council Bluffs, Iowa, and served twenty-five years in prison because Iowa prosecutors had falsified evidence to influence testimony against them.[113] The state of Texas has paid damages in forty-five wrongful-conviction cases, twenty-two of which involved prosecutors withholding evidence from the defense.[114] Prosecutors who withhold evidence to get a conviction are almost never prosecuted. Most don't even lose their jobs.[115]

When there are overzealous police or prosecutors involved, an accusation need not be credible to ruin a life. A girl in Washington State, Donna Perez, told her foster father, Detective Robert Perez, that she had been molested or raped by dozens of people, including most of the adults she knew. Donna pointed out twenty-two locations where the molestations had occurred. She accused passers-by of the crimes, including several homeless people. She also claimed that many of her friends had been molested. Forty-three adults were arrested on 29,726 charges of child abuse involving sixty children. Many were accused of abusing their own kids. When a local pastor criticized the investigation, he was arrested and charged with eleven counts of the sexual abuse of a child. Though prosecutors were unable to supply any physical evidence to support the charges and the main investigator in the case was the foster father of the main witness, many of those charged went to jail because they were homeless, mentally handicapped, or so frightened that guilty pleas could be extracted from them. Ultimately, higher courts overturned every conviction, but not before five of the people had served their full sentences and many had lost their parental rights.[116]

Ed Jagels, a well-known and respected California district attorney, built his reputation on the Kern County child molestation cases of the 1980s, but of the twenty-six convictions Jagels secured, twenty-five were overturned.[117] Kern County has paid nearly $10 million to settle suits brought by those wrongly imprisoned.[118] How did twenty-five innocent people get sent to jail, several for ten years or more? Apparently through instructed child witnesses and persuasive hyperbole. Though appellate judges now say the Kern County sex crimes never happened, witnesses testified that the molesters drank blood and hung children from hooks after forcing them to have sex with their parents.[119] Brandon Smith, a child witness who was sent to a foster home after his parents were incarcerated for sex crimes he testified they committed, later said, "They basically coached me to say that my parents had sexually abused me."[120] His testimony caused his parents to each serve twelve years on molestation charges before a reversal by an appeals court. Said Brandon, "We've put it all behind us, but the one thing I would love is a verbal apology from Ed Jagels for tearing my family apart."[121] Around the time of his retirement, Jagels instead echoed the sentiments of many police, prosecutors, and district attorneys, saying, "If California prisons are overcrowded it's not because we have too many people in prison. It's because we don't have enough prisons."[122]

Police can violate an individual's right to life by using force needlessly. At least twenty men were tortured into confessions by the Chicago Police Department between 1973 and 1991. One of the men, Michael Tillman, was released in 2010 after twenty-three years of imprisonment for a rape and murder he didn't commit. Tillman had confessed after being asphyxiated with a plastic bag and beaten with a telephone book over a three-day period in 1986. Torture was apparently common within that division, known as Area 2. Another victim, Andrew Wilson, was admitted to the hospital after receiving at least a dozen injuries while in police custody, including lacerations to the face and head, chest bruises, and second-degree burns to his thighs. Other defendants claimed they had been had been beaten, cut, shocked, and burned with cigarettes. The People's Law Office documented 110 such cases; 12 men have been released. Four died in prison. In 2008, the Chicago City Council approved a $19.8 million settlement with four of the men who were pardoned.[123]

During the same period, it was also the policy of the Chicago Police Department to arrest and strip-search women for minor traffic violations or misdemeanors like disorderly conduct. According to Ellen Alderman and Caroline Kennedy in *The Right to Privacy*, a thirty-two-year-old woman who had just graduated from medical school was on her way to the Chicago Art Institute with her sister when they got pulled over. Because the driver had outstanding parking tickets, she was taken to the women's lockup across town, where she was subjected to a strip-search and body-cavity search while matrons at the lockup humiliated her, mimicking her cries of disbelief at her treatment. In another instance, Chicago police stopped two women and a man for not displaying the proper registration stickers. When the driver, Mary, tried to explain that it was a borrowed car, the officer arrested all three for disorderly conduct. At the lock-up, while witnessing Lillian, the other woman, being strip-searched, Mary testified that the matron "snatched Lillian's clothes down and shoved her. Then this lady put her hand all the way up inside Lillian. She didn't even wear a glove. I kept telling her she didn't have to do that and to stop. The more I yelled, the more [the matron] kept saying, 'You just better shut up because your turn is coming.' She told me she was going to do the same thing to me and that she was going to let the policemen watch if I didn't cooperate."[124]

Hundreds of women in the Chicago area reported similar stories. Chicago's arrest-and-strip-search policy applied only to women. Men in similar circumstances were subjected to a "pat-down" search. The ACLU filed a class action suit on behalf of the women, charging that the policy violated the Fourth Amendment's guarantee against unreasonable searches and the Fourteenth Amendment's guarantee of equality before the law. Though the city of Chicago disagreed that the policy was unconstitutional, it agreed to change it.[125]

Husband and wife Quinn and Cara Kronen were teachers at New York City's New School for the Arts and Sciences. They were teaching English and social studies, respectively, when a fight broke out in the girls' bathroom. They helped get it under control. Six students were involved, and one was injured. Cara called 911 to get medical attention. When the police arrived, the students had been separated and things were back to normal, but the police demanded to know which students were involved and handcuffed them. When Quinn said he thought that was unnecessary, a police sergeant yelled that he had better "shut the fuck up" or she would arrest him too, and then she did. When Cara protested that Quinn had done nothing wrong, the sergeant said, "That's it—cuff the bitch," and arrested her too in front of their students. The two spent hours under arrest, and both were charged with disorderly conduct. The charges were dismissed at arraignment.[126]

Reverend James Manship, the pastor of a New Haven Catholic church, tried to videotape police officers using excessive force on an Ecuadorean family in their grocery store. Though the tape shows an officer asking, "Is there a reason you have a camera on me?" the police arrested and charged Father Manship with disorderly conduct because they reported he was holding "an unknown shiny silver object."[127]

Shortly after the opening of the Rainbow Lounge, a gay bar in Fort Worth, Texas, six police officers and two liquor control agents used excessive force in a raid in which twenty-six-year-old Chad Gibson suffered a concussion, a hairline fracture to his skull, and internal bleeding after officers slammed his head into a wall and then the floor. Another patron received broken ribs, and a third, a broken thumb. One customer said that the police "were hyped up. They came in charged and ready for a fight. They were just telling people they were drunk, or asking them if they were drunk, and, if they mouthed off, arresting them."[128]

In Austin, in response to a report that children were throwing stones at cars, police chased the children into the lot of an adjacent apartment building, using pepper spray on them. Said resident Tammy Roberts, "They were beating kids with billy clubs." When another resident, Phyllis Williams, asked why police were detaining one eleven-year-old boy, they shoved her in the chest and told her to back up. She protested; they sprayed her, arrested her, and charged her with hindering apprehension and evading arrest. The same with other adults. The people in the building were defending the eleven-year-old because he had multiple sclerosis and was mentally handicapped.[129]

US Customs officials sometimes go too far. When reentering the United States after visiting relatives in Canada, Akif Rahman, a native-born American citizen and owner of a Chicago software firm, was bodily searched with excessive force, kicked, and shackled to a chair for three hours in the Detroit-Windsor tunnel. It was a case of misidentification—the *fifth* time for Mr. Rahman in less than two years.[130]

Use of excessive force most commonly occurs when an officer uses a Taser without sufficient cause. According to a *Sixty Minutes* investigation, Tasers have been used on more than 1.5 million individuals. They are used by more than 16,000 law enforcement agencies in the United States. More than 500,000 officers are armed with Tasers, and police who don't have them "are clamoring for them."[131]

A Taser is an electroshock weapon that incapacitates by causing painful involuntary muscle contractions. It fires two electrodes, propelled by small compressed nitrogen charges, which pierce the skin like darts. To prevent removal once lodged in place, they are barbed. They deliver an electric shock potent enough to interrupt the brain's ability to control the body's muscles, which seize up, causing uncontrollable spasms and an incapacitation that cannot be overcome.

Tasers can be dangerous. The high voltage they produce can cause cardiac arrhythmia, leading to heart attacks and sometimes death. They can impair breathing and respiration, and the effects can be increased by adrenaline or drugs in the bloodstream. Other drugs can diminish the stun effect, prompting police to tase someone more than once, and repeated use can kill. Tasers can also cause injury (including serious spinal injuries) as the person falls. Authorities claim that the Taser is a humane use of force, but it's hard to believe after you've seen someone lurching in pain as they collapse. Michael Todd, chief constable of Greater Manchester Police, England, agreed to be tased to demonstrate that they were safe and not inhumane. After the trial, he said, "I couldn't move. It hurt like hell.... I wouldn't want to do that again."[132] Police officers in at least five states have filed suit against the manufacturer, Taser International, claiming they suffered serious injury after being shocked with the device during training classes.[133]

Tasers are less lethal than handguns, but their effectiveness and ease of use can promote police to use them too quickly, often in cases in which they would never have fired a handgun or used a billy club. Police can use them in traffic stops and in responses to complaints of noise or nuisance. In 2007, police in Jacksonville, Florida, pulled over Christian Allen because his radio was too loud. He jumped out of the car and ran. An officer gave chase, caught Allen, and tased him at least three times. Allen later died in custody.[134] The following year, police tased Baron Pikes nine times, and six of the shocks were administered within three minutes of one another. Pikes's death was ruled a homicide by the medical examiner. During a routine traffic stop, Robert Mitchell, a five-foot, two-inch, 110-pound sixteen-year-old with a learning disability, fled the vehicle. He was tased and died.[135] After police were called to a YMCA in Minneapolis, they tased David Smith, twenty-eight, for refusing to leave. Smith died.[136] In 2011, Dale Burns, twenty-seven, started to vomit after being tased three times. He was taken to the hospital and pronounced dead soon afterwards.[137] In Lake Arrowhead, California, Allen Kephart was pulled over for running a stop sign. According to police, he became combative and forced them to tase him several times, after which he died. Residents of the town doubted the official story since it was wholly out of character for Kephart, who had no criminal record or history of aggressive behavior and was universally known as a person who never lost his temper.[138]

Some Tasers have a "Drive Stun" setting, in which no projectiles are fired. Instead, police activate the Taser and then hold it against a person's body, which causes pain but does not incapacitate the subject. Compliance is sought through pain alone. A study of US police and sheriff departments found that 30 percent of them allowed this technique for gaining compliance in a passive resistance scenario, one in which there is no physical contact between the officer and the subject.[139] "Pain compliance" is a euphemism for torture, which at times has apparently been the goal. Maurice Cunningham, an inmate at South Carolina's Lancaster County Detention Center, was subjected to continuous shock for two minutes, forty-nine seconds. The medical examiner said the experience caused cardiac arrhythmia and Cunningham's subsequent death.[140]

In 2007, the United Nations concluded that using a Taser on someone constituted a form of torture,[141] and to date, 445 people have died after being tased.[142]

Crimes without Intent

In accordance with each person's right to life, criminal law is only supposed to apply when there is *mens rea*, an evil intent, but with so many rules, criminality can be hard to avoid. You can commit a crime by making a mistake or using questionable judgment with regard to bookkeeping, tax filing, bidding on government contracts, stock trading, banking, hiring and firing, privacy law, filling a prescription, or losing your temper.

Omnipresent regulation makes it possible to commit a crime while home asleep in bed. If you are required to file a form with the EPA and forget, and then the midnight deadline passes, it could constitute a crime. Negligence is another way. Say you're putting in a swimming pool and the digging has created a mound of earth. It storms during the night and water runs off of it, flooding your neighbor's basement. You are liable for the damage. Another way: you're an officer of a corporation home asleep when someone in your employ violates an environmental law. You can be charged and convicted under the "responsible corporate officer doctrine." It happened to a man in Alaska: Edward Hanousek Jr. was sentenced to six months in prison when a backhoe operator working for him accidentally ruptured an oil pipeline.[143]

In passing countless laws written in ambiguous statutory language, the federal government has given prosecutors the means to transgress an individual's right to life *within* the parameters of the law. For example, prosecutors can use the criminal justice system to cow citizens. Prosecutors have broad discretion in deciding who to indict. They can choose their cases and interpret malleable laws to fit their purposes. They can pick a highly visible person, charge him with a crime, disrupt his life, humiliate him, and sometimes imprison him as an example to all others of what happens to people who go too far. That the person chosen is scarcely guilty of a crime makes him that much more relatable and instills more fear.

Federal prosecutors can credibly threaten long incarceration. Convictions for violating federal law, which often applies in cases involving drugs or white-collar crime, carry long sentences. According to respected attorney Harvey A. Silverglate in *Three Felonies a Day,* they can use wiretaps, surreptitious tapings, and confidential informants. They can charge mail fraud, wire fraud, securities fraud, or racketeering. They can employ dual or multiple prosecutions. They have the means to pierce attorney-client privilege by indicting attorneys. They can threaten criminal charges to force individuals to testify against friends, family, or business partners. Prosecutors can question endlessly, take hundreds of hours of depositions, and under the federal false statement statute, any white lie, omission, misstatement, or contradiction can bring charges of obstruction of justice and a sentence of up to twenty years.[144]

To avoid the risk of being found guilty and receiving an odious sentence, even when that risk is low, defendants may be forced to plead guilty to "reduced" charges. Then there is the shaming of the defendant. If you ever find yourself forced to confess to a minor crime, be prepared to grovel and show remorse. If you claim that you weren't really at fault or that you were railroaded, all you'll do is lengthen your sentence. This has nothing to do with protecting people's rights; it is government showing the individual, and all who are watching, who is in charge.

Michael Milken was a wildly successful financial entrepreneur and also the symbol of the "decade of greed," as some called the 1980s. Everyone knew Milken was guilty. Otherwise, how could one man earn $550 million in one year trading in bonds? Even wealthy people found the amount unconscionable. But no one could say what Milken did that was illegal. Unlike Dennis Levine or Ivan Boesky, there was no evidence that Milken had committed any clear violation of securities laws. One of the men who prosecuted Milken, Rudolph Giuliani's assistant US attorney, John Carroll, acknowledged that many of the prosecution's theories had to be novel because Milken's actions had never before been considered unlawful. He noted that the prosecutors, including him, were looking "to find the next areas of conduct that meet any sort of statutory definition of what criminal conduct is."[145] Though Milken's guilt was questionable, the press skewered him. One writer called his company "the Cosa Nostra of the securities world."[146]

Milken was indicted on ninety-eight counts of securities fraud and racketeering. To further pressure him, the prosecution threatened to indict his younger brother Lowell. Embattled, Milken finally agreed to plead guilty to six counts that were not part of the ninety-eight-count package but were acceptable to both sides. He pleaded guilty to "stock parking," though a technical violation, a practice that was not unusual in the securities industry and hadn't been prosecuted as a crime. Regardless, Judge Kimba Wood sentenced Milken to ten years in prison (later reduced to two). Milken's real crime, felt many observers, was unabashedly earning $550 million in one year as a trader.[147]

Say you own stock in a publicly traded company. It's a very small holding, comprising less than 1 percent of your net worth. Your broker calls and tells you he just heard that the company's CEO is dumping his personal stock. The broker doesn't know why but finds it suspicious and asks you if you want to sell yours. You think about it for a moment and say, yeah, go ahead and sell. This is precisely what Martha Stewart did; she was sentenced to five months in prison and another five under house arrest for it. Four days after Stewart received the telephone call from her broker and sold her shares, the stock in question, Imclone, dropped 18 percent in one day when it was announced that the FDA had disapproved the company's major product, an anti-cancer drug called Erbitux. Imclone's CEO, Samuel Waksal, who had dumped his shares, was charged and convicted of insider trading in a clear-cut case. Martha Stewart was not an insider—she was not an officer of the company and had no information about its inner workings or why the CEO had sold, but Stewart was worried. She was the wealthy, famous founder and CEO of her own publicly traded company, Martha Stewart Living Omnimedia, and feared a scandal. She was afraid that what she did *might* have constituted insider trading, so, when questioned, she lied to prosecutors about why she sold the stock—and that is what got her sent to jail. Her lie, to cover a noncriminal act, constituted a criminal act.[148] The Stewart affair brought glee to individuals who presume that all rich people are scoundrels.

Comedian Tommy Chong's son Paris ran an Internet company selling bongs, which was legal in forty-eight states. He asked his father to let him use his name for marketing purposes, and Chong Sr. agreed. They didn't know that the DEA was running two sting operations, facetiously entitled Operation Pipe Dreams and Operation Head Hunter, from Pennsylvania—one of the two states in which selling rolling papers, pipes, and bongs was illegal. DEA agents posing as Pittsburgh head shop owners pleaded with the Chongs to sell bongs and pipes to them. Knowing it was illegal, the Chongs repeatedly refused. The agents then promised to come and pick up the order in person, so the Chongs filled it, but the agents never showed up and went back to asking them to mail it. The Chongs again refused, but after eight months, they sent it. Federal agents with guns drawn arrested the whole family. Though Chong's son was the CEO of the company, the DEA went after Tommy Chong. Threatened with a long prison sentence if he fought, Chong pleaded guilty to one count of distributing drug paraphernalia. To keep his wife and son from being prosecuted, Chong also agreed to make antipot television ads in which he advised youths to replace marijuana with salsa dancing.[149] (Shaming?)

Chong was sentenced to nine months in prison. The government spent $12 million on his prosecution, using dubious tactics. The repeated requests for the bongs seemed to many to constitute entrapment. Why did the feds go after Chong Sr. rather than his son, the CEO of the company? Why did Tommy Chong receive a harsher sentence than other first-time arrestees for the same offense? The answers were suggested by court documentation that made specific references to Chong's movies, which featured stoners (often lampooning them) and ridiculed law enforcement, as a consideration in his punishment, a violation of his First Amendment rights. Nevertheless, it was a career-making case for the prosecutor, Mary Beth Buchanon, who was lauded for her work and promoted to director of US attorneys, the most powerful federal prosecutor in the nation. Chong, after being released from prison in Taft, California, where he met many others there on minor drug-related charges, became an activist for the first time in his life. After experiencing how easily anyone can be imprisoned when federal prosecutors choose to go after you, when asked what prison is like, Chong now answers, "You'll find out."[150]

To summarize the chapter, human interaction formed a spontaneous order, which does not require commands, but it does require individuals to refrain from injuring or stealing from one another, which is common law. If no one may harm, coerce, or defraud an individual, then the individual is complementarily protected by a right to life, from which all other rights spring. The right to life protects him from restraint or compulsion from others or from government. It precludes a military draft and prevents police and prosecutors from abusing their authority. Regardless, violations are not uncommon. The cases of Michael Milken, Martha Stewart, and Tommy Chong demonstrate that it's possible to be sent to prison for a trivial or unintentional infraction of the law.

CHAPTER 7
The Right to Liberty

Rules of Organization

Along with common law, a second kind of law restricts the liberty of individuals. Government makes *rules of organization* to facilitate order or to help maintain it on a larger scale. Such rules are required because common law, derived from one-to-one human interaction, does not provide for life en masse—for crowd control, public health and sanitation, transportation safety, emergency procedures, and long-term environmental considerations. A small group might not require these, but a nation does. Rules of organization are necessary struts supporting and extending the order. In prohibiting actions whose neighborhood effects interfere with other individuals' health or safety (their right to life), rules of organization prevent one person from endangering another against his will or without his knowledge. For example, a contractor might be tempted to take dangerous shortcuts to save money. Building codes prevent it. Polluting a stream creates neighborhood effects to the detriment of people downstream; pollution laws are rules of organization. A person may go barefoot on his property, but he loses that choice to health codes in public. He may drive a car, but he must obey the rules of the road. Driving drunk does not necessarily harm others but it directly endangers them, so a law prohibits it. Rules of organization restrict freedom of action in order to protect the rights and valid expectations of others.

A few make the argument that the extended order is not worth taking part in if it means sacrificing any liberties at all, but those who reject all rules of organization must also forgo all benefits of living among other people. Individuals who shun civilization have allowed their dislike of rules to grow into a psychological problem eclipsing their rationality. The wealthiest, most resourceful man on earth could not live as well alone on a desert island as a man earning minimum wage in America, demonstrating that it is not primarily money that provides the necessities and comforts of life; it is the interaction of individuals acting in their interests, the spontaneous order. Nature may seem a paradise, but being without central government is a miserable condition for human beings, as evidenced by the Dark Ages. Thomas Hobbes, writing after a long, bloody period of too *little* government, likened it to a perpetual state of war,[151] in which theft and violence were routine. Montesquieu and John Dickinson both observed that liberty was well described in the Holy Scriptures as a state "when every man shall sit under his vine, and under his fig-tree, and none shall make him afraid."[152] Liberty requires security, which requires both common law and rules of organization.

Rules of organization get made in every community, because they make too much sense not to get made. Good ones allow the greatest compatibility of aims with the least infringement on liberty and fit neatly into the lattice of existing rules. Rules of organization include those that allow government to structure itself and administer common law, rules of taxation, rules that establish required constructions and services, rules to protect public health and safety, and humanitarian efforts.

The scope of government activity and the corresponding burden of taxation are greater than foreseen by the founders, but there is an obvious need for government services and for them to be financed by taxation. Taxes are a sore spot for individuals who feel that their right to property protects them from having to contribute toward government expenditures they don't support. Their feeling is, why should we have to donate based on how someone else wants to spend money? But some sacrifice must be forced on all by government for the maintenance of the order, which means that at least one of the Five Rights must have some give somewhere. The right to property, through taxation, is where. If the majority knows the cost of a public construction or service and is willing to pay it, government can organize collective action and force all individuals to contribute. Tax-coercion is unavoidable because *not* coercing the minority to pay for something wanted by most people forces a standstill on every issue or forces the majority to shoulder the load for all, which violates the right to property and to equality of those in the majority. Tax-coercion of the minority is necessary to avoid worse coercion—that of the larger group by the smaller group. Taxation raises money to pay for common needs. Each individual works for himself but donates a portion of his work to help maintain acceptable ambient conditions.

Taxation does produce three justifiable complaints: different groups are taxed in different ways at different rates unequally under the law. Money is spent inappropriately: in addition to financing public requirements, tax dollars are used to impose government policy or to gain favor with professionally represented interests. And there is no effective way to limit total spending. Before the Depression, spending was curtailed by constitutional limits to lawmaking. When few actions of government were permitted, there was less to spend money on. Today, government can easily spend all it can raise and more.

Rules of organization are used to establish needed services not provided by market forces. When it is unworkable to charge the individual beneficiary of a service (military protection, police, or air purification, for example), the desired benefit cannot be provided by competitive enterprise, only by concerted effort financed by taxation. Tax dollars can be used to provide vital needs like fresh water and roads, or things that are widely desired like waste disposal and snow removal. Taxes can be used to build and maintain highways, bridges, dams, mass transit systems, and airports. Rules of organization created the Federal Reserve, the National Weather Center, NASA, and the Census Bureau. Rules of organization may be used to create libraries, museums, clinics, or public school systems without violating the rule of law, provided the advantages are available to all. Equal treatment does not mean that each individual will benefit equally—almost every measure will help some more than others—it means that every individual must be allowed the same opportunity to benefit. For example, public education is a greater benefit to a family with children of school age than one without them, but if the opportunity is extended to any children, it must be extended to all.

Rules of organization set public health and safety standards. Regulations may involve transportation, product safety, fire safety, sanitation, or crowd control. Also included are rules that require licensing or certification in professions of high responsibility (doctor, airline pilot), restrictions on the sale of dangerous goods (arms, explosives, toxic substances), and regulations regarding the disclosure of ingredients, purity, and production processes.

Rules of organization may be used for humanitarian efforts—to aid those who need help to survive, to alleviate suffering, or to help victims of severe misfortune. In the past, families were expected to take care of the ill or infirm, but since people have become more mobile and families less familiar, social legislation has become part of the culture. Every major government makes some allowance for individuals who cannot support themselves. Should it choose, an affluent nation could afford to provide a floor below which no individual for any reason is allowed to fall. A plan could be instituted constitutionally so long as it affords the same basic needs to all. A minimum level of individual deprivation could be approached as a single line item in the budget, like an insurance policy.[153] The United States does not provide such a floor, though it would likely cost less than maintaining hundreds of overlapping programs at different levels of government based on different criteria, so that some individuals become adept at exploiting multiple programs while others fall through the cracks. The United States could provide shelter, food, and emergency medical treatment to all who require them, but not while financing so many less basic needs. The current system of social legislation is not based on reason or morality, but on a hodgepodge of accumulated political ends.

Rules that attempt to benefit some individuals or groups at the expense of others generally fail because they attempt to rectify a problem impervious to rule changes. For example, individuals who have fared poorly often owe it not to unfair rules but to an inability to act in their interests. If a person is not acting in his interests, he will not likely do so under additional rules, including those favorable to him, and people who have taken advantage of current laws will likely do the same with new ones. Those who function within established rules and customs, or exploit them, rather than ignore or oppose them, will fare best in any case and will actually benefit from increased regulation relative to the rest. This is one reason why rules that seek to redress perceived inequity sometimes produce effects contrary to those intended.

Because every rule of organization costs money to implement and maintain, requiring tax-coercion, and some also employ command-coercion, the total number of rules of organization should be kept to a minimum. Each new rule leaves a bit less up to the individual to decide, and the accretion can eventually reduce him to a component in government's plans, which is why each proposed rule should be scrutinized. Does it violate anyone's rights? Is it workable, enforceable, compatible with human nature? What alternatives are there for people affected by the law? Can it be implemented without disrupting market forces? Is it worth the long-term cost to the order? A rule of organization should not appear just sensible but *essential*. People invented government to provide conditions in which they could live among themselves free of coercion. A government that too easily employs coercion defeats this purpose.

Wrote Adam Smith, "The man of system ... seems to imagine that he can arrange the different members of a great society with as much ease as the hand arranges the different pieces upon a chessboard. He does not consider that the pieces upon the chessboard have no other principle of motion besides that which the hand impresses upon them; but that, in the great chessboard of human society, every single piece has a principle of motion of its own, altogether different from that which the legislature might choose to impress upon it. If those two principles coincide and act in the same direction, the game of society will go on easily and harmoniously, and is very likely to be happy and successful. If they are opposite or different, the game will go on miserably and the society must be at all times in the highest degree of disorder."[154]

Proponents of more government are unable to conceive of order that is not deliberately imposed by man, unable to comprehend the degree to which self-serving actions can mutually coordinate to serve general purposes.[155] Authoritarians and anthropomorphics are driven to "fix" it according to their views. Proper rules of organization define boundaries already suggested by tradition or common law, but they can only augment spontaneous order and not replace it because spontaneous order is a result. Attempting to alter a result without regard for the cause of it is ineffectual, like trying to improve the efficiency of a business by altering its financial records.

It seems like rules of organization should work fine: identify a problem and then make a law that limits people's behavior in a way that helps resolve it. In practice, though, making rules to achieve a particular result frequently fails because each new law promotes all parties close to the matter to adapt and to exploit unexpected consequences. To block that exploitation, more rules are required, whose consequences are exploited and so on. Any new law can initiate a rivulet of them. Government can make rules, but it can't control how they will blend with people's circumstances and priorities to give rise to a new environment. (Note that human responses to laws, rather than the laws themselves, determine the characteristics of an order. For example, prosperity cannot be commanded, but it can result from the voluntary, self-interested action of individuals within a framework of rules conceived to elicit self-interested action.)

Privacy and Self

For there to be liberty, there must be someplace where free action cannot be prohibited by rules of organization. Someplace *not* public. Otherwise, there is nowhere for a person to exercise his right to liberty without being regulated out of that right. According to the Supreme Court, the Fourteenth Amendment's guarantees include "a realm of personal liberty which the government may not enter."[156] This is the protected sphere, the insular area formed around an individual when all others honor his rights. Within his sphere, the individual may match his actions to his will; he cannot violate common law but he may not be forced to serve the ends of another or of government.

The protected sphere has two parts. The outer sphere is private property. The inner sphere is the physical body—everything from the skin and hair in. As a property owner is free to do what he likes with his property, each person is free to do as he chooses with his body, it being his most intimate and inalienable property.

The right to privacy safeguards the protected sphere. The Supreme Court has recognized two kinds of privacy: the right to make fundamental decisions for one's self without undue interference, and the right to keep personal information confidential. The first covers decisions like contraception, abortion, and where to educate children; the second covers the privacy of mail, telephone conversations, and medical records. According to the Court, "privacy" includes all personal rights that are "implicit in the concept of ordered liberty."[157]

Privacy is voluntary separation from other people that limits their access to you or to information about you. Though the word "privacy" appears nowhere in the Constitution, the First Amendment, in guaranteeing freedom of assembly and association, allows individuals to gather as they choose and thus implies the right to exclude. If you are free to consort with people of your choice, then you must be free to decline to consort with some. Hence, privacy is a right constitutionally guaranteed by the First Amendment. The Fourth Amendment pertains to privacy in that it bans unreasonable searches. The Fifth and Fourteenth Amendments uphold unenumerated rights to privacy that have been recognized by the Supreme Court, which include the right to select a mate, to have a family, to choose an occupation, to prevent a pregnancy, to terminate a conception, and to seek medical treatment or end one's life by refusing treatment. When the Court identifies a right, it receives the protection of the Fourteenth Amendment's guarantee of liberty. Giving meaning to "liberty" by specifying unenumerated rights one at a time is what puts the substance in substantive due process. Generally accepted rights become legal rights, while "liberty" becomes better defined.

A right to privacy was first enunciated in 1877 when the Supreme Court found that opening mail constituted a search because it violated an individual's "reasonable expectation of privacy."[158] In 1891, the Court recognized privacy of the body or "inviolability of the person."[159] During the 1920s, the Court ruled that the right to privacy included the freedom to choose where to send children to school. In striking down a Georgia obscenity law, the Court ruled that the individual has the "right to satisfy his intellectual and emotional needs in the privacy of his own home"[160] and "the right to be free from state inquiry into the contents of his library."[161] In *Whalen v. Roe* (1977), the Court established that personal medical data was private. And Congress passed the Video Privacy Act, which prevented individuals from learning and publicizing one another's video rentals and purchases.[162]

The Fourth Amendment, banning unreasonable searches, applies to violations of privacy by government only; it does not defend against violations by individuals, corporations, or private institutions. A recognized tort, invasion of privacy, is the main protection against intrusion by them. Invasion of privacy occurs when an individual's right to be let alone on his property is violated by trespassing, peeking through windows, using binoculars or remote surveillance, or publishing personal information improperly. Invasion-of-privacy cases have included a business that publicized a customer's debt and a television station that broadcast a dying man's last moments against the family's will.[163] For private information to be publishable, it's supposed to be accurate, newsworthy, and according to the Supreme Court, not "highly offensive to a reasonable person,"[164] but unless an invasion-of-privacy tort pertains to private information used very inappropriately, it quickly bumps up against the First Amendment rights of the publisher.

Privacy can refer to solitude. People prefer to do some things alone: bathe, inspect or prepare their bodies, or recuperate from illness, for example. Solitude protects dignity and invites reflection, allowing a person to reconcile new information with accumulated knowledge. Sometimes a person feels like withdrawing without being able to give a conscious reason for it. Other times he may want to avoid others to escape their expectations and judgments. In public, the individual must consider the impression he's making; privacy allows release. If all the men and women are merely players, they can stop acting when alone.

Privacy can refer to intimacy. Sharing thoughts with one person or two allows minimum self-editing. "A friend is someone before ... [whom] ... I can think aloud," wrote Emerson.[165] Intimacy allows low-guard communication because a person's friends indulge him. He can be pedantic, profane, defeatist, prideful, or childishly exuberant; he might criticize people he cares about, omit information, contradict himself, or gossip. Familiarity allows people to say things they don't really mean. Friends accept one another anyway. When lonely, or in need of help to get through grief or heartache, or to celebrate a happy moment, we seek out intimates.

Whereas solitude and intimacy require having few people around, another kind of privacy, anonymity, can depend on being able to lose one's self in the crowd. Anonymity can be freeing. It allows experimentation. It permits a person to investigate other cultures or lifestyles without causing a stir or damaging a reputation. An anonymous person can attend a rock concert, scream at a hockey game, try to meet sexual partners, or buy birth control products because strangers don't know his story and don't care about it. He is identified by others as a fellow human being and accorded the requisite courtesies, but he is not recognized as any particular person and does not have to fit any established character. For this reason, anonymity can be empowering. When teens attend spring break, each is one among many, anonymous, and it feels to them like escape from standing disapproval. In *My Own Country*, Tennessee doctor Abraham Verghese described how gay men leave their home towns and move to large cities in order to live their lives more openly and find freedom in being surrounded by large numbers of diverse people.[166] Janna Smith observed that anonymity also allows individuals to release "incorrect but genuine" feelings—ones they would be ashamed of.[167]

Privacy can also mean confidentiality: the right to keep secrets, to *not* offer information. Confidentiality may be required pending completion of a scientific inquiry or business deal, to surprise someone, to avoid publicity or harassment, or to keep a medical condition quiet. Confidentiality is important in growing a relationship. When strangers talk, each assesses the other, constantly updating the assessments. They feel one another out. Once they become acquainted, they see one another's flaws in the context of their full character, but early on, each is more prone to notice faults and evaluations can be harsh. During the time it takes for commonalities to surface and mutual grudging to give way to mutual regard, discretion reduces misconceptions and awkward disagreements by allowing each person to reveal information about himself as he chooses—which particular things when.

Gays who choose not to reveal their sexual orientation to the general public may still have most to lose when their privacy is violated. Neel Lattimore, who had been Hillary Clinton's press secretary, had revealed only to close friends that he was gay when he was outed on national television by Paula Jones's spokeswoman, Susan Carpenter-McMillan, who accused a male writer of having an affair with him. Lattimore watched the most personal part of his life being discussed on *Meet the Press*. He said it was an "out of body experience. You want to breathe but you can't think about how to bring air back into your lungs again ... it's like watching a storm destroy your house when you're not in it."[168] When Sara Jane Moore tried to assassinate President Gerald Ford in 1975, a Marine named Oliver Sipple saved the president's life by striking Moore's arm just before she fired. The *San Francisco Chronicle* ran a story containing implications that Sipple was gay. Sipple sued for invasion of privacy but lost on the court's dubious assertion that Sipple's sexual orientation was part of the story. The article led to Sipple's estrangement from his family and to depression. Tragically, he committed suicide.[169]

No right is absolute, including the right to privacy. At times, competing interests may overrule it. Reporters need to be able to offer facts, employers need to be allowed to run their businesses, and police need to be able to investigate crimes. Here is how the right to privacy has been interpreted in the courts.

Freedom of Association

Liberty includes the freedom to associate with whom one chooses by mutual consent, to come together or remain apart, and to exclude third parties. The Supreme Court has recognized two kinds of associations: intimate and expressive. Intimate associations include family, friendships, dating, and marriage. Freedom of personal association lets you befriend or avoid whomever you wish. It lets you choose who to invite to your wedding.

Expressive associations include the Boy Scouts, the PTA, the AMA, the Green Party, the Sierra Club, the Red Cross, women's gyms, the YMCA, the NAACP, and gay pride parades. They are so designated because they promote a point of view. Hotels, restaurants, and other businesses that serve the general public are subject to antidiscrimination law, but the organizers of an association can exclude at will. Were it not so, every group would have to accept opponents, undermining its purpose. Freedom of association allows like-minded people to join to promote their common interests and goals. They can meet, form clubs, support causes, start businesses, establish colleges, organize charities, establish sports leagues, demonstrate, and picket. Freedom of association permits small but thoughtful opinions to gather support. In *NAACP v. Alabama* (1958), the Court upheld the right of individuals to assemble anonymously, without which, neither blacks in the South nor gays would have been able to organize a political movement toward equal rights.[170] The civil rights movement owes much of its progress to freedom of association.[171]

Searches

The Fourth Amendment requires that searches by authority be reasonable, which means that probable cause is required and that the invasiveness of the search not exceed its importance. Authorities must have a specific reason for violating privacy. The Court has stated that at "the very core of the Fourth Amendment stands the right of a man to retreat into his home,"[172] adding that "to withdraw protection of this minimum expectation would be to permit police technology to erode the privacy guaranteed by the Fourth Amendment."[173] The Court has tried to maintain the level of privacy established when the Fourth Amendment was adopted, so it has prohibited electronic snooping. Other than line-of-sight enhancements, technology that allows people outside the house to learn what is going on inside constitutes a search and requires a warrant. The Court recognizes that if the individual's "reasonable expectation of privacy" is to be maintained, it must be the principle of probable cause rather than the contest between walls and technology that determines the perimeter of the protected sphere.

An officer in the Oregon National Guard suspected Danny Lee Kyllo of growing marijuana in his house. The officer used a thermal-imaging device to measure the amount of heat coming from Kyllo's house, compared it to those of neighbors, and found that it was warmer. He suspected that the heat was coming from grow lights for the plants. A warrant was issued on the basis of the higher temperature. Kyllo was arrested and charged. Kyllo challenged the use of the thermal-imaging device as an unreasonable search, but an appellate court ruled against him. In *Kyllo v. United States* (2001), however, the Supreme Court reversed, ruling that the use of a thermal-imaging device to ascertain what is going on inside a house constitutes a search and cannot be done without a warrant.[174]

Several data-gathering methods don't require a warrant because they don't constitute a search, such as use of binoculars, a telescope, a night scope, or an overhead view from a helicopter. Taking fingerprints and voiceprints are not considered searches. Requests by government agencies to inspect your telephone or bank records do not constitute searches. A caseworker's surprise visit to the home of a family on public assistance requires no warrant. No warrant is needed when there are exigent circumstances, which means in an emergency or when a crime is in progress. A person under arrest can be searched and any evidence found can be used against him even if it's unrelated to the crime for which he was arrested. No warrant is needed when there is a "compelling interest" to the government, as with metal detectors at airports or auto emissions tests. As part of the War on Drugs, the US Border Patrol does not need a warrant to search a vehicle within one hundred miles of the Mexican border. Police need no warrant to stop and frisk someone since a frisk requires only reasonable suspicion, a lower standard than probable cause. Evidence in plain view does not require a warrant. And garbage or trash set out for collection can be searched without a warrant.

Due to the War on Drugs, privacy rights in a car are now minimal. In *Whren v. U.S.* (1996), the Supreme Court ruled that police can stop and search a car if they have any suspicion whatsoever that it contains contraband.[175] Lamented Justice Sandra Day O'Connor, "When a police officer has probable cause to believe that a fine-only misdemeanor has occurred, that officer may stop the suspect … arrest the driver, search the driver, search the entire passenger compartment of the car including any purse or package inside, and impound the car and inventory all of its contents." Finding anything suspicious permits him to search the trunk as well.[176] The ruling has resulted in hundreds of thousands of car searches and arrests for possession of drugs.

The founders prohibited general warrants that did not list a cause for the search or the object of it because in their experience, general warrants had given law enforcement too much authority to search at will, and they didn't want a nation of checkpoints and security searches. According to the Supreme Court, police cannot set up general roadblocks, but they can establish roadblocks for a stated purpose like checking for drunk drivers or searching for a fugitive. When pulling over motorists individually, anything from speeding to weaving to the driver not wearing his seat belt can be a reason for a stop. Then police may ask for consent to search the vehicle—and usually get it.[177] Saying no implies guilt so almost everyone says yes, including those with something illegal to hide. If you refuse consent for a search, the officer may imply that things will go worse for you—that your refusal will constitute reasonable suspicion, warranting a search, or that you will be arrested and then searched incident to arrest, or that you will be detained until a search warrant can be gotten. In truth, the officer might be unable to get a warrant because that would require demonstrating probable cause to a judge, which is why individuals should generally refuse to give consent for a search. When a warrant is required, there is a separation of power created—a judge must agree that there is probable cause. When no warrant is required, no impartial magistrate is notified, leaving probable cause up to the police officer. A search warrant limits the scope of the search, whereas a consent search is effectively unlimited. Transgressions by authority are less likely under a warrant because the possibility of evidence being excluded is higher.

When making an arrest, a police officer reads the arrestee his Miranda rights, notifying him that he can refuse to answer questions, but in a traffic stop, an officer does not have to inform an individual that he has the right to refuse a search. In South Carolina, police stopped a man for speeding. When the officer asked if he could search the car for drugs, the man asked what would happen if he said no. The officer told him that saying no would make him appear guilty of criminal activity and that he would "call a drug dog right up the road to come down here and let him sniff the car."[178] So the man consented to the search, and the police found drugs and charged him. The district court ruled that consent for a search was given freely; the Fourth Circuit also upheld the search though both courts admitted that the officer had no right to bring in a drug dog because that required probable cause, like the smell of the drugs or a weapon in view, but there was evidently nothing to prevent him from *threatening* to bring in a drug dog. Technically, this may have been a consent search, but it felt to the man arrested and convicted just like the general, mandatory search that the Supreme Court has repeatedly struck down.

The current system permits police to use hostility, intimidation, and deceit, which are forms of coercion. Police should not be allowed to imply that they have the right to search when they don't, for the same reason that individuals are not allowed to imitate police officers—it's wrong to misrepresent one's authority. It should be unlawful for police to say things like, "Do you really want to make me more suspicious?" Instead, police should be required to inform individuals of their right to refuse consent to a search, as with the right to remain silent.

The War on Drugs has generated a need for monitoring, wiretapping, and spying and has reduced Fourth Amendment protections in a home. In 1967, the Court okayed wiretapping for only the most serious crimes like murder and kidnapping, but by the 1990s, three-quarters of all wiretaps were being used in drug cases. Do one thousand simultaneous telephone taps seem like a lot? More than that occurred once in Los Angeles County alone.[179] Police can climb trees to look in windows; use high-powered binoculars, surveillance, and helicopters; put a microphone outside a door or window; look through keyholes; go through someone's garbage; or interview neighbors, all without a warrant or any particular reason.[180] Police require no warrant to initiate a "knock and talk," in which they sometimes try to take advantage of people's fear of being impolite to authorities. (Generally speaking, don't let the police in without a warrant; either don't answer the door, or if you are comfortable talking to them, do it outside and do not go back inside the house until after the police have left.)[181]

Abortion

In 1961, a New Haven doctor and the executive director of the local Planned Parenthood chapter were arrested and fined for advising married couples about birth control in violation of a Connecticut law banning the use of contraceptives or counseling anyone in the use of them. The pair challenged the law successfully. The Supreme Court struck it down in *Griswold v. Connecticut* (1965), ruling that a law banning contraceptives "operates directly on an intimate relation of husband and wife ... a right of privacy older than the Bill of Rights." In the majority opinion, Justice William O. Douglas asked the other justices to consider enforcement of the alternative decision in the case, regulating sexual encounters: "Would we allow the police to search the sacred precincts of marital bedrooms for telltale signs of the use of contraceptives?"[182] To Justice Arthur Goldberg, privacy regarding sexual activity was exactly the kind of right protected by the founders in the Ninth Amendment, an unenumerated right retained by the people. Justice Harlan similarly found the right to privacy not in any specific provisions of the Bill of Rights but historically included in the concept of liberty. In *Griswold*, the Supreme Court placed a new liberty under the protection of the due process clause: the right of married people to use contraceptives. Later, in *Eisenstadt v. Baird* (1972), the Court found that a ban on the use of contraceptives violated the privacy rights of single people too, citing the doctrine of equality before the law.

Griswold led those in favor of legalizing abortion to ask, if the right to privacy protects individuals' choices involving sexual relations and pregnancy on the basis that it's none of government's business, why doesn't it also cover a woman's right to choose to have an abortion? The two are not exactly the same: whereas use of a contraceptive prevents a pregnancy, abortion terminates a pregnancy already in progress. Nevertheless, both matters clearly fall within the protected sphere of the individual. How could privacy rights cover one and not the other?

Abortion has been practiced for millennia. In the United States, most laws banning it were passed during the mid-nineteenth century and were made more lenient during the twentieth century. On January 22, 1973, the Supreme Court struck down a Texas law banning abortion on the basis that the law violated the individual's constitutional right to privacy. *Roe v. Wade* legalized abortion in the United States for the first time in ninety years.[183]

The Supreme Court refused to become embroiled in the debate over when life begins. It ruled that regardless of age, a fetus did not have rights because the word "persons" as used in the Constitution has never been defined to include the unborn. A fetus is a preborn human being that survives through its mother's voluntary and involuntary actions. It is dependent on her, and being dependent, it cannot be considered an individual and cannot have the rights of an individual. The mother can survive on her own; she is an individual with rights, including the right to privacy, within which terminating a pregnancy is her option. However, the Court also ruled that the State had a stake in the "potential for life" inside of each woman. According to the Court, government's interest increases as the fetus develops, permitting it to limit the woman's choices during the last trimester. Justice Harry Blackmun's opinion in *Roe v. Wade* established the classification of abortion rights by trimester. During the first trimester of pregnancy, all decisions about abortion would be between the woman and her doctor. During the second trimester, government could regulate abortion procedures for the health and safety of the mother, and during the third trimester, it was free to restrict or even prohibit abortion. (Ninety percent of all abortions are performed during the first trimester, when both surgical and less invasive medical abortions are possible. A medical abortion is induced by drugs, usually either methotrexate or mifepristone, also known as RU-486; 99 percent of all abortions are performed before the end of the second trimester.)

The Supreme Court has twice wavered on *Roe v. Wade*. The first time was in *Webster v. Reproductive Health Services* (1989). Ostensibly to "encourage childbirth," a Missouri law banned abortions in public hospitals and clinics. The Supreme Court upheld the law in a close decision. Opinions showed that four of the five justices in the majority—Scalia, White, Kennedy, and Rehnquist— favored scrapping the trimester framework established in *Roe* and substituting a doctrine advanced by Chief Justice Rehnquist in his *Roe* opinion that government's interest in "potential life" began at conception—which could allow the highly regulatory conditions of the third trimester to be expanded over the entire pregnancy. (The argument against abortion is rooted in the claim that personhood begins at conception, that a fetus is a person and thus has rights. During *Webster v. Reproductive Health Services,* a brief was submitted to the Supreme Court in which 12 Nobel laureates and 151 other scientists testified that the latest neuroscience suggested that brain functions normally associated with being a person were impossible until the twentieth week of gestation.)[184]

In *Planned Parenthood v. Casey* (1992), the Supreme Court ruled that the framework established in *Roe v. Wade* did not give government enough ability to regulate abortion prior to viability—during the first and second trimesters. The Court scrapped the woman's right to autonomy during the first trimester and near-autonomy during the second. Instead it would allow regulation by the states but strike down any law that placed an "undue burden" on a woman's right to have an abortion. State laws that made abortion more cumbersome or expensive would be upheld unless they presented a "substantial obstacle" to abortion rights. (The ruling in *Planned Parenthood v. Casey* prompted South Carolina to pass laws requiring wider door and hallway widths than usual for abortion clinics in an attempt to impose unnecessary costs on them.) Four of the nine justices—White, Scalia, Thomas, and Rehnquist—favored going further, allowing greater regulation of abortion by overturning *Roe* altogether. One more vote and the right to choose abortion could be in jeopardy. Wrote Justice Blackmun, the original author of *Roe,* "I fear for the darkness as four justices anxiously await the single vote necessary to extinguish the light."[185] In *Stenberg v. Carhart* (2000), however, the Court reaffirmed that women may choose abortion before viability and that states may not make laws to thwart them.[186]

In both *Webster* and *Planned Parenthood,* Justice Sandra Day O'Connor voted to uphold the anti-abortion laws in question but not to tamper with *Roe,* so in both cases hers was the swing vote that prevented a revisitation of *Roe v. Wade.* Justice O'Connor's position is that a woman has a right to choose abortion before viability and that the State has the power to restrict abortion after viability, but like most Supreme Court members, Justice O'Connor hedges by claiming a role for the State in the protection of the fetus too. There is contradiction in writing, "It is a promise of the Constitution that there is a realm of personal liberty which the government may not enter," referring to the rights of the woman, and also claiming that the State has "a legitimate interest in the life of the fetus."[187] In truth, government cannot begin to protect rights until there *is* an individual; meanwhile, it cannot claim to protect the rights of something that can have no rights. Doing so is not reason; it is sentiment. It is the Supreme Court assuming authority by the age-old contrivance of speaking for a nonplaintiff, as when someone claims to speak for God. There is no such thing as the "State's interest in preserving life." There is only the State's duty to protect the Five Rights, one of which is the right to life. Consider the difference. The "State's interest in preserving life" is merely an excuse to abridge a right that the Court is supposed to be protecting: privacy (under the umbrella of liberty). Sperm are alive. Eggs are alive. So are viruses, cancerous tumors, mold, and mosquitoes. It is not *life* that is important and requires preservation. It is the life of an individual—which the woman is and the fetus is not.

To the charge that abortion is murder, the apt reply is, nonsense. Since a fetus is not an individual, it has no rights and cannot be murdered. "Pro-life" is the self-label of many who want to prohibit abortion. Since the adult rather than the fetus initiates the action being considered—abortion—the adult is the subject of the matter. The fetus—the thing affected by the decision—is the object. When a person says he is pro-choice, he is supporting the subject's right to choose whether to terminate her pregnancy. When a person says he is pro-life, he is making no comment on the subject at all. Rather, he is substituting the object of the discussion (the fetus) for the subject (the woman and her rights) and then ignoring the subject. With the two syllables "pro-life," he shifts the issue to the biological condition of the fetus, distracting attention from his attempt to deny a personal choice. It's a handy euphemism. "I'm pro-life" sounds better than staying on subject and having to say, "I favor State management of pregnant women's bodies."

Anti-choice groups sometimes try to ascribe rights to a fetus based on the idea that it must be protected from violence, say, of an irate father-to-be. It's a roundabout way of trying to undermine *Roe v. Wade*. If successful, opponents of the right to choose abortion can claim that if a fetus has rights that protect it from violence by the father, then those same rights protect it from violence by the mother, including abortion. But the fetus is already protected by laws that protect the mother. Granting a fetus rights introduces other complications. For example, if a fetus has a right to life and is known to have a deadly, untreatable illness like Tay Sachs, which generally kills infants within their first few years of life, must it be delivered at term and forced to suffer for those years?

During the time abortion was illegal in the United States, amateur abortions killed an estimated 5,000 women annually.[188] In all, more than 400,000 young women died. Abortion, like gambling, alcoholism, drug addiction, prostitution, extramarital affairs, and unwanted pregnancies, is something that will always happen—legal or illegal—due to human nature. These things can't be prevented by laws; a ban only wastes resources and harasses people. To make their case, opponents of the right to choose abortion often dwell on the mechanics of the operation itself in graphic detail, building to the febrile crescendo, "How can we continue to let this happen? Something has to be done." They ignore that it's not their business to do anything about, only that of the person carrying the fetus. As Justice Blackmun put it, "In a Nation that cherishes liberty, the ability of a woman to control the biological operation of her body ... must fall within the limited sphere of individual autonomy that lies beyond the will or power of any transient majority."[189] If what happens within human skin is not beyond the reach of the State, what is?

The Right to Die

The *Quinlan*, *Cruzan*, and *Schiavo* cases have had the greatest influences on US policies pertaining to the right to die.

In April 1975, after mixing alcohol and tranquilizers at a party, twenty-one-year-old Karen Ann Quinlan stopped breathing for fifteen minutes—twice. She was given mouth-to-mouth resuscitation, which failed. She was taken by ambulance to the hospital, where she was found unresponsive to deep pain. She had suffered brain damage and lapsed into a persistent vegetative state. Several weeks later, when it became clear that there was no hope of a recovery, her father Joseph sought to be appointed her guardian, authorizing him to remove her from life support, since Karen had previously expressed her desire not to be kept alive that way. The physician in charge agreed that there was no possibility of a recovery, but he refused to honor the Quinlan family's wishes because he could find no medical precedent for removing a non-terminal patient from life support. The attorney general of New Jersey intervened, arguing that the State's compelling interest in the preservation of human life outweighed the individual's right to die and that taking Karen off life support would constitute homicide; her respirator must be continued. The Supreme Court of New Jersey ruled in favor of the Quinlans, basing its finding on the right of the individual to privacy as enunciated in *Griswold v. Connecticut* and *Roe v. Wade*. The court ordered the hospital to remove the breathing apparatus, but the nurses, anticipating the decision, had carefully and successfully weaned her off of it. Quinlan was able to breathe on her own—for nine years. She spent her last several years curled in the fetal position. When she died in June 1985, she weighed sixty-five pounds.[190]

In another right-to-die case, *Cruzan v. Director, Missouri Department of Health* (1990), a car accident had left Nancy Cruzan in a complete vegetative state from which she would never emerge. Told that there was no hope, her family asked that her feeding tube be removed. The hospital refused, citing the law that to allow someone to die required "clear and convincing evidence" of the *patient's* wishes, which was lacking. When the Supreme Court upheld the Missouri law, Justice William Rehnquist noted that a competent person could refuse life-saving treatment, but if incompetent, his family could not refuse it for him or her. Nancy would have to be kept alive.

The decision was a tragic outcome for the Cruzan family, but there was an upside to the case. Right-to-die advocates seized on Justice Rehnquist's statement that competent people *did* have a right to end their life by choice—which had never been spelled out before by the Supreme Court. In acknowledging that a person has the right to die by refusing medical treatment, based on the Fourteenth Amendment's guarantee of liberty, the Court affirmed passive suicide. Rights advocates maintained that if a competent person has the right to choose suicide, the means are irrelevant. If a person can end his life by refusing drugs, why can't he also end his life by taking drugs? In either case, a competent person is choosing to end his life. And if he can choose to end his life, why can't he do it correctly by consulting a physician? Of all times, at death, why not be able to enlist the recommendations of a medical professional?

But the courts have not seen it that way. While no state in the nation prosecutes attempted suicide as a crime, almost all of them prosecute doctors in physician-assisted suicides. State laws banning physician-assisted suicide have been upheld. The Supreme Court has been unwilling to grant that physician-assisted suicide is a basic choice covered by the constitutional right to privacy, as abortion is. (The two are not the same. In an abortion, the fetus has a potential for living a life but no right to choose, since that right belongs to the pregnant woman. The terminal person considering suicide is in the reverse situation: he has the right to choose but no potential for life.)

"Physician-assisted suicide" refers to a doctor providing the means to bring about death, usually through pills, which the patient takes himself when he sees fit. "Euthanasia" means actively injecting a drug to cause death. Euthanasia is unpopular in the United States, but about 70 percent of Americans favor legalizing physician-assisted suicide.[191] Euthanasia is not legal in any state, and Oregon is the only state to have ever legalized physician-assisted suicide. The only nation in which both are legal is the Netherlands, where about five thousand people each year opt to die by one or the other.[192]

In a physician-assisted suicide, the patient is active; he must request the prescription and self-administer the lethal dose. Being illegal, a doctor usually does it in practice by prescribing pain-relieving drugs as needed until they happen to kill the patient by respiratory depression. Dr. Michael Irwin, a British physician and a former medical director of the United Nations, is one of many doctors who have admitted to increasing dosages of pain medication with the intended side effect of killing the patient. Dr. Irwin said he has done it at least fifty times and also noted that he has arranged that a colleague do the same for him should he ever require it.[193] It is not uncommon for doctors and nurses to quietly aid in helping people to commit suicide. One *New York Times* article declared, "One in Five Nurses Tell Survey They Helped Patients Die."[194] Individuals too seem inclined to allow physician-assisted suicide, judging by their jury verdicts. Though illegal, Dr. Jack Kevorkian assisted in over one hundred suicides and was seriously convicted only once. He served eight years in prison. In drawing attention to the issue, Dr. Kevorkian did more toward legalizing physician-assisted suicide than anyone else.

In *The Right to Privacy*, Ellen Alderman and Caroline Kennedy told the story of Dr. Timothy Quill and a terminally ill patient named Diane.[195] She had been succeeding in a lifelong bout with alcohol and depression when she learned that she had leukemia. Her longtime physician, Dr. Quill, told her that without treatment, she would live only a few months. Radical treatment—chemotherapy, radiation, and bone marrow transplants—would likely fail but at least offered a glimmer of hope. Diane chose to forgo the intensive therapy, preferring not to spend her final months in hospitals. Dr. Quill was against her decision, but Diane remained intransigent, and over time Quill realized that Diane was not acting out of despondency but out of a wish to end her life as she chose.

As the end neared, Diane feared a lingering, agonizing final few weeks, so she asked the doctor to help her die. There was nothing that Dr. Quill could do legally, but he wrote her a prescription for sleeping pills and told her how many she should take to sleep or to end her life. Later Quill remembered, "I wrote the prescription with an uneasy feeling about the boundaries I was exploring … yet I also felt strongly that I was setting her free to get the most out of the time she had left, and to maintain dignity and control on her own terms until her death."[196] Knowing that she could end her life when she chose freed Diane's mind and allowed her to spend her remaining time at home with her husband and son. Finally, she said her good-byes, asked to be alone, took the pills, lay down, and died peacefully.

Dr. Quill knew that any mention of suicide in his report would result in a police investigation, so he listed the cause of death as acute leukemia. Months later, Quill revealed the truth in an article, admitting, "Although I did not assist in her suicide directly, I helped to make it possible, successful, and relatively painless."[197] Quill wondered how many other physicians had helped patients to die and how many suffering people had chosen to commit suicide in more violent ways, always forced to die alone for fear of involving a loved one in an investigation. After the article appeared, Quill was shocked to find himself charged with second-degree manslaughter. He endured harassment and legal turmoil, but a grand jury refused to indict him.

Some religious groups oppose permitting the choice of physician-assisted suicide on the basis that it violates God's will. Other opponents claim that it undervalues the State's interest in preserving life by making suicide too accessible. They charge that it would allow people who are vulnerable and failing or depressed to choose death too easily. Dr. Quill coauthored a paper in response, writing that physician-assisted suicide should be considered only for a patient "whose suffering has become intolerable and who has no other satisfactory option."[198] Quill recommended that three conditions be met: the patient must be competent and able to make the decision himself; the request must be "enduring," meaning repeated over time; and approval requires an independent second opinion from another physician. If either doctor thinks the patient is suffering from depression, the patient is referred to a mental health professional. Quill also recommended that physician-assisted death be an option not just for terminal patients, but for anyone with an incurable illness. Only a patient with fewer than six months to live is defined as terminal. Someone with ALS (Lou Gehrig's disease), for example, is not considered terminal because he may live for years, but without the option of physician-assisted suicide, he can be forced to suffer for all that time. Wrote Dr. Quill, "The goal is to allow someone to die intact as a person, not to disintegrate before dying."[199]

The US Court of Appeals for the Ninth Circuit accepted Quill's arguments, finding that the decision to end one's life was a basic right of choice covered by the guarantee of liberty in the Fourteenth Amendment, specifically by the individual's right to privacy. The court agreed that the State had a stake in preserving life but found that it shrunk as a person aged, was reduced to negligible as he neared death, and did not outweigh a terminal patient's interest in living or dying. Part of the court's finding is worth noting verbatim: "Under our constitutional system, neither the state nor the majority of the people in a state can impose its will upon the individual in a matter so highly central to personal dignity and autonomy. Those who believe strongly that death must come without physicians' assistance are free to follow that creed, be they doctors or patients. They are not free, however, to force their views, their religious convictions, or their philosophies on all the other members of a democratic society, and to compel those whose values differ with theirs to die painful, protracted, and agonizing deaths."[200] A month later, a three-judge panel in the Second Circuit, which includes New York City, also found that the right to die was a constitutionally protected right but based its finding on the idea established in *Cruzan* that if you can choose to die by refusing drugs, then you can choose to die by taking drugs, and if you can take drugs to die, you should be able to consult a doctor about it.

But the Supreme Court overturned both of the circuit court rulings (*Vacco v. Quill, Washington v. Glucksberg*). It upheld the laws in New York and Washington that made it a crime for doctors to give lethal drugs to dying patients seeking to end their lives. It refused to grant individuals the right to commit suicide with the help of a doctor. The Court subordinated the agony of thousands of suffering patients to "the American tradition of condemning suicide and valuing human life."[201] The decision did, however, leave the states with the power to ban or legalize assisted suicide. According to Chief Justice Rehnquist's opinion for the Court, it was still an open question whether the Constitution recognized a competent but suffering individual's "interest in controlling the circumstances of his or her imminent death."[202]

In 1990, twenty-six-year-old Terri Schiavo experienced respiratory and cardiac arrest and collapsed in her home. Her brain was deprived of oxygen, causing extensive irreversible damage and leaving her in a persistent vegetative state. After three years, her husband Michael entered a do-not-resuscitate order for her, but nursing home staff rescinded it. In 1998, Michael petitioned the court to remove her breathing tube, but Terri's parents opposed him. In 2001, Terri's feeding tube was removed and then reinserted while legal proceedings ensued. Finally, in 2005, after *fifteen years* in a persistent vegetative state, Terri Schiavo's life support was removed and she was allowed to die. Because the main point of contention was that Terri's wishes had been undocumented, the case prompted millions of individuals to establish living wills. Picturing themselves in Terri Schiavo's situation, they did not want to live that way. "Life," to most people, means more than being technically alive—it means to be aware, ambulatory, communicative. To be in a vegetative state or very close to it without hope of anything approaching a normal life is to many a greater evil than death.[203]

The right to die includes the right to make a living will with specific directives, to file a do-not-resuscitate order, and to establish a medical proxy to speak for you if you are incapacitated. You have the right to vigorous pain management. You can refuse or discontinue any unwanted treatment. You can refuse food and water. You can refuse CPR. And if your wishes are not being met, you can change doctors. But your physician cannot legally prescribe a medication for you to end your life, except in Oregon.[204]

The Catholic Church, eternally pro-suffering, is the most powerful group contesting the right to physician-assisted suicide. It denounced Kevorkian. It has spent millions to defeat assisted-death legislation, successfully. The pope has called the idea of permitting individuals to end their lives if they choose, "the culture of death." Due to this mentality, people languish in prisons for doing as their loved ones asked, including a man in Canada serving a forty-year sentence for the mercy killing of his severely disabled twelve-year-old daughter because he couldn't bear to see her suffer anymore.[205]

In the United States, bans on physician-assisted suicide force the individual to choose between a lagging, debilitating decline and a difficult, lonely suicide. In the Netherlands, where euthanasia and physician-assisted suicide have been practiced for thirty-five years, three in every hundred deaths is a voluntary one.[206] Choosing to die, though abhorrent to many, is an exercise in liberty. Some people choose to live precisely because having the option to die deters them from taking it. Giving them a rational choice motivates them to act rationally. Outside of the Netherlands, the first man legally helped to die by a physician was Bob Dent in Australia's Northern Territory, where the practice was briefly legal in 1996. He left a letter in which he wrote, "If you disagree with voluntary euthanasia, then don't use it, but please don't deny the right to me."[207] Personal autonomy must include the freedom to end one's existence. They too are pursuing happiness that choose to avoid pointless suffering.

Near the end of life, the focus should be on palliative care. Pain medication and nerve blocks should be used liberally with minimal concern over high dosage levels. Dying patients should be referred and admitted to hospices earlier, where doctors and nurses are trained to help them manage pain, anorexia, and depression. The goal so late in life should not be longevity. When people expressed their hopes that Benjamin Franklin, in pain during the last two years of his long life, recover soon, he always answered flatly, "I hope *not*," comprehending that death is not a horror to be outrun till the very last moment. Your life is completed when you've had your fill of all it has to offer. For most of us, this time comes and we detach voluntarily. Cicero described it so: "In the same way as apples while green can only be picked by force, but after maturity fall off by themselves, so death comes to the young with violence but to old people when the time is ripe. And the thought of this ripeness so greatly attracts me that as I approach death I feel like a man nearing harbor after a long voyage: I seem to be catching sight of land."[208]

Confidentiality of Genetic Data

A human cell is about one-tenth of a millimeter in diameter, which means that it's visible under a ten-power lens. Each cell is alive, and one hundred trillion cells working in concert make up a living person. Each of us is a machine made out of many machines, each managed from within by a black dot, the nucleus, which contains a tiny computer that tells the cell what to do—a human genome. It is made up of 22,000 genes packaged on twenty-three pairs of chromosomes: twenty-three from the individual's father and twenty-three from the mother. Each chromosome is one pair of extremely long DNA molecules, and many, many rungs, called bases, hold the pair together. A single human genome contains three billion pairs of bases, that is, three billion pairs of four nucleic acids: adenine (A) and thymine (T), which pair up, or cytosine (C) and guanine (G), which also have an affinity for one another. Because these four acids partner as they do, cells replicate, which is life. The four nucleic acids are the alphabet of the computer software language that is organized in three-letter "words." The program is gigantic. If you were to write out each letter of the human genome on one line in letters so tiny they were barely visible, one "A," "C," "G," or "T" per millimeter, you would need a sheet of paper wide enough to stretch from Denver to New York City, about 1,800 miles. And this program fits inside the nucleus of each cell.[209]

Your program has glitches—everyone's does—and your life depends on there not being any glitches in the wrong places. Science writer Matt Ridley provides an example: on chromosome four you have a gene in which the "word" CAG is repeated many times. It may be repeated as few as six times or over one hundred times. Most people have about a dozen repeats, and the word can be repeated up to thirty-five times before it causes any problem. But if CAG is repeated more than thirty-nine times, you will contract an incurable disease, Huntington's chorea. Starting around age thirty-eight or forty, you will become confused and have trouble with your sense of balance. Your limbs will begin to jerk uncontrollably, and you will suffer from deep depression. Eventually you will become incapable of taking care of yourself, and after about fifteen years you will die prematurely. Though the precise schedule varies with the number of repeats of CAG, there is no chance of it not happening and no recourse.[210]

Fortunately, Huntington's chorea is not like most gene-related illnesses. Huntington's is a rare case of predestiny, whereas most genetic information only speaks to predispositions and probabilities. The genome is not a template of our future, nor does a mutation necessarily harm us. Usually it makes no difference at all—the genome has backup systems and corrective capabilities. Or a mutation might increase the probability of contracting a certain illness, but it never happens. Genetic testing can help too, since risks stemming from genetic mutations, once known, can often be reduced through adjustments in diet, or by changes in lifestyle, or with medication. People can now be tested for predisposition toward breast or colon cancer, cystic fibrosis, sickle cell anemia, and muscular dystrophy. Other diseases linked to genetics include Alzheimer's, cancers of the ovary and prostate, and osteoporosis. Attention deficit disorder, alcoholism, obesity, and depression are thought to have a genetic component as well. By testing, an individual can learn if he is presymptomatic or a carrier of a recessive or X-linked disorder that does not affect him but may affect his offspring. Soon, genetic data will affect decisions about reproductive choices; it could become the central piece of information in each individual's medical records, used by doctors in reaching a prognosis and in prescribing medication.[211]

Though human beings share more than 99 percent of their DNA with one another, the letter-by-letter reading of your genome is the recipe that made *you,* so genetic testing provides positive identification. DNA evidence has overturned the wrongful conviction at least fifteen people on death row, and it has gotten at least 220 people released who were serving long sentences for crimes they did not commit.[212] After two centuries of historians denying that Thomas Jefferson sired a child with Sally Hemings, DNA evidence confirmed it to be true in 1998—her second child, Eston, had Jefferson's distinctive genetic markers.[213] DNA testing is commonly used to determine paternity; three hundred thousand tests are done in the United States each year. When a company named Identigene bought billboard space advertising its services with, "Who's the Father? Call 1-800-DNA-TYPE," it received 300 telephone calls a day requesting the service, mostly from single mothers in search of evidence allowing them to demand child-support and from males uncertain if they were the father of all of their children.[214] All fifty states operate DNA databases, and they all require felons convicted of violent crimes to provide a genetic sample before parole. Information is pooled in a national FBI-operated database. Originally, the idea was to databank DNA samples of sex criminals only, but the practice quickly spread to all serious crimes, and now in some states a person convicted of a misdemeanor like disorderly conduct is required to provide a genetic sample to the state. The system will soon include tens of millions of samples.[215]

Genetic privacy is important due to the predilection of those in judgment to feel that genes indicate destiny when they don't. Environmental factors contribute, as well as gene interactions that we don't yet understand. Having a propensity toward a certain disease is not having the disease or even having a likelihood of contracting it, but because genetic testing tags each person for easy categorization, it leads to stigmatizing and discrimination. Being at risk for a serious illness changes how people see you. They presume that you may not be around in the future or that you may be too sick to work; they don't want to rely too heavily on you, especially people with no personal connection to you, like prospective creditors. In a business that offers group insurance coverage, the top 10 percent of claimants use three quarters of all the resources, so employers with access to genetic test results have incentive to use them in hiring and firing decisions.[216]

Because genetic information is often convoluted and long-term in nature and the economics of insurance force companies to concentrate on costs most likely to occur in the first few years of a policy, insurers have so far preferred to base rates on their own experience, but increasing genetic awareness will likely put upward pressure on rates. If people can know the results of their genetic tests, but insurers cannot, individuals can use that knowledge to take advantage of insurers by loading up on coverage in anticipation of a particular illness. This is called adverse selection, and it undermines the statistics upon which rates are set. For an insurer, it's like dealing a hand of blackjack and *then* allowing the players to place their bets. The house's edge is lost. When insurers lack information, they raise rates. If genetic testing is unsupervised and becomes so simplified that it can be done at home and the results known only to the subject, adverse selection could become routine, forcing higher rates.[217]

There is a second, more deep-seated problem for the insurance industry. When no one knew their chances for health or long life, insurance worked as a business because it provided a service to willing customers: risk sharing. But as genetic illnesses become less a matter of blind chance and more one of calculable probabilities, only those at high risk, a small minority, retain the incentive to share costs equally. Given a choice, low-risk individuals would decline, causing market failure and the loss of communitarian benefits. Insurers could sell policies to low-risk individuals at low rates and charge high-risk individuals in accordance with their risk group, like with teenage drivers, but the rates for high-risk individuals would skyrocket. People have no choice in their genetic makeup. If a woman has the BRCA1 or BRCA2 mutation, putting her at higher risk for breast cancer, should she be charged much more for insurance? If not, but she is to be covered, then low-risk individuals must be forced to subsidize high-risk ones, seemingly requiring State-mandated participation like Social Security. The other option: insurance is based on competitive advantage like mating or job seeking, and individuals are left on their own.

Because neither alternative is satisfactory, both insurers and insured have preferred to keep DNA test results out of the mix altogether. More than a hundred bills to protect genetic privacy have appeared before state legislatures. Congress passed the Health Insurance Portability and Accountability Act, which made it a crime to provide genetic information to anyone not authorized to know it. Consider the potential consequences if genetic test results were unprotected by privacy law. DNA material can come from nail clippings, blood, saliva, hair follicles, sweat, sexual fluids, or waste products, so it's not difficult for someone to collect a sample—a used tissue is enough. Private industry has incentive to collect and compile samples because the results—you, neatly categorized—has value for people you do business with, all of whom want to protect themselves. Mortgage companies might deny mortgages based on genetic data. Retirement facilities could require applicants to undergo a test for the ApoE-4 gene linked to Alzheimer's. Schools could require genetic tests in an effort to predict which students are likely to be troublesome. Imagine what political opponents would imply from each other's profile. If genetic privacy is not respected, millions born with a meaningless genetic deficiency might find themselves discriminated against.[218]

Privacy in Public

When a bomb blast killed 170 people in the Alfred P. Murrah Federal Building in Oklahoma City in 1995, the general surveillance tape from a nearby apartment building recorded Timothy McVeigh's rented Ryder truck exploding. The tape helped police charge McVeigh quickly and demonstrated that closed-circuit television (CCTV) surveillance could play a role in catching major criminals. Authorities in Great Britain came to the same conclusion twenty years earlier and acted on it; Britain now has more than five million surveillance cameras in place. People operate some; most are automatic recorders. There are advantages to it for effective government. Nothing has ever worked better to enforce speeding regulations. (When surveillance cameras were installed in the Australian state of Victoria, speeding dropped from 15 percent of all vehicles to 3 percent and fatalities from over 1,000 to under 250.)[219] Proponents of closed-circuit television in Britain see surveillance as an inevitable improvement that promotes compliant behavior, first through the subject's fear of penalty for wrongdoing, and then by habit. Said a representative of the British government, "If this all saves one life, it's worth it."[220]

CCTV doesn't stop crime in progress, however, because there is rarely a way to get someone on the scene in time. It doesn't help capture criminals not in the database, since the face cannot be matched to a name, and it doesn't help catch disguised or well-concealed criminals. The cameras most commonly witness crimes like traffic violations, littering, public urination, underage smoking, drunkenness, loitering, solicitation, small drug deals, or disturbing the peace. In one study, 900 incidents of targeted surveillance of suspicious individuals produced twelve arrests, ten of them for fighting.[221] In most of the scuffles, citizens at the scene had quelled the disturbance by the time the police arrived, and no arrests were made. As noted by Clive Norris and Gary Armstrong in *The Maximum Surveillance Society: The Rise of CCTV*, in life public order is often maintained by the intervention of bystanders, some of who might be less likely to help if they know they're being videotaped.[222]

Surveillance induces conformity through anticipation of penalty for nonconformity, so people avoid unusual actions. What is commonly done becomes what is allowed, not by law, but according to the self-restraints born of constant surveillance. The individual's range of choice shrinks from what is possible to what he calculates is acceptable to the watchers. The cameras intimidate, and that seems in part to be the intent: to use the cameras as a means of control. In South London, police used closed-circuit television in red light districts to videotape men approaching prostitutes. Photographs of the encounter, along with an explanatory letter, were sent to the men's homes. Said Sergeant Maurice Morewood of the vice squad, "It is a tactic on our part and should act as a deterrent."[223]

It is said that technology ignores geographical borders. It also ignores social boundaries. For example, when face-to-face, we do not stare at each other; it's considered rude because it makes people uncomfortable. Empathizing, we look away. One sociologist named this "civil inattention."[224] But the operator of a surveillance camera does the opposite. His job is to stare. Because he is distant and the subject can't see him, manners and shame don't enter into his calculations. He interprets odd behavior as suspicious and zooms in on it, unfazed that he is violating evolved traditions of human interaction in order to catch people violating man-made rules of organization. The camera operators decide who to watch based on the appearance of the subject, which allows discretionary, discriminatory policing known as profiling. The wrong appearance gets you surveilled. The right appearance attracts attention too. While investigating Princess Diana's death, officials discovered that she had visited the Harvey Nichols department store in London days earlier, where the store's security cameras filmed her. A videotape was found in the head-of-security's desk in which the operator had used special zoom features to tape "lingering close-ups" of her bust and thighs.[225]

Closed-circuit surveillance cameras are already in sports arenas, malls, parking lots, airports, and retail stores, and they are also used on the street. At twenty-five frames per second, a ten-camera surveillance system produces twenty-one million pictures in a day, and there is no cost-effective way for human beings to inspect all of them, but the latest software allows image processing and intelligent scene monitoring. Soon, one person will be able to scan hundreds of photos selected by computer out of millions of automated surveillances. A handful of people will be able to exercise visual advantage over a nation. "If you've got nothing to hide, you've got nothing to fear," announced Prime Minister John Major concerning the cameras,[226] but Major's statement pertains to no one, since hiding some things about yourself is part of being human. An individual may have a second job he is ashamed of, or a business affiliation he wants to keep secret, or a bad habit. He may have separate friendships with individuals who don't get along or sexual relationships he wants to keep private. A teenager might want information about pregnancy or sexually transmitted diseases. An undercover police officer or a witness to a crime might want to conceal his identity.

Automated facial recognition systems got a boost at the turn of the twenty-first century, when in Kuala Lumpur in December 1999, a Malaysian surveillance team videotaped Khalid Al-Midhar meeting with several known international terrorists. The Malaysian government gave a copy of the tape to the United States, and Al-Midhar was added to the Immunization and Naturalization Service's "watch list" of potential terrorists—but the process took more than a year and a half. While US and federal agents were trying to learn his whereabouts, a plane hit the World Trade Center, and then another. Then a plane hit the Pentagon; Al-Midhar was on that one, along with sixty-three other people—American Airlines flight 77 from Washington to Los Angeles on September 11, 2001. Soberingly, Al-Midhar had bought his ticket in his real name. A system that automatically checked names and faces against a database of terrorists would have spotted him in the airport. Or, had the US government's database been linked to commercial databases, Al-Midhar might have been apprehended days earlier when he used his Visa card.[227] A legacy of 9/11: the United States now has over thirty million surveillance cameras in place.[228]

Facial recognition works by capturing an image on camera, taking one hundred or more nodal measurements like distance between eyes, width of nose, and depth of eye sockets, and translating them into a numerical code, a face print. Each is compared to stored face prints of known criminals. Some airports use versions of facial recognition technology, and casinos have used it to identify known cheats. It could be used to track less dangerous people, say, to record the identity of each person who attends peace rallies, or speeches of fringe-group speakers. House Majority Leader Dick Armey warned that facial recognition software "could allow the public movements of every citizen in the state to be identified, tracked, recorded, and stored."[229] Biographies and cross-referencing would likely follow. Collected data could be distributed to government agencies or used to compile a database of potential troublemakers, defined as government likes.

The Supreme Court has never acknowledged that a limited expectation of privacy exists in public, but perhaps it should. When you sit on a park bench and chat with a friend, you do not expect that your conversation is being recorded from hundreds of yards away by high-tech surveillance equipment. Outdoors, a person loses privacy to the normal vision and hearing of others. Beyond those limits, it's reasonable for him to expect some consideration, even in public. Zero privacy means being open to recording and tracking devices of every kind.

Drug Testing

How drug-testing laws apply to you depends on whether you are a public employee, a private-sector employee, or a student, since the rules are different for each.

Government can perform drug tests on its public employees in safety-sensitive jobs, on workers suspected of impairment on the job, and after an accident. In *Skinner v. Railway Labor Executives Association* (1989), the Supreme Court upheld drug testing of employees without reasonable suspicion but only when there was a compelling need to protect public health or safety. Tests could be given only to employees who "discharge duties fraught with such risks to injury of others that even a momentary lapse of attention can have disastrous consequences."[230] The Court okayed drug testing of pilots, train engineers, and police, but struck down testing of administrative or clerical workers and blanket testing of all employees. It ruled that a government employer could not institute suspicionless drug testing as an attempt to protect the integrity of the workplace or to cut costs.

Private sector businesses can and do perform drug tests prior to hiring, often prodded by government through transportation regulations or conditions attached to government contracts. In the late 1980s, William Bennett, the director of the Office of National Drug Control Policy, sought to reduce drug use by making it impossible for a drug user to find a job. Said Bennett, "Because anyone using drugs stands a good chance of being discovered, with disqualification from employment as a possible consequence, many will decide that the price of using drugs is just too high."[231] To Bennett, drug users were just weak people in need of resolve, but first they had to be exposed, justifying the need for testing. Most employers didn't mind instituting pre-employment drug testing, since it worked as a loose screening test for them. When a person fails a drug test he knows is coming, it makes him appear either a fool or an addict and he's rejected.

Testers are usually searching for evidence of marijuana, cocaine, opiates, or amphetamines. Testing affects marijuana smokers most because more people use marijuana than all other illegal drugs combined and because it can be detected in urine days after mild use or weeks after regular use. Curiously, urinalysis tells a company nothing about the impairment of an employee. It tests for the presence of metabolites, traces left behind, so it tells what drugs a person took days or weeks earlier but is silent regarding his present ability to do his job. According to the Substance Abuse and Mental Health Services Administration, alcohol accounts for 86 percent of all the costs imposed on business by drug abuse,[232] but few employers test for alcohol, and when they do they test for intoxication rather than general use. Their concern is that the employee is not impaired on company time. With marijuana, it should be the same. Pre-employment tests should be scrapped. If on-the-job testing is done, it should require probable cause, and the test should be for impairment only, since otherwise drug use is a matter within the protected sphere of the individual and none of the employer's business.

A few bold managers have resisted the trend. Wayne Sanders, the CEO of paper goods giant Kimberly-Clark, told the *Dallas Morning News* that he "wasn't about to pee in a bottle" and would never require his employees to do so, calling the idea of urine testing "demeaning and completely alien in a culture based on trust and respect."[233] In Michigan, a librarian with experience in sales was offered a job that he wanted badly, but he refused to take a drug test, calling it invasive and insulting, and the employer dropped the requirement.[234] Because good employees are the resource in shortest supply at any company, when a few of them stand their ground, it makes a difference. If employees think that their bodily fluids are their affair and demonstrate it by taking their labor elsewhere, they can discourage companies from drug testing. In time, businesses may abandon the practice, if permitted.

Students have the least protection. The Supreme Court has a history of curtailing students' privacy rights on the basis that the reasonable suspicion standard cannot be allowed to undermine public schools' custodial responsibility for children. The Court has always upheld the right of schools to drug test suspected students. It has gone both ways when drug tests are imposed on a group—athletes, for example—and it has generally struck down drug testing of whole student populations.

A school district in Vernonia, Oregon, instituted a drug-testing program that was challenged by parents. The Court upheld the program because there was evidence of heavy drug use in the school district and because the drug testing was limited to athletes. The Court noted that without these special circumstances, suspicionless drug testing would be found unconstitutional. But then the Court upheld a drug-testing program in a school district in Tecumseh, Oklahoma, that required any student, not just athletes, wanting to participate in *any* extracurricular activity to be tested. Three students, Lindsay and Lacey Earls, and Daniel James, who had to take drug tests to join the choir, the marching band, and the academic team, respectively, challenged the program. The Tenth Circuit Court of Appeals declared the drug-testing program unconstitutional, but that decision was reversed and the program reinstated by the Supreme Court in *Board of Education v. Earls* (2002). In a five-to-four decision, the Court approved broad, random, suspicionless drug testing of students.[235]

In defending the *Earls* decision, Justice Clarence Thomas opined that students had a reduced expectation of privacy, that drug testing was a "negligible" intrusion, and that because drug abuse was a problem, the program was acceptable.[236] Justice Thomas saw it as a deterrent, but his rationale placed government's role as a progenitor of policy ahead of that as the protector of individuals' rights. Justice Anthony Kennedy found the ruling reasonable because the program had an element of consent.[237] In Kennedy's view, any student who wanted to protest the policy could do so by boycotting extracurricular activities. Justice Ruth Bader Ginsburg posed an excellent question in the dissenting opinion: why test debate team members at all? The drug testing of athletes can be justified by the risk of sports-related injury. What is the reason to test choir and band members, who had not sacrificed their personal privacy as athletes in locker rooms do? Justice Ginsburg found the decision "perverse" in that testing would turn away students who wished to participate in extracurricular activities, known to help keep kids away from drugs.[238] Justice David Souter criticized the decision too, pointing out that in the past there had always been a special need whenever random suspicionless drug testing had been upheld, but there was no such need in *Earls*.[239] One writer correctly noted that the *Earls* decision gave "the inside of students' bodies less protection than the insides of their backpacks."[240] According to *Earls*, in the same buildings in which twenty-three million students are taught that they have rights to liberty and privacy, they can be shepherded into lavatories for samples of their urine and penalized for what they've been doing on their own time. Students put off by the drug testing at the Tecumseh school rejected extracurricular activities. Rather than bond with teammates, supervised, on school grounds, both users and nonusers had a few more hours to kill each day.

Suspicionless drug testing does more than limit a minor's Fourth Amendment rights: it ignores them. You take your pet to the veterinarian, have tests done, and act on the results because he is your responsibility—you own him. Government similarly tests individuals, but government doesn't own individuals. People are not the State's to be sorted by what's in their blood or urine into groups of acceptable and unacceptable. Urinalysis cannot be justified. It protects no one's rights. If it violates rights to extract information from a person against his will, then it must violate rights to extract tangibles like blood or urine. An infringement of the inner protected sphere, drug testing is more invasive than any search imposed on Americans by the British during the eighteenth century—the searches that produced the Fourth Amendment.

Monitoring of Employees

The main privacy protection on the job is the common law, which defines an invasion of privacy as an intentional intrusion on an individual that a reasonable person would find offensive. For instance, the monitoring of restrooms and locker rooms by employers has been ruled a violation of privacy. A company can invade privacy by publishing private matters, disclosing medical records, or using an employee's name or likeness for commercial purposes, but in

111

most other cases, judges have ruled in favor of employers. Company representatives can search an employee's desk, his work area, and anything on his computer without a warrant, or probable cause, or any individualized suspicion of wrongdoing, as established in *O'Connor v. Ortega* (1987). A company can monitor employees by video camera or electronically; it can require them to carry handheld computers; it can review e-mails, web-page visits, and downloaded files; and it can monitor employees online. In some jobs, each employee's work day is monitored: number of keystrokes per minute, number of calls per hour, time per call, and so on. A company can use the Global Positioning System to monitor the speed and direction of traveling employees, recording stops, addresses, and time spent at each.[241]

To insulate themselves against invasion-of-privacy lawsuits, companies tell new hires to expect no privacy on the job. The employer is given a lot of latitude because he owns the equipment and pays the employee for his time. Companies want to make sure that employees are not sharing proprietary company information with outsiders. Safety and workplace theft are also given as reasons to monitor employees. But a company might *have* to monitor for another reason: to protect itself against potential lawsuits stemming from internal communications—racism, sexism, threats, or defamatory statements. Government forces each company to police its employees by making the employer liable for discrimination or harassment that takes place on his property.

Take the case of sexual harassment. There are two kinds. The first occurs when one person makes repeated unsolicited, unwanted sexual advances toward another at work or when a superior ties a raise or promotion to sex. Either of these constitutes quid pro quo sexual harassment, which is always intentional and directed at someone. The second kind occurs when someone creates a "hostile environment" in the workplace, a standard based on people's sensibilities, which differ. What is a bawdy remark or innocent bedroom humor to most may qualify as "creating a hostile environment" to some. And unlike quid pro quo harassment, which must be directed at someone, this form can be unintentional. To prevent what might be construed as a hostile environment, companies restrict speech and behavior by prohibiting dirty jokes and pictures and suggestive expressions or gestures. Downloading pornography at work does not violate government's laws, but it can create a sexual harassment liability if the porn is circulated or left on the screen where others can see it. At work, Big Brother himself is not watching, but through hostile-environment legislation, he has forcibly deputized employers.

Free Speech

The first federal law violating the right to free speech came in 1798 when, overreacting to the libel of President John Adams, Congress passed the Alien and Sedition Acts, making it a crime to criticize the president. Ten people were convicted before the law was repealed. Similar laws were passed during World War I. The Espionage Act and the Sedition Act outlawed "disloyal, profane, scurrilous, or abusive language" about the United States government and resulted in the conviction of more than one thousand people, most for speaking out against the draft. Freedom to criticize US military action had grown by the time of Vietnam: the Supreme Court upheld the publication of the Pentagon Papers, though it was certain to increase opposition to the war.[242]

Even during peacetime, the right to freedom of expression does not protect every spoken word or publication. Voltaire's *Candide* was banned by US customs as obscene in 1929.[243] Other books banned in the United States at different times and places include *The Grapes of Wrath, Tropic of Cancer, Ulysses, Lady Chatterly's Lover*, and *The Naked Lunch*. When the X-rated film *Deep Throat* was screened in New York theaters in 1972, authorities confiscated prints mid run and charged exhibitors with violating obscenity laws. The film *Carnal Knowledge* was also considered obscene for a time. Films banned in US localities for religious objection include *Monty Python's Life of Brian* and *The Last Temptation of Christ*. Regarding electronic communication, Attorney General Janet Reno tried but failed to ban "indecent" speech on the Internet.[244]

It's government's job to uphold the Constitution and to maintain law and order, but what if these goals are contradictory? For example, the First Amendment guarantees the right to free expression, which can threaten peaceful order. In Nigeria in 2002, fashion writer Isioma Daniel was addressing Muslims opposed to an upcoming beauty contest. When charged that the contest was immoral and asked what Mohammed would think, she said, "In all honesty, he would probably have chosen a wife from one of them."[245] The comment triggered violent religious riots that left more than two hundred dead, one thousand injured, and eleven thousand homeless. The publisher's offices were set on fire and the Islamist government of Zamfara, in northern Nigeria, issued a fatwa against Isioma Daniel, declaring, "It is abiding on all Muslims to consider the killing of the writer as a religious duty."[246]

One particular method of expression that galls in the United States is the burning of the American flag. There is a difference between speech alone, as in a newspaper editorial, and speech mixed with actions of protest like marches, rallies, or flag-burning. In the late 1960s, a young man named David O'Brien and three others burned their draft cards on the steps of the South Boston courthouse before a crowd, in violation of a 1965 federal provision. The Supreme Court ruled against them. "We cannot accept the view," wrote Earl Warren, "that an apparently limitless variety of conduct can be labeled speech whenever the person engaging in the conduct intends thereby to express an idea."[247] The First Amendment protected wearing a symbol, like an armband, but not burning draft documents.

In 1969, Sidney Street heard on the radio that civil rights activist James Meredith had been wounded by a sniper's bullet in Mississippi. Infuriated, he burned an American flag at an intersection in Brooklyn, shouting, "We don't need no damned flag," defying a New York State statute that banned defiling "either by words or act" any flag of the United States. The Supreme Court overturned Street's conviction on the grounds that the statute was unconstitutional because it banned both words and actions and that the First Amendment protected Street's words at least. Whether flag burning was legal was left open.[248] In *Spence v. Washington* (1974), a college student had affixed a peace sign to both sides of an American flag with black electrical tape and hung the flag upside down from his dorm window to protest the Vietnam War. He was convicted of violating a Washington law, but the Supreme Court held that the law violated Spence's freedom of expression. Spence's flag was privately owned and was being displayed on private property in a way that did not breach the peace and in a way in which flags have traditionally been used to convey ideas.[249]

During the Republican National Convention in 1984, Gregory Johnson doused an American flag with kerosene and lit it while leading the crowd in the chant, "Red, white, and blue, we spit on you." Johnson was convicted of violating a Texas law prohibiting "the desecration of venerated objects." The Supreme Court ruled that Johnson's actions were "sufficiently imbued with elements of communication" to warrant First Amendment protection. Wrote Justice Brennan, "The Government may not prohibit the expression of an idea simply because society finds [it] offensive or disagreeable."[250] Justice Anthony Kennedy concurred, remarking, "The flag protects those who hold it in contempt."[251] Four justices, including Chief Justice Rehnquist, offered strong dissents, and the ruling permitting flag burning was immensely unpopular. Veterans groups denounced it. President George Bush deplored it. A *Newsweek* poll found that two thirds of the people disagreed with it, and by a vote of ninety-seven to three, the US Senate passed a resolution expressing "profound disappointment" with it.[252] Members of Congress called for constitutional action to overrule the Court. Opposite, civil libertarians and the American Bar Association urged strict preservation of First Amendment rights.

In 1989, Congress passed legislation to criminalize desecration of the American flag. The Flag Protection Act required up to a year in jail and a $1,000 fine for anyone who knowingly "mutilates, defaces, physically defiles, burns, maintains on the floor or ground, or tramples on any flag of the United States." The law did not last long, though. The Supreme Court struck it down as an unwarranted restraint on symbolic expression, a violation of the First Amendment. Justice Brennan wrote for the majority that the Flag Protection Act banned a form of free expression out of concern for its likely impact. He noted that government can create and promote national symbols and advocate their respectful treatment, but it cannot outlaw their disrespectful treatment without violating a person's liberty. What the flag represents—a republic in which each person can say what he pleases—is what's special, not the piece of cloth. Better to have free expression sacred than the icon, at the expense of the real thing.

One challenge to free speech comes from watchdog groups who monitor television and seek to censor advertising and scenes in TV shows that don't plug into their values like a Tetris block. OneMillionMoms.com is an online project of the American Family Association based in Tupelo, Mississippi (not associated with the Million Mom March organization). According to its website, the American Family Association is a "nonprofit conservative, pro-family organization" and "a well-respected member of the pro-family and pro-life community," which "exists to motivate and equip citizens to change the culture and reflect Biblical truth." Through e-mails, members of OneMillionMoms.com protest against shows they find too un-Christian. Some of their targets have included the television shows *NYPD Blue, The Shield, Medium, Brothers and Sisters, Pretty Little Liars, South Park,* and *Desperate Housewives.* Some of the companies they have targeted include Disney (for airing the movie *Little Manhattan*); Abercrombie and Fitch (for offering small bikini tops for underage girls); NASCAR (for "indecent language" making it onto the air); Procter & Gamble (for a character in a Febreze ad who said, "Oh my God," offending Christians); the drugstores Rite Aid, Walgreen's, and CVS (for offering adult toys on their websites); Dodge (for sponsoring a "lingerie bowl"); and Levi Strauss (for an ad campaign that exhibited "disrespect and chaos with no consequences"). The group also took exception to an ad for Dentyne Ice in which two young people were making out and the girl stopped and asked the guy if he had anything, apparently referring to a condom. He said yes and took out a pack of gum. The commercial's tag line was "practice safe breath."[253]

Some of their calls to arms are unintentionally amusing. One implores, "When is it okay to sell v*br*tors, d*ld*s, and other s*x toys on a drugstore's website? (An asterisk is used to insure our e-mails get through to those who have signed up for our alerts. Otherwise, specific words referenced would be blocked by some Internet filters.)"[254] The irony of being unable to communicate with one another due to their own censorship is lost on them. (The same situation exists at the other end of the political spectrum with regard to racial issues.)

OneMillionMoms.com directs its greatest ire at the sponsors of television shows that depict gays and transsexuals as normal people. The group targeted the show *Glee* for encouraging gays to accept who they are, as opposed to teaching that sexual orientation is a matter of choice. It denounced the TV show *Degrassi* because one character, an "openly gay football captain and starting quarterback, declined reparative therapy for his homosexuality." It targeted the show *Dancing with the Stars* for "announcing Chaz Bono as the first transgendered contestant" and for having "the audacity to give a definition of what that means for anyone who is not aware." In addition, OneMillionMoms.com has gone after Old Navy (because they "carry 'gay' shirts,"), J. Crew, for an ad that "blatantly celebrates transgendered children" (by showing a young boy wearing pink toenail polish), and Target, for sponsoring the Trevor Helpline and for helping to publicize its motto, "Be proud of who you are." In contrast, one of the headlines on the OneMillionMoms.com website is, "June 4 Gay Pride Day at Disney—Disgusting Tradition Continues!"[255]

Religious groups and parents trying to shield their young have long advocated censorship, but more recently, challenges to free speech have come from the hostile-environment component of antidiscrimination law, which rather than protect the Five Rights, tries to protect feelings by regulating communication. The reasoning: if words or pictures can create a hostile environment, then the words and pictures must be controlled. This would seem to contradict First Amendment rights. How can there be laws against hurting peoples' feelings *and* free speech? Important as they are, the issues of race, ethnicity, religion, gender, and sexual orientation must be determined within the Five Rights, not in spite of them. The effort to eradicate discrimination in businesses, universities, and membership organizations has produced laws targeting real racism and sexism, but the laws can be applied to unsuitable speech and exploited by professional offense-takers, including third parties.

Every time a person makes a choice, he discriminates; he picks one alternative and rejects others. To select is to discriminate, and since everyone does it routinely, it can always be accused. To hire capable workers is to discriminate against goof-offs. To loan only to family is to discriminate against friends. Sometimes we can't even say why we choose as we do. Prohibiting discrimination—something immutable in human nature—makes every individual guilty to some degree, and so in any argument, whoever has the best claim to being offended can use antidiscrimination law as a club to get his way. More than any other legislation, it invites claims of victimhood. A mother sued the San Francisco Ballet for height and weight discrimination when it declined to accept her daughter into its program.[256] Under pressure from Native Americans, Denver officials refused to issue a permit for a Columbus Day parade unless the organizers agreed to ban any reference to Christopher Columbus.[257] A federal judge held that gender-related terms like "foreman" and "draftsman" were discriminatory and constituted sexual harassment.[258] Another judge ruled that classified ads for homes with an "ocean view" and with "family rooms," discriminated against the blind and singles, respectively.[259]

Employers, to avoid legal fees and bad publicity, usually try to settle even opportunistic claims of discrimination, which makes the charge an effective weapon for a scheming employee. In one case reported by Tammy Bruce, an experienced, respected corporate manager was assigned to help improve the people skills of an up-and-coming but abrasive junior executive, a woman who had a pattern of antagonizing coworkers. At one point, he suggested that she "could be a little nicer." The woman filed a sexual harassment suit against him, claiming that he was soliciting her. The case failed, but the incident caused the manager's suspension and ultimately forced him to leave the company.[260] On being promoted to manager of her Dairy Mart in Wellsville, Ohio, Dolores Stanley removed *Playboy* and *Penthouse* from the store's shelves because they offended her as a Christian. When she refused to replace them, the chain fired her, and she sued for sexual harassment (for creating a hostile workplace environment). Though the chain had a First Amendment right to sell the publications, it settled the case before trial for a sum "well into the six figures."[261]

Sexually suggestive e-mails need only offend someone who hears about them to constitute harassment. *The New York Times* fired twenty people for sending such e-mails, citing a need to protect itself from liability. Employers, who are as biased and politically motivated as anyone else, are conscripted as listeners and correctors to monitor and regulate communications, often overreacting because they too are unsure of what constitutes a hostile environment. The general rule has become, anything you would not say in front of young children, do not say at work. You could trigger a lawsuit and lose your job by repeating a line from a network sitcom if it offends a fellow employee.[262]

Editors and television producers view their mediums as vehicles through which the enlightened enlighten. They say what they think people need to hear, and their most ubiquitous lesson is that discrimination is bad. Hypersensitive to the charge themselves, they are highly selective about how news stories are reported and what details are omitted. If unbiased full disclosure of a story can conceivably cause accusations of racial or sexual bias, the story is edited to correct for it.[263] A journalist cannot make any statement that calls a stereotype to mind without risking his career. National Public Radio fired senior news analyst Juan Williams for admitting that people on airplanes dressed "in Muslim garb" sometimes made him nervous.[264] Williams later apologized. It's also dangerous to make any comment that gives pause for not matching the prescribed presumptions. CNN fired journalist Rick Sanchez after he opined that Jewish people in America today were not oppressed. Sanchez apologized.[265] *Meet the Press* host David Gregory was reviled for referring to a hypothetical leader of the Republican Party as its "grand wizard," and he apologized.[266] When NBA star Jeremy Lin, who is Asian, had an off night after several great performances in a row, sports writer Anthony Federico noted that Lin's nine turnovers might show "a chink in the armor." ESPN fired Federico immediately. Pundits applauded the firing, many of them referring to the use of the familiar phrase as "heinous."[267]

None of these remarks were intended to offend, but all did because, as pious third parties with too much time, we live to be offended. And since indignation sells, whatever the group, editors and producers focus on its mistreatment, covering any comment that "raised eyebrows" in excruciating detail as national news, always presuming a deliberate insult to help generate the greatest possible ire. The editorializing *is* the story, but it plays as real news because, since the 1980s, when racism replaced communism as the "ism" you had damn well better hate, nothing has been more PC than to exhibit outrage at every unfortunate choice of words. To not object calls one's values into question, so writers robotically accuse racism while employing emperor's-new-clothes timidity themselves, and we take our cues from them. Thirty years of tiptoeing now has us referring to Klaus Barbie as "a person from Germany."

The we-aren't-biased bias affects hiring too. Editors of major US newspapers have admitted to relying on quotas and favoring less qualified minority candidates to fill positions and that race, ethnicity, and gender influence who covers what stories.[268] *The New York Times* has interviewed prospective interns at graduate journalism schools on a "minorities only" basis, precipitating complaints of favoritism.[269] Other newspapers have put freezes on hiring white men to hire more women and persons of color.[270] In journalism, to oppose racial preferences is considered bigotry.

At colleges too, it is apostasy to say or do anything that can possibly be interpreted as discrimination. To prevent a hostile environment on campus, public universities impose speech codes to censor views potentially offensive to women, racial minorities, or gays. Expressing a politically incorrect opinion—saying something like, "Men seem to be better than women at poker"—can get you expelled. The University of Maryland's sexual harassment policy prohibits "idle chatter of a sexual nature, sexual innuendoes, comments about a person's clothing, body, sexual activities, weight, body shape, size, or figure, and comments or questions about the sensuality of a person."[271] Saying to a friend, "I like the way girls look in granny glasses," could constitute sexual harassment. Swarthmore College issued a student manual calling sexual innuendo "acquaintance rape."[272] From the *Yale Daily News*: "We are dedicated to eliminating sexism … we now refer to female first-year students as 'freshwomen' and to mixed-sex groups as 'freshpeople.'"[273] At the University of California, a fraternity had T-shirts made to promote a "South of the Border" party. The shirts depicted a man wearing a sombrero sitting on a beach watching the sun set, bottle of tequila in hand. Latino activists charged that the shirt demeaned Mexicans. The university forced the students to destroy the shirts, apologize in writing, engage in community service, and attend two seminars on multiculturalism.[274]

Indoctrination begins in preschool. Groups decide what words and characterizations bother them and complain, and those words and pictures disappear from textbooks and television. At government's behest, more than four hundred words and phrases have been banned by major publishers of educational materials for being demeaning to some group. The list includes "airman" (banned as sexist), "Americans" (banned for being geographically chauvinistic, to be replaced with "people of the United States"), "the blind" (banned as offensive, to be replaced by "people who are blind"), "bookworm" (banned as offensive), "brave" (banned as offensive when referring to Native Americans), "brotherhood" (banned as sexist), "cowboy" (banned as sexist), "cleaning woman" (banned as sexist), "councilman" (banned as sexist), "craftsmanship" (banned as sexist), "crazy" (banned as offensive), "cult" (banned as ethnocentric), "crippled" (banned as offensive), "crotchety" (banned as a reference to older people), "deliveryman" (banned as sexist), "dialect" (banned as ethnocentric), "doorman" (banned as sexist), "dwarf" (banned as demeaning, to be replaced by "person of short stature"), "early man" (banned as sexist), "economically disadvantaged" (banned as ethnocentric), "the elderly" (banned as ageist), "Eskimo" (banned as demeaning), "exotic" (banned as demeaning), "extremist" (banned as ethnocentric), "fanatic" (banned as ethnocentric), "feebleminded" (banned as offensive), "fellowship" (banned as sexist), "fisherman" (banned as sexist), "founding fathers" (banned as sexist), and "fraternity" (banned as sexist).[275] You get the idea, and these examples are from just the first six letters of the alphabet.

Antidiscrimination law is an attempt to protect the members of a group, which is a flawed philosophy. The rights of the individual must be respected over those of any group, because every person is an individual. The category omits no one. Defining people by group always excludes some people, creating faction and rivalry. Antidiscrimination law, in protecting each collective according to its clout, makes each an interest group, each competing to get its way *from* individuals, many of whom find the special treatment of groups tedious and wonder, is it really necessary to restrict what people can say to each other to protect them from the damage of hearing ugly words when the cost is the liberty to speak freely?

People take offense when they perceive they're being stereotyped or prejudged, even by a friend. When someone prefaces a bit of news with, *"You'll* appreciate this," usually, you don't, because you're busy wondering, "Why did he think *I* would appreciate this? Boy, he has me all wrong." No person wants to be thought of as a predictable stimulus-response mechanism. Each wants to be considered an individual with unique thoughts and reasons. When the presumption appears related to nationality, religion, gender, or sexual orientation, the offense carries extra weight.

Many comments taken as racist or sexist are innocent, but since no one is sure of the rules, conversation is fraught with charges of wrong speaking and the requisite apologies for it. People who know that they're espousing the right views in the right language—television and the Internet have told them so—can be among the most intolerant. They know that the proper response to any dissonant remark is scorn. No words are wasted on debate; they wince with disapproval, label the cretin a religious nut or racist, and icily dismiss him, affronted. To gasp and label is not an argument, but it's the prescribed ad hominem response to any comment even mildly reminiscent of those that television writers put in the mouths of their most loathsome characters to exhibit their malignance. (Television teaches us that battery, though wrong, is at least not a slur.) And so, fearing disgrace, people self-repress and parrot. Undesirable qualities are imputed to people who say undesirable things, so they don't, making discourse synthetic.

Recently, the clearest violations of First Amendment rights have involved laws prohibiting "cyberbullying," defined by the National Crime Prevention Council as the transmission of "text or images intended to hurt or embarrass another person."[276] A bill introduced in the US House of Representatives empowers the federal government to send to jail for up to two years any person who makes any electronic communication deemed intended to "harass, intimidate, or cause substantial emotional distress to a person."[277] Upset someone and go to jail. People's feelings aren't just hurt. They're *lacerated.* And the wound can only be healed by exacting some concession from the offender. Ultrasensitivity has moved from the realm of emotional blackmail to that of real extortion.

At least forty-four states have cyberbullying laws, generally intended to protect teens from one another's cruelty. Legislatures pass them easily. When an antibullying bill came before Massachusetts lawmakers, though the bill clearly disregarded First Amendment rights, legislators passed it *unanimously* in both the house and senate,[278] indicating the level of political necessity that attends "protecting the children." Some schools now monitor all e-mails, ostensibly to protect students.

"Bullying" in this case is an emotion-laden misnomer intentionally chosen by the parents of the victims and by lawmakers. It does not refer to one student blocking another's path or shoving him into a locker, but to ridicule, which cannot be banned. Antibullying laws place the power to bully individuals (in the true meaning of the word: to intimidate or coerce) in the hands of authorities, who can impose their personal standards arbitrarily. They can interpret teasing or name-calling as hate speech or defamation, making it a matter involving school officials, police, and prosecutors. It's wrong to use words or pictures to inflict distress on someone, and it's unfortunate that some young people may be especially vulnerable, but that does not invalidate other students' First Amendment rights. If the use of electronic communication to humiliate is to disappear, it must happen through early education, not through laws and penalties, which are less helpful anyway because they *follow* the incident.

Honoring the First Amendment requires thicker skin. As the saying goes, freedom *of* speech is a right, but freedom *from* speech is not. There is no right to go through life unoffended. Such a right would allow anyone to cry foul at any perceived slight. Freedom of speech requires that even the ugliest words be allowed, for if a single word is made actionable, soon there would be many; this strategy also backfires, since banishing a word makes it more potent. Even the most offensive word in the English language, "supernatural," must be permitted. One can ignore words or respond to them, but he can't silence them. By what they say, people are considered wise or foolish, and this reality rather than law must govern their choice of words.

The Right to Bear Arms

Attempts in the seventeenth century by British monarchs Charles II and James II to disarm Protestants and suspected political opponents led to the establishment of a right to bear arms. Sir William Blackstone, in his *Commentaries on the Laws of England,* wrote that the right to bear arms was a part of "the natural right of resistance and self-preservation."[279] In the American colonies, the right to keep arms had fewer qualifications than in England, broadening the right. Gun ownership was encouraged: guns were needed for game hunting and defense, and a colony without a sufficient number of armed men was unlikely to survive. In the 1760s and 1770s, the American Revolution began with acts of rebellion by armed citizens, and when the nation was formed, the right to bear arms was included in the Bill of Rights, in the Second Amendment.

By the start of the twentieth century, a tentative balance had been reached between the right to have arms and the power of government to limit that right, but after World War I, Prohibition brought organized crime and open violence to the streets of many major US cities, along with a new weapon, the Thompson machine gun, the first fully automatic weapon widely available to civilians. In the 1920s and 1930s, the "Tommy gun" aided the rise of gangsters like John Dillinger, "Pretty Boy" Floyd, and Bonnie Parker and Clyde Barrow. The new talkies brought the violence of automatic weapons to the screen, leading to the National Firearms Act of 1934, which effectively outlawed fully automatic weapons, sawed-off shotguns, and most silencers. It also established a federal licensing system for gun manufacturers and dealers. The urban riots and the three major US assassinations of the 1960s gave rise to the Gun Control Act of 1968, the first gun legislation that affected large numbers of Americans. It limited the purchase of firearms through the mail and the importation of surplus military rifles, and it prohibited felons from purchasing firearms. The 1993 Federal Firearms Act, called the Brady Law, introduced waiting periods and background checks to determine eligibility of gun ownership. Guns were denied to buyers who were under restraining orders or had been convicted of domestic violence, stalking, or harassment. The Assault Weapons

Ban outlawed nineteen semiautomatic weapons and large capacity ammunition feeders.

In general, the Rocky Mountain and southern states have the most lenient gun laws, and the northeastern states have the toughest. At least fifteen states require the purchaser of a handgun to obtain a license. Most states have permissive licensing, which allows anyone to buy a handgun unless they fall into a prohibited category (convicted felons, domestic abusers, drug users, fugitives from justice, and illegal aliens). Other states have restrictive licensing, in which a license is granted only if the candidate can show a special need, leaving it up to local authorities to decide who gets a license. In some states, sheriffs and police chiefs can issue concealed weapon permits as they see fit, allowing them to use the permits as political currency. The discretionary system used in New York City, for example, results in permits for the wealthy, celebrities, and friends of high-ranking police, while people without connections are denied.

Despite the regulations, Americans own at least 250 million firearms; about 80 million are handguns, the rest are rifles and shotguns.[280] Tens of millions of individuals take pleasure in hunting, sport shooting, and gun collecting. There are more than nine thousand outdoor shooting ranges in the United States.[281] There are more magazines about hunting than cars, and with a greater circulation.[282] Hunters enjoy their sport as a throwback, an escape, a commune with nature. Since hunters are licensed by state fish and game commissions, they pose no threat to endangered species, and they pay special taxes to fund conservation efforts.

In the United States, however, guns are second only to car accidents as a cause of nonnatural death. On average, thirty-five people are shot and killed each day. About 90 percent of those are assaults, and 10 percent are accidents. A greater number of people—about forty-five each day—commit suicide with guns.[283] (Factor in suicides by all other methods and the number comes to an average of eighty-eight people each day, which means that for every two people shot and killed by someone in the United States, five people kill themselves. The ratio suggests that perhaps one person shooting another is less a problem than the failure of so many to attain happiness.) Because attempted suicide by other methods, especially drug overdose, commonly fails, and attempts with a gun usually succeed, having a gun contributes to suicide—not by increasing the likelihood of an attempt but the efficacy of one. For the same reason, an armed criminal is more likely to commit murder than an unarmed one. Because guns are deadlier than other weapons, the United States has the highest homicide rate of all industrialized Western nations.[284]

Some have suggested that the Second Amendment should be repealed. Others have tried to interpret the Second Amendment as guaranteeing nothing to individuals, claiming that the right to bear arms is a "collective right," meaning that it applies only to organized militias, like the National Guard. But the right to bear arms is guaranteed to "the people," as in the other amendments, and in none of those does the phrase refer to a collective. Each right belongs to each person. Not until the twentieth century did anyone claim that the right to bear arms was a "collective" right, which is no right at all if you are not considered part of the collective in question. Individuals, not just certain groups of them, have a right to free speech and to bear arms. Arguments to the contrary are contrived to fit a desired end.

Other proponents of strict gun control assert that the need for guns has become obsolete. The right to bear arms was intended to allow individuals to protect themselves and their families from harm by other individuals, and to provide an armed body from which a militia could be drawn, if necessary, to defend the nation from outside aggressors or from a government turned tyrannical. Are these reasons still valid?

The first one is. It's still a big country with a lot of empty space, a certain number of bad guys, a limited number of police, and a delay in response time. With about 1.4 million violent crimes in the United States each year, self-defense is not an obsolete concern. Over a person's lifetime, there is a 50/50 chance that he will be a victim of a violent crime (by definition, one in which the victim interacts with the criminal), and the most likely location is in or near his home, where he would be most likely to have access to a gun. Police admit that they can rarely intervene before a victim is injured or his property taken. Police investigate *after* a crime, but they do not protect individuals from harm up front, leaving people dependent on themselves. During a riot, during a blackout, or after a natural disaster, it can be days before order is restored and looting often happens—except to the people who stand guard over their property, armed.[285]

Guns make it easier for people to kill one another, but they also let vulnerable people protect themselves. A gun can make up for a difference in physical size. A New York woman named Linda Riss asked the police to do something about her unstable boyfriend, who had repeatedly threatened, "If I can't have you, no one else will have you, and when I get through with you, no one else will want you." Soon after, he paid a man to throw lye in her face, blinding her in one eye and scarring her for life. Riss sued the city but lost.[286] The City of New York had refused to provide protection for her while forbidding her to arm herself. Prohibiting small arms fortifies the physically dominant.

What about guns as a last resort against tyrannical government? In theory, if government does not honor the Five Rights, it's up to the citizenry to resist and change it, and they must possess the means. Can armed individuals on their home turf hope to threaten a modern army with smart bombs and satellites? It is at least possible, but a better reason for permitting arms in private hands is to *deter* severely unconstitutional action by the State. Three institutions keep the federal government in check: the Supreme Court, the ballot box, and private gun ownership. An unarmed populace provides little threat to an established government, but when many hold arms and the State is always under the implied threat of a militant response, it has a concrete reason to behave. "The power of making war often prevents it," noted Washington.[287] For this reason, as a nation, we hold weaponry. We don't trust another nation to hold it for us because we'd be in trouble if it turned on us. As individuals versus the State, the reasoning is the same. We are governed by our consent more so than individuals in other nations, in part, because we are armed.

The implied-threat element of gun ownership has value among individuals too. There is a kind of "free market" for aggressive behavior in which some people try to gain advantage through bravado and intimidation. When people own guns, combatants in any quarrel have reason other than the legal system to fear escalation. Gun

127

ownership can quietly halt aggression by other means: harassment, blackmail, thievery, stalking, or assault. In a free market, people often want something but refrain because it costs too much. When considering an act of aggression, the same is true. The fact that handguns are present in four out of ten homes is unquestionably a deterrent to criminals.

The Supreme Court has taken a restrictive view of the Second Amendment, limiting the right to bear arms and stipulating the legality of weapons and the conditions under which they may be kept, but the gun control movement would like to see the Court go much further. It seeks to reduce the number of guns in circulation, though statistics suggest that more guns do not necessarily translate to more crimes. It may sound counterintuitive, but for fifty years, while the number of handguns in circulation has boomed, the number of gunshot deaths has been decreasing. Twenty years ago, there was an average of 24,100 murders annually in the nation.[288] In recent years, the number has been around 16,300, a drop of one third, despite a 50 million increase in human population and a doubling of the number of guns.[289] Twenty years ago, there were about 1.9 million violent crimes annually. Recently, the number has been around 1.4 million, and they tend to be concentrated among an underclass of criminals.[290] On television, armed killers include the eminent doctor, urbane architect, all-American astronaut, family matriarch, larcenous art dealer, and long-suffering wife of a licentious lizard, but in life, men with a criminal record commit most gun murders. Wanting fewer guns in circulation may satisfy personal desires, but the data suggest that keeping guns out of the wrong hands is more important.

Opposite the gun control movement, the National Rifle Association (NRA) fights doggedly to preserve the right to own firearms. It has been criticized for taking extreme positions, for example, opposing regulations on the sale of armor-piercing "cop-killer" bullets. The NRA takes the view that every gun control proposal is a step toward confiscation, as happened in the United Kingdom. While the fear is not unfounded, it makes a poor slippery-slope argument in the face of reasonable gun control measures, like screening to limit the ability of people with criminal records or a history of mental instability from purchasing firearms. To achieve this, waiting periods and background checks are not a lot to ask. Robyn Anderson, the woman who bought guns for Eric Harris and Dylan Klebold, the perpetrators of the high school massacre at Columbine, testified that she had bought the weapons at a gun show from a private seller rather than a Federal Firearm Licensee because no paperwork or background check was required. "It was too easy," she said. "I wish it had been more difficult. I wouldn't have helped them buy the guns if I had faced a background check."[291] A comprehensive registration and licensing system may come in the future (for guns or ammunition or both), but confiscation is unjustifiable. Self-defense remains a valid reason to own a gun. A government that can only defend the right to life after the fact cannot claim to disarm individuals for their protection.

Speaking generally, any liberty that can possibly be permitted should be, and private gun ownership obviously can be permitted.

On the whole, liberty is messy and often unpopular. It allows self-destructive behavior; it permits extremes, annoyances, and tragedies. It lets fools sound off. If we could step outside of our actions and see them from a distance, we would see spontaneous order chugging along as always. Since that perspective eludes us, we try to correct the discordant behavior around us. Liberty allows variety and disarray, and our aversion to disarray puts liberty forever at risk. German philosopher Bernhard Rehfeld called the making of deliberate rules man's most perilous invention, a greater threat than fire or gunpowder.[292] Nevertheless, seeking ideally arranged order, we apply legislative cures like medieval doctors at work on a patient with the sniffles. Liberty is an abstract principle and less gripping than the desire to legislate against a wrong that is fresh and vivid and works on our passions, which is why, unless diligently guarded, liberty is sacrificed to the concern of the moment.

CHAPTER 8
The Right to Property

The property line sets the outer boundary of the protected sphere. It separates public from private; it's the line between majority rule and free choice. Property is a mini sovereignty in which the owner is autonomous, able to answer the tugs of his personality without regard for others' views, to act on his whims without asking permission or giving explanation. In setting clearly defined boundaries within which liberty has teeth and the State does not, property shields the individual from government's tendency to treat every issue as a public concern.

Common law is universal, but rules of organization do not normally apply on private property. Since their purpose is to sort things out when one person's rights collide with another's, and in a person's protected sphere, *that* person's rights prevail, rules of organization have no place. There is one exception. Because people may reasonably expect that others do not foul the water on their property, that noise is not excessive, and that their neighbors are not warehousing explosives, rules of organization like pollution laws and zoning ordinances are valid. Even within his home, an individual may not endanger or disturb neighbors. A displeasing choice of architecture, landscaping, or color of paint doesn't violate anyone's rights. To warrant a violation, neighborhood effects must be measurable externalities like noise, vibrations, smoke, or odors, all of which are covered by nuisance law.[293] Government may not arbitrarily ban personal actions on private property. If the behavior has no appreciable neighborhood effects, there is no reason for rules of organization.

Possession of a thing means the ability to manage, move, alter, or sell it. An owner of physical property has the right to use it as he sees fit within preexisting general rules; to exclude others; to lease, subdivide, or grant easement; and to keep any income derived from the property. Property can include a business, money, cars, art, a trademark or brand name, a patent or copyright, or a mailing list. An idea can be property; so can a right to take a certain action. Property rights include the right to earn, inherit, and keep or allocate money, and to make contracts and hold parties to their agreements.

Here is how property relates to the concepts of liberty and justice. A person's property comes from his labor, which took his time, his liberty. Property is past liberty used productively. Property and liberty are interchangeable by mutual consent. A person trades his liberty for property when he takes a job. He trades property for liberty by paying someone else to do a job or by buying a product from him. Military power is the ability to get what one wants through armed conflict. Political power is the ability to get government to mandate what one wants. Economic power lets one buy what he wants. Only the last requires the consent of all parties involved, and voluntary exchange requires the concept of property.

Regarding justice, if property is just in that it gives a person his due, then as Locke observed, "Where there is no property there is no justice, is a proposition as certain as any demonstration in Euclid."[294]

Familiarity unites us to things we have long enjoyed. We favor objects that have been useful to us or that call up agreeable memories. Since prehistoric times, when an individual had something he regularly used, it was understood that it was wrong for another to take it from him. Ownership began with traditions and conventions that eventually became rights. Agriculture could not exist without property rights—what would insure that the individual who planted and tended the crops would be the beneficiary of them? Ownership entered recorded history around 2200 BCE in the area surrounding the Mediterranean Sea near Crete, and among the Myceneans, according to the Greek historian Strabo.[295] In the eighteenth century BCE, a thousand years before the Bible, the Code of Hammurabi dealt with theft of property.

Modern property rights stem from the feudal system of the Middle Ages. Before the rise of strong central government, each landowner produced what he needed, and all stole from one another in raids. The master of a property had to defend it. He needed help from men with military skills, who were available, but they had to be paid. The lord couldn't pay in cash—currency and precious metals were scarce and of little use since there were few merchants or stores—so he paid his soldiers by giving them land, which helped attach them to him geographically. Included in the deal between the lord and the professional soldier, or vassal, were serfs to work the land while the vassal defended his lord and raided other properties for him. When a vassal died, the lord often made the same arrangement with the vassal's son. Over generations, the property became thought of less as the lord's and more as the vassal's—by both parties. The longer any person or group makes improvements to a piece of land, the more it comes to be theirs in sentiment—this was a motivation behind the American Revolution. Vassals inherited land, left it to others, used it as dowries, and sold it to one another. The traditional terms of these arrangements became property rights.

Mutual respect for property rights had big advantages. People didn't have to spend so much time guarding against interlopers and thieves. Without ongoing raids, they could enjoy their belongings and use their spare time to create surpluses to exchange for other things they wanted. Commerce made it more useful to know how to produce, transport, or manage assets than to fight; people started to get rich not by stealing but by making and trading. Individuals' efforts to improve their circumstances brought the rise of a middle class and the wide dissemination of private property and eventually caused the feudal system to be replaced by something that could better protect property rights: strong central government.

Early in thirteenth-century England, King John's attempt to violate property rights led to the Magna Carta, which declared that the king could not seize provisions without making compensation, that individuals could not be dispossessed of their property without due process, and that the king could not raise taxes without the consent of a body representing the people, which became Parliament. Magna Carta also declared that individuals were free to seek employment or to establish a trade. As interpreted by Edward Coke, the premiere legal scholar of his age, Magna Carta guaranteed the rights to life, liberty, property, and equality before the law.[296] Thus, four of the Five Rights were first guaranteed in writing eight centuries ago. The right to pursue happiness would not join them until the Enlightenment and the Declaration of Independence.

Europeans of the time feared democracy, associating it with mob rule. With the majority in charge, what would prevent the numerous poor from overthrowing established institutions? Property was the answer. Property rights "render men fit members of society by making them abstain from the possessions of others," wrote Hume.[297] Property anchors people and unites them in a sentiment of preservation. Widespread ownership brings community and stability, and promotes peaceful order. People don't fear the loss of what they don't own. They don't take extra care in its management. Renters, sharers, and borrowers have no incentive to take the long, prudent view; they are motivated to extract as much from a property as possible. Ownership inspires planning, investment, and conservation—often pride and affection too.

Private property also standardized fair dealing. It sanctioned the transfer of a possession from one person to another, generating a contract complete with price, date of delivery, and other terms. A contract imposes a legal obligation to follow through on resolutions; it forces people to keep their word. The practice of honoring agreements and performing up to expectations spread, allowing people to make plans based on each other's actions. Individuals acting predictably, reciprocally, are the moving parts of spontaneous order.

In the 1640s, the refusal of James I and Charles I to recognize more rights as they increased taxes and Charles's attempt to undo some long-established rights led to the English civil war, after which the term "property" came to include not just tangible assets, but nontransferable, inalienable possessions including a person's life, body, and reputation. Dutch jurist Hugo Grotius popularized this view, and Locke and Hume expanded on it. William Blackstone published his *Commentaries on the Laws of England,* in which he constructed on Locke's ideas a sound legal foundation for the sanctity of property rights. Blackstone defined property as "that sole and despotic domain which one man claims and exercises over the material things in the world in total exclusion of the right of any individual in the universe."[298] He considered the right to property so great "that it will not authorize the least violation of it; no, not even for the general good of the whole community."[299]

Blackstone's *Commentaries* was one of the half-dozen books that most influenced the authors of the US Constitution, but the American colonists didn't start out revering property. At Plymouth, for the first seven years, assets were common to all, and each person received a daily distribution from the public store. The problem with a communal system is that working harder does not benefit the individual. He can shirk his duties and get the same. Whippings were administered to slackers, without success. After several years of barely surviving, the settlers abandoned communal ownership for private property, and the colony flourished. Wrote founder James Wilson regarding Plymouth, "[T]he introduction of exclusive property immediately produced the most comfortable change in the colony by engaging the affections and invigorating the pursuits of its inhabitants."[300] There were fewer claims of illness and incapacity. Noted Wilson, "What belongs to no one is wasted by everyone. What belongs to one man in particular is the object of his economy and care."[301]

Ownership begins when one uses his labor to separate something from common. Locke used the example of a public fountain, noting that the water in the fountain belonged to all, but once someone had filled his pitcher from it, that particular water was his.[302] A person makes an apple his when he picks it from the tree. In a newly discovered land, a person makes a piece of property his by seeding and harvesting it. The colonists crossed the Atlantic to avoid religious persecution and martinet landlords, and property was their means. They felt that they owned themselves, their time, and what they produced with it. When the colonists rebelled, their anger over the Stamp Act and the tea tax had nothing to do with the costs, which were minuscule. Their reaction owed to their rigid belief in the rights and privileges associated with property.

Among the founders, the import of property was never in dispute. Gouverneur Morris of Pennsylvania noted that property and not liberty was the main goal of society, because man had had liberty in a state of nature yet he chose to form government to secure his property. Wrote James Madison, "[T]hat alone is just government, which impartially secures to every man, whatever is his own."[303] During the Revolutionary War, Arthur Lee of Virginia wrote, "The right to property is the guardian of every other right, and to deprive the people of this, is in fact to deprive them of their liberty."[304] John Adams, as usual, was more succinct: "Property must be secured or liberty cannot exist."[305] In defending the controversial Jay treaty in 1795, Alexander Hamilton declared, "No powers of language at my command can express the abhorrence I feel at the idea of violating the property of individuals."[306] The founders included in the Constitution four provisions to protect property rights: the due process and takings clauses of the Fifth Amendment, the prohibiting of bills of attainder, the privileges and immunities clause, and the contract clause.

John Marshall, chief justice of the Supreme Court for the first third of the nineteenth century, was as suspicious of government constraints on property and business as the founders had been. Marshall found suspect any law that inhibited commerce, since it impeded free choice and the most productive use of assets. The Marshall Court only permitted government to use its police powers when essential. Following Marshall, the Supreme Court of Chief Justice Roger Taney (1836–1864) let government legislate when it thought it could advance the public interest. The Taney Court allowed states to ban industrial uses of residential property and to demolish privately owned buildings to stop the spread of a fire. It okayed the licensing of liquor sellers, bakers, and auctioneers. Graveyards were regulated to prevent health problems associated with overcrowded interment, and privately owned wharves could be regulated.[307] But on the whole, property rights were respected.

What someone earned, that person owned. People who needed help were largely ignored. Responded one nineteenth-century journal to the suggestion of welfare, "Property has no intrinsic duties of charity. It is the poor who have duties, not the rich; and it is the first duty of the industrious poor not to be poor."[308] President Grover Cleveland vetoed an emergency relief bill to aid Texas farmers, criticizing paternalistic government in his veto: "I do not believe that the power and duty of the general government ought to be extended

135

to the relief of individual suffering which is in no manner properly related to public service or benefit."[309] A politician could not make this statement today without sounding callous, but in the nineteenth century, people were serious about the "general" in "general welfare." Government didn't take from some to give to others. Most individuals saw property as the reward of living a commendable life and the lack of it as resulting from alcoholism, indolence, or foolish waste.

After the Civil War, states passed laws to regulate prices charged by railroads and grain elevators, seemingly violating property rights, but the Supreme Court upheld them. In *Munn v. Illinois* (1877), Chief Justice Morrison Waite noted, "[W]hen private property is devoted to a public use, it is subject to public regulation."[310] In *Fertilizing Company v. Hyde Park* (1878), the Court ruled that government could breach an existing contract if necessary to abate a nuisance.[311] In *Stone v. Mississippi* (1880), it ruled that a state could outlaw an action it had previously approved.[312] The rulings increased the police power of state legislatures, who made more laws. In *Mugler v. Kansas* (1887), the Court upheld the right of a state to outlaw alcoholic beverages, legalizing prohibition in any state that chose to impose it.[313] The Court upheld safety regulations in mines, employees' rights to sue employers if injured on the job, and states' rights to establish fish and game rules. A state could order the slaughter of diseased cattle, regulate railroads, establish workplace standards, limit the height of buildings, and force the vaccination of children.

Twentieth-century problems included overcrowding in urban areas, factory and residential zoning, food purity, air pollution, contamination of waterways, and inadequate waste treatment and related health problems. Women's rights and public education were ripe for reform too. Along with social change, progressives sought economic equality, considering it wrong for some to have so much and others so little. Concentrations of wealth were seen as immoral. Whereas the first part of progressivism was intended to protect individuals at work or to lessen industrialization's toll on the environment, the second part sought to redistribute income. The first tried to establish safe circumstances in which all individuals could compete; the second tried to alter outcomes of the competition considered unjust. Both cost money to implement, and it was during this two-pronged trend that the first regular income tax came to exist in 1913.

In *Block v. Hirsch* (1921), the Supreme Court upheld rent control in the District of Columbia on the premise that a housing shortage temporarily warranted it. Being a direct State-mandated transfer of wealth, rent control is one of the more pernicious violations of property rights. It places a ceiling on what landlords may charge, an amount lower than the market rent, so demand for the housing always exceeds supply, exacerbating shortages. In a free market, price increases eliminate shortages by enticing more supply, but when law fixes rents, there can be no price rises, so no new supply is produced. The buildings fall into disrepair because a landlord has no incentive to refurbish them. Since no one wants to buy rent-controlled buildings, money goes elsewhere while they dilapidate. Rent control inexorably worsens the problem it was mean to address: lack of housing. Over time, it becomes ruinous. Vietnam Foreign Minister Nguyen Co Thach declared that rent control caused more destruction to Hanoi than the entire American bombing during the Vietnam War.[314] Regardless, rent control is still dangled before voters by big city politicians, since it promises big benefits for a few lucky people, like a lottery does.[315]

With the Depression came disillusionment and mistrust of business. Economic hardship made creditors into villains. Debtors petitioned government for debt relief legislation and got it. After protecting contracts for 147 years, the Supreme Court, under Chief Justice Charles Evans Hughes, ruled that the contract clause could be violated, that the right of individuals to contract with one another was "not an absolute one and is not to be read with literal exactness."[316] The Court's finding in *Home Building and Loan Association v. Blaisdell* (1934) confirmed that states could interfere in private contracts and could cancel debts at the expense of the creditor.[317]

From 1933 to 1937, the Court could not simultaneously uphold property rights and New Deal programs that were their antithesis. Something had to give, and it was the Court's regard for property. When President Roosevelt threatened to remake the Court, it relented, and since then, government has had the final say in asset distribution. It was what the majority wanted. Frustrated by what they saw as the failure of free market forces to function as advertised, they felt that government could do a better job (or at least a conciliatory one). In *Nebbia v. New York* (1934), the Court found that "a state is free to adopt whatever economic policy may reasonably be deemed to promote public welfare."[318]

Property rights took two more blows in 1937 and 1938. Social Security had been created in 1935, and Congress's power to tax both employees and employers to provide pension benefits was challenged in *Helvering v. Davis* (1937). Social Security was upheld. The Supreme Court, in finding that government could create such a fund, broadly expanded government's power to tax for the "general welfare." Social Security is not compelled thrift. The dollars collected today are paid out to the Social Security recipients of today, making it a direct transfer of funds. Before the 1930s, it hadn't occurred to anyone that government could take income from some and give it to others—it seemed such an obvious breach of property rights and of the right to equality before the law. After the 1930s, it became routine.

The second blow to property rights came in *United States v. Carolene Products Co.* (1938) in which, through the most opaque and significant footnote in US judicial history, the Court implied that property rights were less important than other rights. The *Carolene Products* footnote allowed regulators to go from a walk to a run. State legislatures took it to mean, act as you think best provided you don't pass any laws that discriminate by race, religion, or national origin, or violate civil rights. Congress took it to mean, tax and spend as you like provided you don't violate those same rights. Interest groups took it to mean, since government will be allocating as it sees fit, beef up your lobbying, dress your desires as the public interest, and get your share of the pie. The footnote demoted property rights—an unthinkable act to eighteenth- and nineteenth-century jurists. Chief Justice Rehnquist noted that property rights have since been treated as "a poor relation" to the other four rights.[319]

Carolene Products demonstrated the Court's new willingness to uphold any law that was "rationally related to serving a legitimate state interest." For a law to be struck down, property owners had to show that it served no conceivable public purpose. Otherwise, it would be granted a "presumption of constitutionality." For example, in *Williamson v. Lee Optical Co.* (1955), the Supreme Court upheld a special interest Oklahoma law that imposed an unnecessary cost on consumers. Justice William O. Douglas, while acknowledging that the law "may exact a needless, wasteful requirement in many cases," voted to uphold it on the basis that state lawmakers must have suspected something amiss or they would not have made the law. Wrote Justice Douglas, "It is enough that there is an evil at hand for correction, and that it might be thought that the particular legislative measure was a rational way to correct it."[320] It was a Supreme Court affirmation of paternal government.

Takings

Government's power of eminent domain permits it to acquire land to build a highway, airport, dam, or national park. A taking is a sale compelled by government in which the property owner is reimbursed. Government gets the land it wants, the owner gets a check, and the State must limit its number of regulatory takings and prioritize them according to its budget. Taxpayers finance takings, which is apt since government can't force "some people alone to bear the burdens which, in all fairness and justice, should be borne by the public as a whole."[321]

When government suppresses a nuisance or bans an action dangerous to neighbors, it's not a taking and no reimbursement is made. Also not compensable are costs imposed by environmental laws, health codes, zoning laws, and regulations pertaining to workplace safety. They are valid rules of organization because they protect individuals *other* than the owner from the actions or negligence of the owner. Any occupation of private property constitutes a taking. All physical intrusions are takings, even minor ones: in one case, a one-half-inch-wide cable running across a property owner's roof was ruled a compensable taking.[322] The gray area involves regulation that substantially devalues a property. What if government restricts the use of a property to the degree that its value is cut in half? Oliver Wendell Holmes established the general rule in *Pennsylvania Coal Co. v. Mahon* (1922) that, "[W]hile property may be regulated to a certain extent, if regulation goes too far, it will be recognized as a taking." Holmes never defined "too far," but he emphasized that a limit must exist; otherwise it was the tendency of regulators to add rules "until at last private property disappears."[323] The Court has ruled that if a regulation wholly denies the owner the use of his property, it constitutes a taking, but it has also said that *only* when "all but a bare residue of the value of the parcel has been destroyed has a taking been established."[324] Restrictions that reduce the value of a property by 50 or 60 percent do not qualify as a taking, and the losses are not reimbursed.

If a property is designated a landmark or historic site, it can be strictly regulated. In 1978, New York City designated Grand Central Station a historical site though it was privately owned. When the action was challenged, the Supreme Court upheld the right of New York to restrict the uses of a building or to convert private buildings for public use without the owner's consent and without reimbursing him. In *Penn Central Transportation v. New York* (1978), Justice William Brennan wrote for the majority that although the value was greatly diminished, it had not been destroyed and the building still had uses, so it was not a taking; Justice Rehnquist, in dissent, argued that a taking had occurred and that individual property owners should not be penalized for public endeavors.[325] How many historically significant buildings do you think there are in New York City? One hundred? More? Because the city could preserve historic sites at individuals' expense, over the next two decades it designated more than 21,000 buildings historical landmarks, five times more than any other city.[326] Though uncompensated, each owner is barred from renovating, adding on, tearing down, or building overhead.

As noted by author James DeLong in *Property Matters*, a similar usurpation of property rights commonly occurs in the federal control of wetlands. Wetlands were formerly called swamps and considered health hazards. Tax dollars were spent to drain them as a public service; converted wetlands became farms.[327] The Watershed Protection and Flood Prevention Act continued to encourage drainage as late as 1954, but awareness of the environmental function of wetlands increased during the second half of the twentieth century. Wetlands can provide habitat for endangered species; tidal wetlands are important to fishing; river valley wetlands provide flood relief; and wetlands can serve as sinks for pollutants. During the 1970s, in another stretch of the commerce clause, Congress reasoned that since waterways were navigable and thus commerce-related, small streams and tributaries emptying into them could also be regulated, including bogs, swamps, and ponds, no matter how far upstream. The Supreme Court upheld this interpretation in 1985, and in the Wetland Resources Act of 1986, government started penalizing wetlands conversion. The former swamps became "the nation's wetlands inventory," and spurred on by environmentalists, the Army Corps of Engineers, who regulates wetlands, seeks to maintain or add to the inventory.[328]

Since part of the Fifth Amendment reads, "nor shall private property be taken for public use without just compensation," one might expect government to compensate owners for wetlands takings, but wetlands authority comes from the Environmental Protection Agency, and losses caused by environmental regulations are not compensated. If the Army Corps of Engineers designates a property a wetland, it cannot be changed. The owner can still walk on the property, but he can't build additions, plow fields, repair fences, cut trees, or clear brush; he cannot legally move a shovel full of dirt. Though he maintains technical ownership, he loses it by many definitions of the word. If all of his land is designated as wetlands, it's a taking and he's reimbursed, but the Corps, knowing this, tends to avoid determining all of a property wetlands; government has no reason to preserve wetlands in a way that requires it to pay property owners when it can do it in a way that does not.[329]

To insure enforcement, the Army Corps of Engineers requires a 404 permit, which it does not issue without inspecting the property. Assessments are subjective; some wetlands are dry; parking lots have been designated wetlands. The determination is made solely by the Corps and can be changed by them at will. Their findings affect a lot of land. Wetlands comprise 11 percent of the nation. Excluding Alaska, which has more wetlands than all other states combined, there are about 100 million acres of wetlands in the United States, and about 90 percent of them are located on private property. If designated a wetlands, the unlucky owners are stuck with the property and the stringent regulations. Some examples from *Property Matters*: in Delaware, the Turner family was told that they could not install a new roof on their house because the six-inch eaves would cast a shadow on a wetland.[330] Near Reno, Nevada, the Army Corps of Engineers designated a small portion of the Double Diamond Ranch as wetlands; development was permitted on the rest. But three years later, pressured by conservation groups, the Corps reassessed the wetlands as ten times larger than before. It ordered the owner to continue to irrigate, at his expense, land that had been dry before he had irrigated it, because it now harbored wetlands plants.[331] William Ellen, an environmental engineer working in Maryland on the estate of Paul Tudor Jones II, went to jail for six months for moving two truckloads of dirt from one part of the property to another. The property's owner, Jones, was able to avoid prosecution by paying a million-dollar fine and donating another million dollars to the National Fish and Wildlife Foundation.[332]

Lucas v. South Carolina Coastal Council (1992) marked the first time the Court invoked Justice Holmes's rule of seventy years earlier that a destruction of virtually all viable economic value was a taking. According to James DeLong, in 1986 David Lucas bought two adjacent beachfront properties in South Carolina for $975,000, planning to build a single family home on each; neighboring lots already had houses on them. Eighteen months later, the state passed a law to help protect the beach and dune system from eroding. The Beachfront Management Act barred Lucas from building, and the value of his investment collapsed. Lucas claimed that depriving him of all economically viable use of the property constituted a taking under the Fifth and Fourteenth Amendments. The state supreme court ruled in favor of the South Carolina Coastal Council, finding that no taking had occurred because the state could regulate against "harmful or noxious uses" of property without compensating owners. But six years later, the US Supreme Court overturned the decision on the grounds that Lucas was not receiving equality before the law, since the state was banning a use of the property by him that was normal for the neighborhood. The Court found that Lucas's plans for the property did not violate nuisance laws or fit the definition of "harmful or noxious use." And since the law denied him "all economically beneficial or productive use of the land," the state's action was ruled a taking, and South Carolina was forced to compensate Lucas. Justice Scalia observed in *Lucas* that government, when it did not have to compensate property owners, tended to press private property "into public service under the guise of mitigating serious public harm."[333]

Lucas has a telling addendum, which DeLong related as follows: after writing Lucas a check, the state of South Carolina owned the land. In 1993, the state received an offer of $315,000 for it, which it turned down although the buyer was willing to promise not to build on the property. Soon after, the state received an offer of $392,500 from a buyer who would not pay the amount without a specific guarantee that he *could* build on the property. They accepted it. Consider the situation. When Lucas owned the property, the state was willing to devalue it by almost a million dollars to prevent development. When the state owned the property, it sold the right to develop it for the $77,500 difference between the two prices offered.[334] The Council, when it owned the property itself, changed its mind about the harm of development.

Preservation of endangered species' habitat is a third area in which uncompensated takings occur. In the late 1960s, a Department of the Interior report identified eighty-three species of animals whose populations might be dwindling, bringing about the Endangered Species Act in 1973. It became illegal to "take" a member of an endangered species, meaning to kill or capture. There was little opposition to protecting endangered species; wildlife conservation had long been subject to rules of organization.[335] But then government expanded the meaning of the word "take" to include disturbing a creature's *habitat,* a much stricter standard. It prohibited any significant change on a property that could interfere with behavioral patterns like breeding or sheltering. Trimming trees, for example. (Note the definition of "take" when applied to individuals by government vs. the one government uses for itself. When charging the individual with an endangered species crime, nearly *anything* is a taking; when government devalues property, only *everything* constitutes a taking.) The Endangered Species Act pertains to all lands and bodies of water, public or private. If a person's land is designated a critical habitat for a bluetail mole skink or a Stock Island tree snail, the owner is forbidden to develop or disturb the property. The individual must host his permanent feral guests, who may not be burdened or made to be disenfranchised. Few human tenants have such an accommodating arrangement.[336]

The US Fish and Wildlife Service and the National Marine Fisheries Services enforce regulations. Endangered species include familiar animals like the bald eagle, whales, bighorn sheep, grizzly bear, and whooping crane, but they are the stars. Of the 1,100 animals now on the endangered species list, excluding the rodents, only 51 are mammals, less than 5 percent of the total. Listed are nine bats, eight rats, ten mice, eleven snakes, and twelve salamanders. There are over a hundred species of fish listed. Invertebrates include thirty-one snails, fifteen beetles, twelve spiders, and seventy-two species of endangered clams.[337] Moving is the plight of the besieged bivalves.

Animals are added to the endangered species list, or the "threatened" list, which is similar, "without reference to possible economic … impacts."[338] If the costs of saving the habitat of a certain kind of cricket are $10,000 per cricket, so be it. Consequent to this extremism, the Endangered Species Act has cost property owners billions and forced businesses to shut down operations. During the construction of the Tellico Dam in Tennessee, $53 million had already been spent when work was halted by federal order after a small fish present, the snail darter, was found to be endangered. The dam was completed several years later when it was discovered that the snail darter wasn't really endangered—several other populations were found. In 1990, the listing of the northern spotted owl cost the timber industry millions of acres of unused timberlands and contributed to a recession in the Pacific Northwest. In one Oregon case that made property owners jittery nationwide, a district court issued a logging moratorium on a ninety-four-acre plot of privately owned land because two spotted owls were found nesting 1.6 miles *from* the property.[339]

An owner of a three-thousand-acre ranch in Riverside County, California, was told that eight hundred of the acres were inhabited by an endangered species, the kangaroo rat, and that the area couldn't be developed. The restrictions cost the owner over $100,000 per year, and she is not entitled to reimbursement.[340] In Maryland, the Bannister family wanted to build a stone revetment at the base of a cliff on their property to prevent erosion. Government prohibited it because the action could have disturbed tiger beetles on the property. While fighting the matter in court, the section in question eroded and fell away.[341] Ronald Rollins, an Idaho farmer, applied pesticide to fifty acres of feed alfalfa growing on his farm, as he had for many years, but this time geese landed, ate the alfalfa, and died from the pesticide. Though Rollins had used approved pesticide and applied it correctly, he was found guilty of a criminal act because the Migratory Bird Treaty Act makes it a crime for anyone to kill a migratory bird.[342] Viola Allen, a seventy-two-year-old woman in Lynwood, Washington, wanted to sell the eight-acre piece of land that she had owned for forty-four years, but a tiny stream on her property was judged to be vital to salmon, a federally protected species. Ms. Allen has never seen a salmon in the stream in her forty-four years there, and it's a dry ditch for part of the year. No one wants the property due to the restrictions. Of the environmental groups who sued to get Ms. Allen's land restricted, none offered to buy it after its severe devaluation, but one tried to persuade her to donate it to them.[343]

Part of the environmental movement in the United States is less about conserving natural habitat than about thwarting commercial development, and the Endangered Species Act provides a means for nature zealots who see man's existence as an act of aggression against plants, animals, and minerals. Wrote one environmentalist, "We humans have become a disease, the humanpox."[344] They search the endangered and threatened lists to see which species might be around; if they can find one on or near the property, they can take the owner to court and possibly prevent him from development. If they win, they can recoup their legal fees from the owner. Environmental groups oppose reform because they know they have a good thing. Why ask all people to contribute their fair share of the cost of protecting endangered species and risk rejection in a vote when individual property owners can be forced to pay the bill?

The administrators of environmental programs can be fervid. Peter Douglas, the executive director of the California Coastal Commission, was unabashed about his views on the rights of property owners. Environmentalism to Douglas was a "struggle against dehumanizing, amoral corporate capitalism and imperialism at all levels around the planet, and environmental destruction resulting from greed and materialism."[345] When George and Sharlee McNamee installed a canopy, barbeque, shower, and picnic tables in their back yard, the Commission under Douglas ruled that the objects conveyed an unwanted "perception of privatization." It ordered the McNamees to remove them or pay $6,000 per day in fines. Kenneth Healing bought a piece of land in Santa Monica. He wanted to build a three-bedroom house on it and applied to the Commission, which stalled him for seventeen years before okaying it.[346] Secretary of the Interior Bruce Babbit, his reasoning tied to the idea that in Genesis, Noah saved two of *everything* and not just preferable species,[347] rejected the idea that the Endangered Species Act should be held in check by something as pedestrian as costs. It was analogous to an FBI director proclaiming that every crime must be solved, no matter how small and regardless of the cost in dollars or in rights. Environmental regulation is unquestionably necessary, and enforcement has made the United States a less polluted country than it was fifty years ago. Similarly, who could argue against preserving wetlands, endangered species, or historic buildings? But as with all programs, each must be limited by the Five Rights.

When the EPA prohibits pollution or orders a clean-up, it forces the owner to take responsibility for his actions and to incur the costs, rightly, but wetlands and habitat regulations penalize property owners who are not contaminating the environment, who only want to live as they choose on their property. What if, rather than the federal government, an individual wanted to limit a property owner's rights? He would have to purchase an easement: pay the owner for it. Government should have to do the same. Reimbursement for partial takings would honor property rights and, by charging the costs to taxpayers, limit the scope of government action.

Forfeiture Laws

Historic preservation, wetlands restrictions, and protection of endangered species habitat devalue a property by restricting usage. In a forfeiture, property is confiscated outright. There are two kinds: criminal forfeiture and civil asset forfeiture. A criminal forfeiture involves property whose owner has been convicted of a crime, and the forfeiture is part of the sentencing. It's the other one—civil asset forfeiture—that often produces violations of property rights, since assets can be seized without a conviction; credible suspicion is enough. Government can confiscate an asset that is contraband and illegal to own (drugs, weapons, smuggled goods), property that was used in the commission of a crime (cars, boats, planes, houses), or money or property that has come from the proceeds of a crime. Over 90 percent of seizures are civil asset forfeitures.[348]

The founders made no provision for government to take the property of citizens except by taxation or through eminent domain. The power to pass forfeiture statutes is not one of the "foregoing powers," nor is it one of the "other powers vested by this Constitution." It was usurped and upheld on the basis that Great Britain once did it under their common law.[349] Few Supreme Court opinions are as meandering and unsatisfactory as the one upholding the practice of forfeiture in *Calero-Toledo v. Pearson Yacht Leasing* (1974), in which a yacht was seized because one marijuana cigarette was found aboard. Individuals are surprised to find that government can confiscate their property. As House Judiciary Committee Chairman Henry Hyde noted, "People take their due process rights for granted ... they have no idea these [forfeiture] laws exist." He added, of government, "They don't have to convict you. They don't even have to charge you with a crime. But they have your property."[350]

Forfeitures increased after a ruling allowed law enforcement authorities to keep seized assets to finance their own operations. Asset seizures became ends in themselves, tempting police or federal agents to target assets rather than criminals. States had their own civil forfeiture programs, so there was competition among agencies to confiscate property. In most confiscations, there was no parallel prosecution or conviction. A study of five hundred federal cases by the *Pittsburgh Press* concluded that assets were seized without a conviction 80 percent of the time.[351] Often, no charges were filed. Yet over $1 billion worth of assets were seized each year by the federal government, and the same by state and local authorities. Nationwide, police departments came to rely on forfeiture as part of their budgets, with some raising millions of dollars per year for their own use through seizures, making them autarkical.

Abuse of asset forfeiture laws was most common during the

1990s. Willie Jones was a landscaper who went to Houston to buy shrubberies, bringing $9,000 with him. Police stopped him in the airport, found the money, and held him for several hours on the suspicion it was related to narcotics trafficking. They released him but kept his money on the presumption that it was drug-related. It took Mr. Jones over two years to get the money back.[352] In another case in Houston, the US Attorney's Office seized a Red Carpet Motel in a rundown part of the city, claiming the owner had not done enough to discourage use of the hotel by small-time criminals, that, for example, by not raising his room rates he had "tacitly approved" of drug dealing on the property.[353] In Alabama, an elderly doctor named Richard Lowe remembered the Great Depression and was distrustful of banks, so he had stockpiled $317,000 in cash in his home. Finally deciding to trust the system, he deposited the money in a bank. Spotting the large deposit and assuming foul play, government confiscated Mr. Lowe's life savings and other property, assets of $2.5 million.[354] (He was able to get it back.) Rudy Ramirez drove from Texas to Missouri to buy a Corvette he had seen advertised in a magazine, bringing $7,300 in cash with him. He was pulled over by police, who found the money and detained him for hours while they used drug-sniffing dogs to search the car. No drugs were found, but the police confiscated $6,000 of his money, calling it a forfeiture in line with the federal war on drugs. Mr. Ramirez did not contest the matter in court because the legal costs would be twice the amount confiscated.[355] Michigan police seized a car belonging to a woman accused of no crime, but the Supreme Court upheld the seizure because her husband had used it to solicit a prostitute.[356] In some cities, people arrested for drunk driving automatically forfeited their cars, once resulting in over four thousand cars being confiscated in New York City over an eighteen-month period.[357] In California, police still confiscate the cars of unlicensed drivers and impound them for thirty days, permitting the state to raise about $40 million per year, shared by municipal governments and tow operators.[358]

To curb government abuse of forfeiture laws, Congress passed the Civil Asset Forfeiture Reform Act, which allowed owners to recover their property if they could demonstrate that it had been used without their knowledge; it scrapped the requirement that the property owner post a bond during the recovery process; and it forced government to notify property owners of the seizure. Government, however, was still free to seize property without a conviction.

Forfeiture statutes give authorities the means to sidestep due process, presume guilt, and impose a sentence. Police like forfeiture, seeing it as a direct transfer of wealth from the bad guys to the good guys, which in many cases it undoubtedly is. But government's reason for being is to protect the security and property of individuals. How confiscating property does this requires a circuitous explanation. Forfeiture statutes sacrifice principles to utility. It would be helpful to researchers to test new drugs on people without their knowledge, say on the institutionalized mentally ill, but principles prevent it. Likewise, one doesn't violate property rights simply because it's handy.

Commerce in Human Organs

On December 23, 1954, Dr. Joseph Murray made the first successful transplant of a human organ, a kidney, from one identical twin to the other. Then, and for the next thirty years, all transplanted human organs came from living donors. Anyone needing a transplant had to enter the hospital with the donor of the replacement organ. By the 1980s, improvements in surgical technology, tissue matching, and immunosuppressive therapy allowed the transplantation of cadaveric organs. Cyclosporine, especially, increased the survival rate. About 60 percent of all organ donations now come from cadavers and 40 percent from living donors. Still, supply has not kept up with demand. There are about 30,000 organ transplants performed in the United States each year, but that leaves 105,000 people on the national organ transplantation waiting list and 4,000 new patients are added to the list each year. Worse, waiting list numbers understate the shortage because no one can get on the list until they can demonstrate their ability to pay for the operation. Each year, 7,000 Americans die while waiting for an organ.[359]

The two most commonly needed organs are kidneys and livers. Since the liver is a vital organ, every transplanted liver must come from a cadaveric donor. Although 2.5 million people die in the United States each year, less than 20,000 of them yield recyclable organs.

The deceased may voluntarily donate cadaveric organs upon death, or procurement agencies can persuade a decedent's family to donate his organs. Other sources for cadaveric organs include China, where the government harvests organs from executed prisoners for sale on the world market, and in all nations, morgue attendants and others with access to fresh corpses illegally remove and sell organs. Cadaveric organs must be used immediately.[360]

The supply of live donors of a kidney is understandably small. Other than to save the life of a close, dying family member, living people rarely choose to donate a kidney—but it does happen. Imagine yourself in this unfortunate situation: you only have one kidney and it's failing. Without a replacement, you have less than a year to live. You can afford the operation, but you'll likely become one of the 7,000 people who die each year while waiting for an organ. Meanwhile, in a hospital in Mumbai, a teenage boy needs a life-saving heart operation, but the boy's father can't afford it and the boy is going to die. Through the Internet, the boy's father and you become aware of each others' needs and make a deal: he sells you his kidney to pay for his son's operation. If the kidney is compatible, the transaction will save two lives: yours and his son's. But the transaction is illegal in the United States and in most Western nations. According to the law, you and the boy will both have to die.

Since the penalty for obeying this law—death—is more severe than the penalty for breaking it, if you were in this situation, you would likely find an unlawful way of completing the transaction. The result is a global black market for human body parts. Kidneys and other organs from live donors come mostly from desperate people in third-world countries, as in the example. Most organ sellers come from India and probably Brazil after that. Both countries banned the sale of human organs, forcing the trade underground. A kidney can cost the buyer several hundred thousand dollars, though the donor might receive as little as one thousand dollars. Intermediaries get most of the money, as in all black markets. Prohibiting the sale of an in-demand item rewards people willing to break the law. For them, a ban acts like protectionist legislation, outlawing competition, creating market inefficiencies, and multiplying their profits.[361]

A doctor in Virginia tried to help alleviate the organ shortage in 1984 by establishing a service that matched cadaveric kidneys to patients willing to pay for them, but government, spurred on by religious groups, quickly outlawed buying or selling human organs. The National Organ Transplant Act, sponsored by Congressmen Al Gore and Orrin Hatch, banned commerce in human body parts other than replenishable resources such as hair, blood, sperm, or ova. Since the ban, procurement efforts have intensified, but the shortage has persisted. Hospitals and drug companies circumvent the ban by charging for their services rather than for the organ itself. The doctor who removes the organ, brokers, couriers, insurers, health care facilities, pharmaceutical companies, the doctor who transplants it, and those who do the follow-up all benefit financially, and of course, the recipient of the organ benefits mightily, while the donor and his family get little or nothing because they cannot legally sell an organ.

John Moore survived cancer of the spleen. While he was being operated on, scientists took some of his leftover cancer tissue to grow a cell line to be used for further research. His cells contained a rare cancer-attacking protein called GM-CSF, making the cell line potentially worth hundreds of millions of dollars. When Moore learned of it several years later, he filed suit against the University of California, two researchers, and two corporations, all of whom stood to profit substantially from his cells. But the California Supreme Court ruled against Moore. It refused to grant him property rights to his cells, tissues, or body parts, though it effectively upheld the same rights when possessed by the university, the researchers, and the companies. In similar cases since, no supplier of cells has received any remuneration other than a nominal fee for test subjects. Researchers found a family in Nebraska that had a genetic trait that gave them high bone mass. If the gene could be isolated and identified, it might lead to a treatment for osteoporosis, a condition afflicting half of all women over sixty-five. While the professionals involved stood to get rich, the family members born with the trait, who gave blood and donated their time to the project, got next to nothing.[362]

The prohibition on buying and selling human organs has exacerbated shortages, increased prices, prolonged suffering, and caused tens of thousands of premature deaths. For a kidney, the average wait is 2.6 years, a painful period of dialysis and decline that makes the patient less able to withstand the operation should a kidney become available.[363] To help meet the demand, it has been suggested that dying people be allowed to sell their organs as a means to increase the supply. This would make each organ a property, which sits uneasily with many. Regardless, human body parts *are* property. They fall within a person's protected sphere, they are used exclusively by that person, they are wanted enough to have a monetary value, and ownership can be transferred from one person to another by mutual agreement. That's a property.

Professional medical associations, organ procurers, and transplant centers don't want to admit that an organ is property, because if they do, it's clear who the rightful owner is: the person in whom it formed. They oppose a market solution to the organ shortage because it would force them to pay the owner. Current law allows the medical community to confiscate a valuable commodity while waxing moralistic and charging that it's offensive to consider the financial end of things. They claim that a market system would be exploitive, while the current one relies on sweet-talking bereaved families into giving away a precious asset, on persuading the surviving relatives of recently deceased accident victims to donate organs (on behalf of another) at an emotional, impressionable time.

People with religious objections to commerce in organs claim to be acting in the name of a higher power. Others who oppose trade in body parts make the Kantian argument that each human being has dignity by virtue of being human and that dignity is not a saleable item.[364] It's true that some things can't have a monetary value attached to them or be traded in a market. One is justice, which must stand apart from monetary considerations. Nor can humans themselves be bought or sold. But a body part is not a person. It has no rights. Dignity cannot be claimed for a cornea, kidney, or liver.[365] Like food, housing, and clothing, human organs are vital necessities for which markets form. The dignity argument would be better suited to oppose selling one's self into slavery.

A system in which an individual could contract to sell his organs for future delivery (presuming he dies under circumstances that permit transplantation) and direct the proceeds as he chooses would allow him to help his family financially while saving other lives. It would increase the supply of organs and make them cheaper. Fewer living donors would be needed. Thousands of people would get to live longer. Using market forces to increase the supply of organs does not mean that organs would have to be allocated on a strict ability-to-pay basis. If desired, they could be allocated as now, within the guidelines of the United Network for Organ Sharing.

In the prestigious British medical journal the *Lancet*, a group of transplant surgeons from Harvard Medical School and hospitals in Canada and England endorsed legalizing organ sales. Wrote one of them, Nicholas Tiney, a Harvard Medical School professor who had formerly been against the sale of human organs, "We debated the issue for two years ... All of us transplanters, and I'm sure the public, have this tremendous gut reaction against it.... And then, when we all got around and really thought about this and talked about it, our thinking began to change."[366] Physicians were tired of seeing their patients die for lack of an organ that would be available but for misguided laws. They asked which is more distasteful: commerce in human organs, or thousands of needless deaths each year?

In the future, it's likely that animal, cloned, or synthetic organs will be used in transplants. Meanwhile, as people live longer, the market for human organs will likely grow, and transactions that serve both buyer and seller work too well *not* to get done. Governments can criminalize them or accept and regulate them. From a standpoint of rights, trade in human organs should be legalized. An individual owns himself from DNA strand, to bone marrow, to liver and kidneys. If there is something every individual has a proprietary right to, it's his or her own body and its parts.

Seat Belt Laws

Government required car manufacturers to install seat belts, then a few years later, shoulder belts too, giving all drivers the option of using them. Today, about 80 percent of Americans wear seat belts. It makes sense. In an accident, you're about half as likely to be injured or killed as if not using it. Since car accidents are the greatest cause of nonnatural death in the nation, not wearing a seat belt is foolish. About half of the states have primary seat belt laws, which permit police to stop a vehicle and issue a ticket for a seat belt violation. In other states, there is secondary enforcement, in which the police only issue a ticket for not wearing a seat belt if the vehicle is pulled over for some other reason. New Hampshire is the only state with neither law. The federal government gives millions of dollars to states with primary laws, and when a state upgrades, compliance increases by about 10 percentage points. Federal officials claim that an additional 1,400 lives each year could be saved if all fifty states adopted primary seat belt laws.[367]

The trouble is, seat belt laws violate rights. They pertain to a choice taking place within private property that endangers no other person. Seat belt laws are valid on airplanes and public transportation; in an accident, you could be thrown and injure someone, but in your car, alone, seat belt laws have no place. In an accident, your broken body is not going to injure anyone in another car, so there are no neighborhood effects. Roads are public, but your car is your property, and what takes place within it may not be regulated unless it directly affects or endangers *others* (driving while intoxicated, for example). There is an important difference between laws that protect individuals' health and safety from the actions of others and laws that protect a person from himself. The first are rules of organization; the second are directives of policy.

A law can be both life-saving and wrong. Eyes roll; teacups hit saucers. But it's true. Most who favor seat belt laws fail to realize that you can favor seat belt use, use them yourself, and still be against their mandatory use. No one is anti-seat belt, but some people are against being *coerced.* Vociferous proponents of seat belt laws—including former nonusers who got into a car accident, were reborn, and became resolute about illuminating others—accuse those who wish to be able to choose for themselves of somehow *causing* the deaths of others. Said one state representative about people against mandated usage, "They have to get tired of having the blood on their hands." [368] Activists refuse to let each person take responsibility for himself. Self-determination could allow a wrong choice. Enter governmom. One television public service spot called New York State's seat belt law "tough love," demonstrating the state's view of its relationship to the citizens.[369]

The idea that government can regulate any action, regardless of where it takes place or who is affected, is incompatible with the rights to liberty and to property. Purely self-involving choices on private property are not subject to regulation. Common costs would decrease if more people wore seat belts, but financial concerns don't allow government to breach the Five Rights either. More than three hundred people each year die from falling in their showers.[370] By the same reasoning as that on which seat belt laws are based, each home should have a shower harness installed, and its usage should be mandated. Insuring compliance would require enforcement—perhaps periodic inspections. Seat belts and shower harnesses save lives, but permitting free choice on private property supersedes improving personal safety or lowering costs. Greater use of seat belts should be accomplished through education and example. If achieved through coercion, the cure is a greater malady than the illness.

The Importance of Property

Property gives liberty a place to exist. It clarifies boundaries, civilizes, and entices upkeep and stability. It inspires productive effort. The trading of property generates contracts that compel the performance of promises. Since the individual is likely to outlive his ability to work, he must put away more than he needs at present, creating pools of savings that finance growth. Wealth building may seem a crude motivator, but it motivates without commands. Nations of property owners tend to defeat or culturally usurp others because owners work harder for themselves. When Persia, the greatest empire of its age, had conquered its region as far west as Egypt, and then tried to take on the city-states of Greece, it was defeated by people who owned their own land and manned their own government.

Propertyless societies have been advocated, usually by utopian planners of other people's lives like Plato or misanthropes like Rousseau. Marx and Engels in their *Communist Manifesto* wrote, "The theory of the communists may be summed up in a single sentence: Abolition of private property." Seventy years later, the Bolsheviks seized all private holdings under the slogan, "Loot the loot,"[371] leaving the people destitute and subject to government's will. From the seventeenth century until recently, Russia was a totalitarian state that literally owned its citizens. Historian Richard Pipes, author of several scholarly works on the Soviet Union, attributed the degree of injustice to the lack of property rights, allowing the State to claim unlimited duties and services from its subjects. In Western Europe, "the authority of kings stopped at the boundary of private property,"[372] noted Pipes. After examining the relationship between property and liberty in Russian history, Pipes concluded, "what a man is, what he does, and what he owns are of a piece, so that the assault on his belongings is an assault also on his individuality and his right to life."[373] After seventy-three years of totalitarianism, the Soviet Union shed absolute authority in one day. On February 7, 1990, it repudiated Article 6 of the Soviet Constitution, reversing itself and officially permitting property ownership.

The right to property is the greatest means yet discovered of tapping individual ingenuity. Creative capitalists include Benjamin Franklin, George Washington, Robert Fulton, John Deere, Alfred Nobel, Alexander Graham Bell, Cyrus McCormick, Elisha Otis, Levi Strauss, Elias Howe, John Jacob Astor, John D. Rockefeller, J. P. Morgan, Adolphus Busch, Cornelius Vanderbilt, Thomas Edison, Nicola Tesla, Andrew Carnegie, George Westinghouse, William Boeing, Henry Ford, George Eastman, Edwin Land, David Sarnoff, William Randolph Hearst, Howard Hughes, Alfred Sloan, Walter Chrysler, Daniel Ludwig, Andrew Mellon, Bernard Baruch, Walt Disney, H. J. Heinz, J. Paul Getty, Stephen Bechtel, Ray Kroc, Harlan Sanders, Forrest Mars, Thomas Watson Jr., Ben Graham, William Hewlett, David Packard, Igor Sikorsky, Arthur Rock, Andrew Grove, Robert Noyce, Gordon Moore, William Levitt, Warren Buffet, Akio Morita, Sam Walton, Ross Perot, Ted Turner, Sumner Redstone, Henry Crown, Coco Chanel, Fred Smith, Phil Knight, Philip Anschutz, Sir James Goldsmith, Rupert Murdoch, Allen Paulson, Steve Wynn, Steve Jobs, Steve Wozniak, Jack Welch, Bill Gates, Paul Allen, Richard Branson, Scott McNealy, Larry Ellison, George Lucas, Jeff Bezos, Li Ka Shing, Michael Dell, Michael Bloomberg, Steve Case, Carlos Slim, and Mark Zuckerberg. The ongoing industrial and technological boom that began in eighteenth-century Europe and nineteenth-century America is in part the result of well-conceived property and patent laws.

Regarding property rights, government can tax, it can make laws forcing individuals to accommodate their property to others' rights, and it can buy property for public use. When it goes further, each new rule makes the owner a bit less the king of his castle and a bit more a tenant of the State, as does each tax increase. When the individual is permitted to spend his money as he chooses, he buys what he wants. When government takes and allocates his earnings, he is forced to serve the ends of others.

CHAPTER 9
The Right to Pursue Happiness

The phrase "pursuit of happiness" was around long before Jefferson. Aristotle used it in the fourth century BCE. In the first century, Epictetus wrote, "The people have a right to the truth as they have a right to life, liberty, and the pursuit of happiness."[374] During the eighteenth century, David Hume, Adam Smith, Burlamaqui, and William Blackstone all used the phrase. George Mason used it in the Virginia Declaration of Rights. Also prior to the Declaration of Independence, John Adams used it in his "Thoughts on Government," written in January 1776.[375] The right to pursue happiness permits the individual to act in ways disapproved of by others. It allows fun and foolishness.

When government violates the individual's right to pursue happiness, it usually does so through a directive of policy. Though called laws and invariably claimed to be needed rules of organization, directives of policy stem from government's purposeful pursuit of a goal, limiting liberty in deference to a presumed greater good. Whereas rules of organization involve the neighborhood effects of individuals' actions, establishing boundaries, directives of policy don't deal with how an action affects others but with what most people *think* about the action, punishing people who engage in a criticized activity whether or not rights are violated. In short, directives of policy are arbitrary curbs on freedom. They come from customs or religious beliefs so well entrenched that they have gradually acquired State backing or from attempts to improve the order through the wrongful use of coercion.

Command-coercive directives of policy, in prohibiting private actions unlikely to harm others, violate the individual's right to do as he pleases with his body, time, or property. Such directives may include military drafts, bans on an individual's right to sell his organs or to end his life, laws restricting abortion, policies inequitable to gays, and regulations that breach the rights of property owners. Also included are some laws pertaining to drinking, smoking, drugs, censorship, gambling, nude dancing, pornography, and prostitution. *Tax-coercive directives of policy* violate the individual's right to spend his earnings as he chooses and, when seeking privilege for some at the cost of others, the right to equality before the law. These include programs designed to transfer wealth and compulsory State management of the individual's money.

To enforce common law and rules of organization, government employs coercion reactively: it penalizes people who violate others' rights. Directives of policy are different: government coerces to achieve a goal. Directives of policy are intended to make people safer, healthier, or more productive or to force some individuals to contribute to others. But these virtues—self-improvement and generosity—cease to be virtues when they're imposed. A virtuous order is made up of virtuous individuals, not servants to the virtuous intents of leaders. To determine a free order requires making commands, but commands make it unfree, so government can only nudge the inner disposition of human beings over time such that they *choose* to alter their actions. It can publicize factual health and safety data and prompt change through education. Each person chooses what behavior to imitate, consciously or not. Since successful behavior is most often imitated, successful attitudes, habits, and traditions survive.

But government is inclined to go beyond chaperoning organic order and dispensing justice tit-for-tat. It penalizes disfavored personal choices, sacrificing the individual's right to pursue happiness to its aspirations for society. As a living being, an individual has a purpose: to continue living. Society is an overview, a *perception* of the whole. To ban real freedoms of individuals in an effort to improve the general appearance of things is an absurd reversal of priorities, like slaughtering several species of animals to make biological classification come out more orderly.

Directives of policy serve "the public good" rather than "individuals," because "individuals" is too confining a term. A directive of policy cannot be in the interest of *all individuals* when its passage results in the taxing, fining, or imprisoning of some who have not harmed anyone. And a directive of policy cannot favor some individuals at the cost of others without violating the right to equality before the law. Serving "individuals" lays bare the invalidity of a directive of policy. By substituting "the public good," representatives serve a phrase definable as something different from what free action has produced. Government and its promoters tend to interpret the public good as the general health, safety, manageability, and wholesomeness of the order, which they feel can and should be improved by coercing some individuals. If the good of the individual and the public good were considered the same, or very similar, there would be no reason for directives of policy, because there would be no model civilization for which to strive. With no tax-coercive directives, each person could keep the money he earned less his portion of the common expenses of the order, and with no command-coercive directives, each could live according to his desires within common law and rules of organization. Perfect protection of the rights of each person isn't possible, but that should be the goal, as opposed to the public good, an aim that furnishes a pretext for eternal regulation. Only when the goal is to protect individuals' rights is legislation finite and will it tend toward equilibrium, because no person's rights can be extended beyond those of another.

A similarly invalid reason to coerce is, it's for your own good. Since each individual gets pain and pleasure input for only him, each can make decisions for only himself. Nature's setup makes the pursuit of happiness personal. Along with the visible diversity among individuals, physiological differences include structural differences in the brain that influence happiness. For example, some individuals are born with too few dopamine receptors. Dopamine is a brain chemical that allows a person to experience joy, and having too few receptors makes him insensitive to routine pleasures like breathing fresh air or watching a sunset and makes him crave *something*. People with an insufficient number of receptors know precisely what is being referred to here. According to Dr. Nora Volkow of Brookhaven

National Laboratory, "It's like living your life in gray. If other stimuli aren't powerful enough to activate those reward circuits, you're going to get something that will."[376] These individuals seek pleasure in less socially acceptable, more destructive ways, commonly abusing food, drugs, or alcohol, all of which cause dopamine to be produced. Though the substance being abused and the will power of the individual matter, addiction is often a chronic medical problem with a physiological cause. A century and a half before dopamine receptors were understood, Lincoln perceptively wrote of alcoholism, "In my judgment, such of us as have never fallen victims, have been spared more from the absence of appetite, than any mental or moral superiority over those who have."[377] What produces happiness for most does not work for some and might be a hell for others. For this reason, government cannot ordain a pursuit of happiness.

Fun sometimes involves danger. "It's for your own good," could be used to justify bans on skiing, boxing, wrestling, hang-gliding, skateboarding, bicycling, car racing, running marathons, firecrackers, BB guns, mountain climbing, spelunking, horseback riding, rodeos, surfing, archery, hunting, auto racing, cliff diving, skydiving, deep-sea diving, sailing, ballooning, motorcycling, circuses, air shows, all small aircraft, working with wild animals, bungee jumping, sunbathing, and swimming where there is a strong current. There are safer alternatives to these activities. "It's for your own good" could be used to regulate any substance considered dangerous: fuels, cleaning supplies, drugs, alcohol, tobacco, marijuana, and narcotics. All guns could be confiscated and other potential weapons restricted: knives, shovels, pool cues, two-by-fours, tire irons, hammers, and baseball bats, as well as dangerous mechanical devices like lawnmowers, wood chippers, meat slicers, space heaters, and barbecue grills. Seat belt and helmet use could be required in all forms of transportation. Foods high in fat or cholesterol could be banned or their processing and distribution controlled. Red meat could go. Sex can be dangerous for some people. Should this risk for the sake of pleasure also be regulated?[378]

The drive to protect people from their own folly can be used to justify regulation of the individual down to his cells because, when coming from the State, whatever words precede "It's for your own good" constitute a command. At its most benevolent, it is a parental intonation to which the proper response is, *I* choose my good. It cannot be left to anyone else, because lawmakers by the nature of their task tend not to see people as individual beings each with inviolable rights, but collectively, as problems to be solved, which makes it easy to forget that human actions are ends in themselves and not means to be utilized by government to achieve a desirable end.

One such reversal of priorities took place in the United States starting in the 1890s, as progressives and religious fundamentalists pressed for social reforms, including the prohibition of alcoholic beverages. Temperance movements combined to form the Anti-Saloon League, "an army of the Lord to wipe out the curse of the drink," and enlisted civic-minded reformers and discipline-oriented educators. School boards often had prohibitionists on them; high school science textbooks of the time warned of the permanent damage done to the human body by one drink.[379] Alcohol was portrayed then as heroin is now: severely addictive and destructive in all cases. School children were made to repeat verses each day in which they swore they would never touch a drop. Twenty years later, they became the teetotalers behind Prohibition. Fire-and-brimstoners had been preaching against drinking since the Civil War, and their perseverance had helped convince people that alcohol, if not the scourge they claimed, was a vice that America was better off without. Prohibition would be for the peoples' own good.

The movement accelerated after the turn of the century when economic experts, led by Professor Irving Fisher, lent academic support to a ban. Fisher assured that "American Prohibition will go down in history as ushering in a new era in the world, in which accomplishment this nation will take pride forever."[380] Mechanization had made many jobs more dangerous, and it was felt that Prohibition might be necessary to worker safety. The age of heavy construction, automobiles, and automated assembly lines didn't mix well with drunkenness. Henry Ford said, "The country couldn't run without Prohibition. That is the industrial fact."[381] Ford was one of many who assumed that with no alcohol around, drunks would sober up and employees would miss less work and be more productive. The rent money wouldn't get spent on liquor. Men would remain home with their families, and there would be fewer domestic disputes. Crime, immorality, and illness would decline. Prohibition served less noble motives too, including prejudice against foreigners. The Drys disliked the regular intake of wine or beer customary to many European immigrants. Puritans thought immigrants would make better citizens if sobriety were forced on them. Sensational, fabricated tales circulated among the Drys of immigrants getting liquored up, going crazy, and raping women. The Drys used propaganda successfully to persuade undecided Americans that *they* weren't part of the alcohol problem; it was others who required discipline, so supporting the Drys were people who were personally wet.

National prohibition was proposed in 1917 but took almost three years to ratify. In 1918, an influenza epidemic killed 30 million people worldwide, including 675,000 Americans, making it the worst outbreak of infectious disease in US history. No matter what cure was tried, each victim's lungs filled with liquid, and he or she died about three days later. Hundreds of thousands were children. It was a grim time: the number of dead equaled the number of American combat deaths during just-ended World War I times six, and the influenza victims died in one year on native soil—so many, so suddenly that there weren't enough coffins. Prohibitionists claimed it was God's wrath for drunkenness, and in their grief, some believed.

In January 1920, when Nebraska became the thirty-sixth state to ratify it, the Volstead Act banning alcoholic beverages became law. The Eighteenth Amendment prohibited "the manufacture, sale, or transportation of intoxicating liquors within, the importation of thereof into, or the exportation thereof from the United States." Note the two words used to describe what was being banned: "intoxicating liquors." Many who supported Prohibition thought this intentionally chosen phrase referred to distilled spirits only, 80 proof and higher, but the bill's Bible-thumping author, Minnesota Senator Andrew Volstead, clarified after the bill's passage that "intoxicating liquors" referred to all alcoholic beverages containing more than one half of 1 percent alcohol, which included beer, wine, and all other recreational alcoholic beverages. Though drinking had been a human custom for millennia and, for many people, one engaged in for all of their adult lives, laborers and returning World War I veterans would be denied even beer. There was an uproar from those who felt they had been lied to, but Volstead's interpretation held up due to the support of evangelists and their followers and to the prevailing anti-German, anti-beer sentiment from the just-ended war.[382] On the eve of Prohibition, the evangelist Billy Sunday exclaimed, "The reign of tears is over. The slums will soon be a memory. We will turn our prisons into factories.... Men will walk upright now, women will smile, and children will laugh. Hell will be forever for rent."[383]

Hoping the new laws might not be enforced, saloon owners stayed open after January 28, 1920, the first day of Prohibition, until they were shut down, which took several weeks. When shuttered establishments tried to reopen, federal agents destroyed the liquor and also the fixtures and furnishings of the saloons, to the delight of the reformers.[384] Brewers, distillers, bottlers, distributors, and everyone else in the previously legal beer, wine, and liquor industry were out of work, their jobs exported to people in other nations. Government could prohibit liquor, but it couldn't abolish the market for it, since markets are the result of what individuals want, which can't be changed by law. To supply the United States market, distillers in Canada, Mexico, and Europe transported liquor on oceangoing vessels to just outside the three-mile limit off both US coasts to supply the motor boats of bootleggers.

Crime generally doesn't pay because the risk/reward ratio is poor. A person who steals something risks imprisonment and the possibility of injury or death during or after the theft, and the reward is minimal because the stolen item will only bring a fraction of its wholesale value; the criminal is at the mercy of the illegitimate, disinterested cash buyer. But when law prohibits something popular, a seller does not have to discount it to move it. On the contrary, demand allows him to mark up the product several hundred percent, making the risk/reward ratio favorable. His profits are more than enough to cover the costs of product, security, payoffs, and whatever else is necessary to protect his operation. Though he may eventually be caught, in the meantime his success inspires enough imitation to attract other suppliers to the market. Government, when it prohibits a product or service in demand, makes crime pay.

Dealing in contraband, though itself criminal, generates crime of much greater consequence. When a product is illegal, the police and the court system are off limits, leaving no way to enforce contracts or settle disputes other than extortion, assault, and murder. All along the supply chain, ruthlessness wins the greatest market share. Before 1920, criminal alliances were rare—gangs were limited to family members and cronies—but when they were handed a market with forty-five million customers, thugs were given a pie so large that they had no choice but to consolidate, initiating organized crime.[385] Disputes were settled publicly and bloodily on purpose to harvest fear as a warning to witnesses or competitors. Chicago alone averaged more than four hundred Prohibition-related murders per year. A handful of crime bosses financed the violence with resources that formerly went to peaceful people earning honest livings. To John Torrio, the first modern gangster and Al Capone's boss and mentor, Prohibition was a godsend.[386] Torrio's biographer, Robert Schoenberg, wrote that Torrio had spent his life striving "to turn crime into a regular business; now the fools had obliged him by making a regular business criminal."[387] Major gang leaders like Torrio and Capone earned over $10 million a year. Capone was worth an estimated $100 million when he was indicted—over $2 billion today.[388] The net result to the nation, as the writer Andrew Sinclair observed: "National prohibition transferred $2 billion a year from the hands of brewers, distillers, and shareholders to the hands of murderers, crooks, and illiterates."[389]

During the first year of Prohibition, crime jumped 24 percent in the nation's major cities.[390] By the second year, the federal prison system was operating at 170 percent capacity.[391] In 1923, when police were still taking enforcement seriously, *Time* magazine, then in its first year of publication, reported that Prohibition cases comprised 44 percent of the work of United States District Attorneys. Swamped, judges offered "bargain days" on which courtrooms full of suspects were allowed to plead guilty if they paid a token fine.[392] Enforcement loosened but Prohibition violators still choked the court systems and filled the jails—more prisons had to be built.

The speakeasies remained packed. The war and the influenza epidemic were fading memories, and the US economy was booming—it was a good time for America, and drinking was a part of the fun. That it was illegal made it that much better. New York City had 16,000 saloons before Prohibition, but more than double that number of speakeasies after.[393] One reason: it's easier to run an establishment by your own rules than by those of government. The saloons had been regulated, but anyone with access to liquor and a private space in which to serve it could start a speakeasy—there were no liquor licenses or health inspectors, no one checking ages, and no mandatory closing times. More so than usual, people in speakeasies drank to get drunk. When out-of-towners had access to one, they didn't know when they might have the chance again, so they binged. The speakeasies made women feel welcome, inducing them to drink in public, which was new, so there were drunken women in bars for the first time. Ironically, the evangelists helped create the Roaring Twenties, a period during which an atmosphere of abandon, created in part by the natural fellowship of those willing to break the rules together, was not conducive to moderation of any kind.

In rural areas, there were thousands of private stills. People supplemented their incomes by bottling and selling moonshine or bathtub gin. Brewing beer was less common, so availability forced many drinkers to switch to liquor, the consumption of which hit an all-time high during Prohibition, probably explaining the dramatic increase in the incidence of cirrhosis of the liver during the decade. One reason for the switch to hard liquor, as noted by the writer Mike Gray in *Drug Crazy*: whenever something is contraband it must be kept secret, which means hiding it, creating a preference for small and powerful over bulky and hard-to-transport.[394] Beer drinkers couldn't hide beer easily, so they shifted to flasks of liquor. Never had so many people been willing to break the law. Drinkers tipped flasks at theaters, socials, picnics, and baseball games. During Prohibition, drinking at home became acceptable, then habitual. The US per capita intake of liquor increased throughout the decade to 1.3 gallons of pure alcohol annually by 1929 and never returned to pre-1920 levels.[395]

There is no Food and Drug Administration approval for an illegal substance. Several hundred people died from adulterants like methanol in the homemade liquor. Thousands tried to make wood alcohol safe to drink and were blinded or poisoned by it; others met the same fate when it was fraudulently sold to them as grain alcohol. In rural areas, many in search of alcohol imbibed the fluid extract of Jamaican ginger, known as Jake, which was used as a digestive aid and readily available in pharmacies. Jake remained legal during Prohibition because it was classified a medicine and because regulators thought that its awful taste would discourage people from drinking enough of it to cause drunkenness, but it was 70 percent alcohol, so many did. Drinkers in states that had outlawed liquor before Prohibition had used Jake as an alcohol substitute for years. In late 1929, a wholesaler in Boston added a cresol compound that he had been assured was a safe adulterant, but it was TOCP, a liquid plasticizer. Sold by his Hub Products in two-ounce bottles, the tainted Jake paralyzed at least 30,000 people.[396]

Prohibition severely corrupted law enforcement. Since police and other officials didn't see Prohibition violations as major crime, they frequently became appendages to the liquor industry. A police officer could earn six months' pay with a single tip-off to a bootlegger. A typical speakeasy in New York paid several hundred dollars a month to the Prohibition Bureau, police, and district attorney's office. The Wickersham Commission appointed by Hoover to study the effects of Prohibition and to parade its success instead confirmed that corruption was rampant: police, mayors, sheriffs, prosecutors, and judges were on the take. All law enforcement agencies were involved, as were US Customs and the Coast Guard. By 1929, one out of every four federal agents had been dismissed for bribery, extortion, or conspiracy.[397] The agents' common sense prevailed; since supply and demand were finding each other anyway and people weren't being hurt by drinking (except by their own hand), accepting a payoff to ignore it seemed more like a politeness than an immoral act. Rather, interfering seemed wrong, for good reason.

In response to the failure of law enforcement, government put more money into the effort and increased penalties, some of which were multiplied by ten; by the end of the decade, a person could go to prison for five years for selling one drink.[398] Prohibition broadly undermined respect for authority. When millions tread over a law, they don't stop at the next one. The unjustness of Prohibition became an excuse to ignore any laws thought unfair. Crime increased and prison overcrowding grew. The federal system was operating at 170 percent capacity; the penitentiary at Leavenworth had a capacity of 1,500 and a population of 3,600.[399]

Henry Joy, an accomplished man in several fields and one of the founders of the Packard Motor Car Company, had been one of the largest financial supporters of Prohibition but later wrote, "I made a mistake. I was stupidly wrong.... America must open its eyes and recognize that human nature cannot be changed by legal enactment."[400] Pauline Sabin, a wealthy socialite and an early supporter of Prohibition, said, "I felt I should approve it because it would help my two sons ... I thought a world without liquor would be a beautiful world,"[401] but by 1930, she had had enough and testified before the House Judiciary Committee that "women played a large part in the enactment of the Eighteenth Amendment. Many were women who had unhappy experiences as a result of drunkenness among those close to them. They are now realizing with heart burning and heart aching that if the spirit is not within, legislation can be of no avail." She added, "They thought they could make Prohibition as strong as the Constitution, but instead they have made the Constitution as weak as Prohibition."[402] Before Prohibition, she said, her children had no access to alcohol. Now they could get it easily.[403] Mrs. Sabin's testimony was interrupted by applause several times.[404] By 1932, both presidential candidates, Hoover and Roosevelt, favored repeal. Though it required another amendment needing confirmation by two-thirds of both houses of Congress and three-quarters of the states, and no amendment had ever been abolished, in 1933 the Eighteenth Amendment was repealed by the Twenty-First, ending fourteen years of national alcohol prohibition at a cost to the taxpayers of over $1 billion.[405]

"No folly is more costly than the folly of intolerant idealism," wrote Churchill of Prohibition."[406] What Hoover had called "the Noble Experiment" didn't just fail; it backfired so badly that it should have served as a timeless example that prohibiting an item in demand is more destructive than the item itself. Prohibition exhibited the pattern of all such interdictions. Each starts with a high-minded intent backed by enough righteous fervor to persuade many to sacrifice other peoples' choices to the goal. Following the ban, supplies get spotty.

The price rises and buyers and sellers find one another. Connections form and grow into supply networks, complete with specialization and competition. Arrests are made, but only a tiny fraction of the illegal trade is prevented because each exchange of product and cash takes place in secret, and there is no one to protest to the police that a crime has been committed. Law enforcement is corrupted. Funded by the illicit, tax-free profits, organized crime expands. Turf wars and violence escalate. Finally, when it's clear that the ban is doing more harm than good, political pressure grows until it is lifted. The process can take years or decades.

Prohibition violated the Five Rights, most severely the rights to liberty and to pursue happiness. When Henry Joy and Pauline Sabin testified that they had turned against Prohibition because it had failed, they also testified unintentionally to their lack of regard for other people's rights, for if they respected rights, they could never have supported Prohibition. But like many responsible individuals, they felt that their accountability allowed them to coerce less responsible people for the good of the order. Reformers are often blind to the rights of others. Supporters of Prohibition assumed that individuals would spend their dollars more wisely, which turned out to be untrue—price increases caused *more* money to be spent on alcohol—but the reformers had no business taking mind of other peoples' expenditures. Individuals can spend their money as they choose. It was thought that people would spend their time more productively, but as with money, one's time is his own. It was thought that Prohibition would make people healthier, reduce employee absenteeism, and reunite families—admirable goals, none of which were achieved and none of which has anything to do with protecting individuals' rights, government's reason for being. Instead, Prohibition sacrificed rights to State goals, as all directives of policy do.

Prohibition was not the only US attempt to impose morality. In 1986, the federal government decided to stamp out pornography. A commission led by Attorney General Edwin Meese, relying on anecdotal evidence and roundly criticized as biased, found that pornography contributed to sex crimes. None of several previous studies had reached the same conclusion, but the Justice Department formally accepted all of the commission's findings and used racketeering laws (RICO) to close adult book and video stores. To harass and bankrupt pornographers, the Department's Obscenity Enforcement Unit launched simultaneous prosecutions and brought charges in several different states, forcing each business to fight multiple cases.[407] (After a separate crackdown in New York City in 2007, Mayor Rudolph Giuliani declared, "I took a city that was known for pornography and licked it.")[408]

Prostitution is a crime everywhere in the United States, except for a few counties in Nevada. In Missouri, Colorado, and Oklahoma, television stations have displayed the names, addresses, and photos of men arrested for trying to solicit a prostitute. One Kansas City show was called *John TV*.[409] There are plenty of people of both sexes, however, who enjoy casual sex and don't feel that prostitution is wrong. Both parties have normal needs and aspirations and want the liberty to act on them. Most prostitutes don't find their profession any more degrading than that of any other service provider. They like the flexible hours, the independence, the money, the not having to wait tables. Nor are the johns generally deviates. They go to prostitutes for a sex act that their partner will not perform, or because they like the convenience, variety, temporary companionship, lack of emotional involvement, avoidance of rejection, or illicit nature of the encounter.

Kant considered prostitution immoral for the same reason as trade in human body parts: he opposed any sale of the body, writing, "Man is not his own property and cannot do with his body what he will." Nonsense. The body is the one property every person owns, and he can do with it what he pleases. Puritans claim that prostitution is immoral, which is their right, but to criminalize it violates others' rights and protects no one's rights. Some groups claim that prostitution is a form of violence against women, but when a woman chooses to render a service and accept payment for it, she has not been the victim of violence. Like taking drugs or choosing to sell one's organs, the decision to give sex to get money is personal, and anyone can decline. Prostitution is legal in several European countries, where three-quarters of the people see it as a job like any other. Said one Dutch woman who was not a prostitute, "It doesn't even cross my mind that it should be illegal."[410] As for prostitution being a "crime against society," that's a meaningless phrase invoked by people with insufficient regard for others' rights. If the phrase had any substance, its speaker would not have to employ the flaccid noun "society" as the object of the "crime."

Drug Prohibition

Starting in Jamestown in 1607 and for the next 307 years, government was not in the business of prohibiting foods or drugs. Drugs were like ideas, people thought. Whatever ideas someone chose to put in his mind, and whatever chemicals he put in his body, were his affair. That changed with the Harrison Narcotic Act in 1914, the first federal attempt to end the nonmedical use of drugs. In 1930, as Prohibition was unraveling, tough compliance officer Harry Anslinger was appointed commissioner of the new Federal Bureau of Narcotics. For the next thirty years, he ran the agency like Hoover ran the FBI, outmaneuvering political rivals. Anslinger was the first in a line of government officials to use his office to demonize drugs and users. He declared marijuana "an evil as hellish as heroin."[411] To win congressmen to his cause, he repeated stories of teens smoking pot, going insane, and committing murder. His favorite tale was that of Victor Licata, who had smoked pot before killing his family with an ax. Anslinger never mentioned that Licata had been diagnosed as severely mentally ill. Anslinger routinely made up facts and figures, released them to reporters, and then quoted himself as a source.[412] He was instrumental in persuading the federal government to pass the Marijuana Tax Act in 1937, which required a $100-per-ounce fee for the transfer of marijuana, effectively outlawing it.

New York mayor Fiorello LaGuardia thought Anslinger a fanatic, and wondering if pot was really so dangerous, he commissioned the New York Academy of Medicine to perform the most comprehensive study of marijuana ever done. The study continued for six years during World War II. When released, it supported none of Anslinger's claims. It concluded that marijuana did not cause violence or crime, was not being used by children, and did not cause harder drug use or lead to addiction in the medical sense of the term. These things were clear in 1945. Anslinger was unfazed. Authorities often tie something they want people to hate and fear to something they already hate and fear, and as the cold war took hold, Anslinger successfully tied marijuana use to communism. His efforts led to the Narcotics Control Act of 1956, which increased the power of police and prosecutors and doubled many marijuana penalties. In 1968, President Johnson formally transformed drug use from a public health issue to one of law enforcement when he created the Bureau of Narcotics and Dangerous Drugs under the Department of Justice. The Controlled Substances Act of 1970 divided drugs into five categories, called schedules, based on their perceived harmfulness and addictive potential. Marijuana was placed in Schedule I, the most serious category, where it remains along with heroin and LSD. Cocaine is in Schedule II.[413]

President Nixon launched the War on Drugs in 1971. "We have the moral resources to do the job," he said. "Now we need the authority and the funds to match our moral resources."[414] Nixon created the Drug Enforcement Agency and, like Anslinger, tried to produce data to demonize drugs, but when he appointed a commission to find a scientific basis for tougher drug laws, it couldn't. Though comprised of hard-liners, the Shafer Commission found that there was no basis for tougher laws, especially regarding marijuana, which it determined did "not constitute a major threat to public health" and seemed to pose little danger to users. The Shafer Commission concluded, "It is unlikely that marijuana will affect the future strength, stability, or vitality of our social and political institutions."[415] It recommended that penalties for smoking marijuana in private be dropped. Since the findings did not conform to the Nixon administration's views, it buried the report. Thirty years later, ten million people had been arrested on marijuana charges, and usage had multiplied regardless.

As marijuana use grew, people noticed that smokers did not seem to be deranged ne'er-do-wells bent on mayhem. By 1978, eleven states had decriminalized possession. Others routinely dropped the charges for possession of small amounts. Jimmy Carter became the only president to state the obvious, that "penalties against possession of a drug should not be more damaging to an individual than the use of the drug itself."[416] The Americans, Canadians, British, and Dutch performed separate marijuana studies, and all concluded that pot was roughly as intoxicating and dangerous as alcohol and perhaps less so. The United States government ignored the recommendations, but the Netherlands acted more pragmatically, deciding that if people wanted pot and it was safer than other recreational drugs, it would permit pot. If marijuana users could get their supply from licensed distributors, they would be less likely to be exposed to other drugs, so the Dutch government made it a legal but regulated business: marijuana sellers could offer no hard drugs, serve no one underage, and couldn't advertise. Today, the Netherlands has a lower rate for both marijuana use and hard drug use than the United States.[417]

In the 1980s, President Reagan resumed the War on Drugs. Penalties were increased, and new drug paraphernalia laws were passed. Some states mandated therapy for people charged with possession of marijuana. Others suspended an arrestee's driver's license even if the crime did not involve a car.[418] The Omnibus Crime Bill of 1984 lengthened prison terms. Federal employees were required to take drug tests, and then any corporation that wanted to qualify for federal contracts had to institute them. Testing became routine—it now affects at least forty million people. Following Reagan, President Bush escalated the War on Drugs, doubling its budget in a single year. Then President Clinton spent more money on the drug war during his first term than had been spent during the preceding twelve years.[419]

Penalties for possession became draconian. Under New York's Rockefeller drug laws, possessing more than four ounces of marijuana drew a *minimum* sentence of fifteen years in prison—the same as for second-degree murder.[420] In Michigan, possession of cocaine brought a life sentence without possibility of parole.[421] Mark Scott, a Dallas man, was convicted of possession of an amount of cocaine dust equivalent to two grains of salt, but having two priors, he was sentenced to thirty years in prison.[422] Customs agents seized one man's $140,000 fishing boat after finding 1.7 *grams* of marijuana in a crewman's jacket pocket.[423] Alabama tried to pass a law mandating a one-year prison sentence for anyone convicted of possessing any amount of marijuana. In Oklahoma, William Foster was sentenced to ninety-three years in jail for growing ten plants and fifty-six clones in an underground shelter on his property.[424]

The US criminal justice system treats drug users harshly because our culture has branded them deviants. Drug use is perceived as *wrong*, the act of a despicable person. People are labeled citizen or junkie, with the latter to be spurned. Drug use is seen as contemptible and users thought of as throwaway people not worthy of freedom; they *deserve* to go to jail. Criminalization also demonizes in a circular way: if only criminals use something, then obviously it should be illegal.

Kids are taught in school that only losers use drugs. To shore up the message, there is DARE: Drug Abuse Resistance Education. DARE concentrates on fifth and sixth graders, paying police officers to tell children dark parables about lives ruined by drugs and teaching them the three R's: "Recognize, Resist, and Report." The DARE officer is trained to present himself as "a trusted friend interested in their happiness and welfare," and students are encouraged to turn in friends or parents because they "are sick and need help." Students respond by reporting people they know, sometimes leading to arrest, jail, and foster homes for the children.[425] A Maryland girl told her DARE officer that her parents were growing marijuana, and each spent thirty days in jail. After a Dallas boy reported his parents and the police arrested them, he said, "At school, they told us that if we ever see drugs, call 911 because people who use drugs need help. I thought the police would come and get the drugs and tell them that drugs are wrong. They never said they would arrest them."[426] When a Texas high school encouraged students to report drug use and some turned in their best friends, the principal declared proudly, "We have positively brainwashed our student body."[427]

What about drug users who are not addicts but normal functioning people? Drug czar William Bennett once declared, "Users who maintain a job and a steady income should face stiff fines ... have their names published in local papers ... be subject to driver's license suspension, employer notification, overnight or weekend detention, eviction from public housing, or forfeiture of the cars they drive."[428] Said Bennett on another occasion, "The casual adult user is in some ways the most dangerous person because that person is a carrier."[429] Nancy Reagan went a bit further, once declaring, "If you're a casual drug user, you're an accomplice to murder."[430] Another tough-lover, Los Angeles police Chief Darryl Gates, announced that "casual drug users should be taken out and shot" and was applauded for the remark.[431] (Gates founded DARE.)

Contrasting views were not allowed. Dr. Tod Mikuriya, former director of marijuana research for the nation, said, "I was hired by the government to provide scientific evidence that marijuana was harmful. As I studied the subject, I began to realize that marijuana was once widely used as a safe and effective medicine. But the government had a different agenda, and I had to resign."[432] The DEA withholds information regarding any possible attributes of marijuana, claiming that there is no "public benefit" to releasing the data. It tells the public what is best for itself: tales of dissolute addicts, depraved drug pushers, and how the DEA protects the public from them.[433] In 1988, Congress declared the *consideration* of legalizing drugs "an unconscionable surrender in a war in which, for the future of our country and the lives of our children, there can be no substitute for total victory," and Congress proclaimed it "the declared policy of the United States to create a drug-free America by 1995."[434] When 1995 came and went and drug use continued as ever, Walter Cronkite remarked, "It's surely time for this nation to stop flying blind, stop accepting the assurances of politicians and other officials that if only we keep doing what we are doing, add a little more cash, break down a few more doors, lock up a few more [people]," then "victory would be ours."[435] But nothing changed. Following 9/11, the Office of National Drug Control Policy bought commercial time during the 2002 Super Bowl to accuse marijuana users of aiding terrorists.[436] The word "terrorism" appears frequently in DEA requests for budget increases.

Effects of Drug Laws

Since half of all US adults have tried marijuana and tens of millions smoke it regularly, and it's a crime, hundreds of thousands are arrested. In the most recent year for which there is data, just under 900,000 people were arrested on marijuana charges, nine of ten of them for possession.[437] More people are arrested for it than for all violent crimes combined.[438] Thanks to the drug war, more than a million nonviolent criminals sit in America's prisons.[439] In 1970, there were 200,000 people in US prisons. There are now two million, *ten times* as many.[440] For every farmer in the US, there are two people in jail.[441] During the 1990s, the states built a total of 350 new prisons, an average of seven per state.[442] If you include all those currently on probation or parole, there are now 6.6 million Americans in trouble with the law.[443] The United States has 4.3 percent of the world's population and 20 percent of its prison population.[444] No democracy has ever had such a large percentage of its citizens behind bars. Our incarceration rate is seven times as high in as in European countries.[445] Six of every ten federal inmates are incarcerated for drug offenses. We have more people imprisoned on drug offenses than the total prison population of all twenty-seven countries in the European Union combined, due largely to Europe's more sensible policies toward marijuana. While there is no penalty for possession in the Netherlands, Italy, Spain, Switzerland, Ireland, Portugal, and parts of Germany and Austria, here in the United States, the War on Drugs has established an American gulag system. And still usage has boomed. When marijuana was last legal, in 1936, the US population was 128 million and there were perhaps 60,000 marijuana users nationwide; that's one person out of every 2,133. Today there are 300 million Americans and at least thirty million users: one in ten.[446]

Over the past four decades, more than ten million people have been arrested on marijuana charges in the United States and nearly two million on other drug charges.[447] A drug arrest is a thoroughly unpleasant experience: jail, charges, embarrassment, scandal, job loss, financial ruin. For most people charged with possession, it's their first entanglement with the law, and they make easy targets for overcharging attorneys. Penalties for selling are of course more severe than for possession, and though you may not think of yourself as a dealer, for legal purposes, a drug dealer is anyone who shares his drugs, gives them to friends for later use, or possesses a sufficient quantity so that he can be charged with intent to distribute.

A conviction can be a nightmare. Imprisonment is dead, demoralizing time. Even a sentence of thirty days becomes an ingrained, dog-eared memory. Incarceration should not be meted out casually, and it should never be used to punish people for self-harm. Nor should people be thrown in jail on the notion that it is somehow better for them than drug use, as if imprisonment is a relative good.

Along with fines and incarceration, the State has other ways to punish marijuana users. It can revoke benefits and deny eligibility for federal programs. It can deny education grants, student aid, federal loans, and job training. It can evict families from federal public housing. It can revoke child custody. Professional licenses can be revoked from doctors, lawyers, plumbers, and teachers. Government can discharge individuals from the military. It can force people into a mandatory drug treatment program. A drug conviction can result in the loss of food stamps and temporary assistance. Noncitizens arrested on drug charges can face deportation *after* serving their sentences. In some states, convicted rapists and murderers can drive a car, while convicted marijuana smokers cannot. Due to drug laws, four million Americans have permanently lost the right to vote.[448]

Drug law enforcers tend to ignore mitigating circumstances, like medical conditions. One end-stage renal patient on kidney dialysis three times a week was smoking marijuana and growing it for medical use. Police in flak jackets stormed his house, arrested him, and charged him with felony cultivation for growing one plant.[449] A Florida couple both suffering from AIDS were growing two plants and using the marijuana to relieve their symptoms. Twelve armed men broke down their door, held guns to their heads, and took them to jail. They were convicted on three felony charges.[450] A paralyzed Oklahoma man smoked marijuana to relieve uncontrollable muscle spasms. Police raided his home and found two ounces. Because the wheelchair-bound man had two pistols in his bedroom, he was convicted as an armed drug offender and sentenced to life imprisonment, later reduced to a sentence of ten years.[451] In California, a drug squad arrested a seventy-year-old man for growing pot for use by his girlfriend, a fifty-eight-year-old woman suffering from chronic pain. Because they weren't married, authorities tried to make her testify against him. To avoid it, she committed suicide.[452] Roy Sharpnack was a fifty-five-year-old user of medical marijuana (for Meniere's disease, an inner ear disorder) who tried to cultivate it and to help others get it legally. He obtained notarized authorization from doctors in the Sacramento area to protect himself under California's proposition 215, so when he was arrested, the state found no wrongdoing, but the federal government charged Sharpnack as a grower and sentenced him to four years in prison.[453]

Along with the people who languish in jail, the people who have suffered most from the drug war are those who need potent painkillers and can't get them because doctors are afraid to prescribe them in the needed amounts. Jim Klimek got into a bad car accident. When he came to, his legs had frozen. They had to be amputated. Gangrene set in, forcing several more amputations, leaving him with just his torso, head, and arms. Though he had nothing below his navel, the severed nerve endings were still intact and he was in anguish; he constantly felt that his lower half was still being sawed off. But in the state of Virginia, he was unable to get morphine for the agony.[454] In another case, also in Virginia, a police officer from upstate New York who had been hit by a bus threatened to commit suicide if he could not get better pain medication. A month later, he did, but he first taped a message that was shown on *Sixty Minutes*, in which he said, "Suicide was not what I wanted. Pain treatment and control is what I wanted."[455]

Drug law enforcement can harass or traumatize innocent people. In one case, two young men were arrested for possession of cocaine and held in jail for forty-eight hours before police confirmed that their white powder was, as they had claimed, yogurt.[456] New York narcotics officers threw a concussion grenade into an apartment and then handcuffed the four members of a family, including a mentally handicapped girl they had pulled from the shower, before realizing they had the wrong address. In Bangor, Maine, six masked police officers on a "special response team" forced their way into a home to search for marijuana. They found none, but they did find paraphernalia and $500 cash. They also traumatized five children, ages three to ten.[457]

Innocent people can go to jail on drug charges. A Michigan grandmother gave a ride to a friend of a friend, who was carrying cocaine. Under state law, that made her a drug courier, for which she received a sentence of life imprisonment without parole.[458] While a homeowner sold cocaine to undercover agents in his living room, a plumber worked on the kitchen drain. The agents arrested the seller and the plumber. Despite the fact that the plumber had nothing to do with the drug deal, no knowledge of it, and no criminal record, he was charged with conspiracy, convicted, and sentenced to fifteen years in prison.[459] Richard Anderson, a forty-nine-year-old longshoreman with no criminal record, gave his friend a ride to Burger King, which made him an unknowing participant in an undercover deal involving a hundred grams of crack. Forced to sentence Anderson to ten years in prison without possibility of parole, US District Judge William Schwarzer, in tears, noted that it was "a grave miscarriage of justice."[460]

Innocent people get killed too. Accelyne Williams, a seventy-five-year-old retired minister, died of a heart attack after police chased him around his house in Massachusetts after a no-knock raid. No drugs were found; police had the wrong apartment.[461] New York police stopped a car in which Cory Ephriam was a passenger, thinking the car stolen. There was marijuana in the car and Ephriam had been arrested for pot possession once. He panicked and fled. The police pursued by foot and shot him in the back. The car was not stolen and Ephriam was unarmed.[462] Don Scott owned a $5 million ranch in the mountains above Malibu, California, that was desired by a number of parties, including the National Park Service, but he had refused to sell. It was rumored that Scott had marijuana plants growing on his property, and he had married a woman who had been charged with possession once. Early in the morning of October 2, 1992, when the two were hung over and groggy, thirty heavily armed officers raided Scott's home. In the pandemonium, Scott grabbed his gun and stepped into the hallway, where he was shot and killed by a deputy sheriff. No marijuana was found, no plants anywhere on the property, no illicit drugs. Afterward, the DA said, "Clearly one of the primary purposes was a land grab by the Sheriff's Department."[463]

DEA agents in San Diego acting on the tip of a paid informant shot Donald Carlson, puncturing his lung. Carlson, who was found "wholly innocent," was awarded $2.75 million in damages, paid of course by the taxpayers.[464] An undercover officer in New York shot and killed an innocent, unarmed security guard, mistaking him for a dealer in a sting operation. The man's funeral sparked racial violence.[465] Houston police shot and killed an innocent man, Pedro Oregon Navarro, at his home on a false tip that he was a drug dealer.[466] When a dorm counselor found a Purdue University freshman in possession of cocaine, the student killed the counselor and then himself.[467] Rob Pace, an eighteen-year-old senior in high school, was caught carrying drugs in his backpack on a school trip. The associate high school principal refused to allow him back on the bus because the school did not allow drug-using students to participate in school activities. Abandoned and afraid, Pace killed himself by jumping in front of a train. He left a note apologizing to anyone who had been let down by his behavior.[468]

Drug laws kill many more drug users another way. If your best friend overdoses on a prescribed medication, you take him to the emergency room, but if he were on an illegal drug, you'd try to find another alternative or maybe do nothing and hope for the best. An overdose can result in death due to fear of arrest. It happened twenty times in one Dallas suburb alone.[469] It played a part in the death of basketball star Len Bias in 1986.[470] Consider the reasoning at work: because drugs can be dangerous they are prohibited, but because they can relieve pain and give temporary pleasure, they are desired, purchased, and ingested. When on occasion someone needs emergency medical help, drug laws effectively say, you made your bed, now lie in it. And if you die? That proves drugs are unsafe and need to be illegal. The War on Drugs causes the deaths of hundreds of people each year this way. Harsh drug policies also induce pregnant women to shun prenatal care available to them. Anticipating the possible loss of her child, no pregnant addict is foolish enough to admit her drug use.

Competitors in an illegal enterprise cannot call the police or use the court system, so disputes must be settled by force. Drug laws create violence among sellers. Milton Friedman estimated that ten thousand people worldwide each year are killed by the violence born of drug prohibition.[471]

Drug laws corrupt law enforcement. To support a bust, police can lie about drugs having been in plain sight or the suspect having given consent for a search. Drug laws can prompt entrapment. In a crackdown in Raleigh, North Carolina, police posed as students at local high schools, infiltrated suspected groups, and repeatedly prodded the students to sell them marijuana. One officer posing as a senior gave a younger boy a ride home after school each day in his pickup truck. After several days, the student got him some pot for $45. The officer arrested him; eighty-four others were also arrested.

All were suspended for the rest of the year, and some of the students received felony convictions.[472]

Drug laws also entice vengeful informing. They provide a means to harass adversaries by reporting them for some drug-related crime, real or invented. Undocumented informants with an axe to grind underlie many drug busts and asset confiscations. Cheated in a drug deal? Drop a dime on the guy. Get canned at work? Send an anonymous letter to the local police about the cocaine in your boss's desk drawer. Neighbor a pain? Throw some pot seeds in his yard, wait a few months, and tip off the cops. Know about a wild party to which you weren't invited? Tell the DEA it's a drug-fest. Is a trashy mom refusing to do anything about her out-of-control son? Write a letter to social services accusing her of letting her kids have pot parties. A small Texas aviation firm was nearly bankrupted when one of its planes was confiscated and held for nine months on a tip that it was carrying drug money out of the country. Agents found no drugs or money. A rival company had made the false accusation. Ex-husbands, ex-wives, angry in-laws, do-gooders—everyone knows someone they'd like to see in trouble, and drug laws provide a means.

The federal War on Drugs first topped $1 billion in 1981 and burgeoned to $18 billion by the turn of the century.[473] It now exceeds $20 billion with about as much spent at all other government levels combined, for a total of $40 billion annually, to little positive effect and much despair.[474] Year after year, billions are wasted—money that could have been spent on, say, breast cancer research. Due to drug laws, most states spend more money on prisons than on higher education.

While the British and Dutch governments have tried to accept and manage the problems associated with drug use, ours has remained aloof, proselytizing and punishing. US government officials continue to claim that stiff penalties are useful deterrents, though researchers in Canada and Switzerland found otherwise.[475] Criminalization has been injurious: millions of people arrested, hundreds of thousands imprisoned each year, lost opportunities, lost savings and careers, drug testing, searches, secrecy, and mistrust. As young people discover firsthand the exaggerations and lies regarding marijuana, they lose regard for government and law in general—all while pot has gotten more potent and prevalent. About half of adult Americans have tried marijuana at least once, and 10 percent of them—tens of millions of people—use it at least once a month.[476] Prohibiting drugs has worked no better than Prohibition did.

Drug Law Beneficiaries

Regardless, the War on Drugs has many backers. It has produced more agencies, administrators, police, prison guards, and parole officers than ever, all of whom have a vested interest in continued criminalization. Rational arguments for legalization make no impact on most drug warriors because, as with all of us, self-interest infuses their perspective. Another group—drug producers, processors, importers, and dealers—profit from the direct sale of illicit drugs. The first group has political and administrative clout to protect the status quo; the second has money. A third group has both: the big drug companies. Pharmaceuticals prospered during Prohibition because they could sell their products in alcohol's place. Today, the drug companies, cigarette manufacturers, and alcohol producers are allied against marijuana because all fear losing customers to it if legalized, so they help fund the drugs-are-evil message. Anheuser-Busch, Philip Morris, RJR Reynolds, Johnson & Johnson, DuPont, Hoffman-LaRoche, Merck, Procter & Gamble, and many other familiar names are among the biggest contributors to "Partnership for a Drug Free America," which portrays drug users as anything but ordinary people, like a privately funded DARE.[477]

Incidentally, with regard to high prices for prescription drugs, of course the drug companies are greedy—they're in business to make all the money they can—but exorbitant drug prices don't come from greed. If they did, every product would be expensive. They come from market failure. Some prescription drugs cost $20 per *pill,* or $50, or $100 or more, because in 1984, Congress passed the Hatch-Waxman Act, protectionist legislation that granted drug companies a legal monopoly on their successes. The US Patent and Trademark Office grants an exclusive patent, and the Food and Drug Administration grants exclusive marketing rights for a new drug for several years. Through various tricks, drug companies stretch the period of exclusivity to a decade or more. For all of that time, generics, costing a fraction of the price, are banned. No competition, monopoly prices.[478]

Prosecutors love marijuana laws because they insure a steady flow of guilty defendants, a lot of easy wins, and an occasional public relations coup. Lawyers benefit too. A marijuana bust for possession costs about $7,500 in legal fees, and a bust for cultivating or wholesale distribution can cost $25,000 to over $100,000 to defend. Attorneys collect legal fees of between $1 and $2 billion annually from marijuana cases alone.[479]

Because people like to alter their consciousness and will take risks to do it, no campaign to end drug use can succeed. The American people have concluded that drug policy must change, but well-represented interest groups have obstructed the way. California legalized medical marijuana in 1996, and in 2000 it passed proposition 36, directing drug offenders to treatment rather than incarceration, but in 2008 a bill to reduce marijuana penalties and establish treatment programs for harder drug users was defeated. It had the support of the California Nurses Association, the California Society of Addiction Medicine, and the California Academy of Family Physicians, but it had stronger opponents, including the California State Sheriffs' Association, the California Narcotics Officers Association, the California Peace Officers' Association, the Police Chiefs of California, and prison guards.[480] Legalize drugs and you lose at least a third of all criminals in the United States, to the detriment of those who make their living arresting or confining people.

How Drug Laws Violate Rights

Drug prohibition violates the rights of the individual to liberty, to property, and to pursue happiness.

No one takes drugs trying to feel worse, only to feel better, and even if his reasoning is flawed and his method fails, he is pursuing happiness, as is his right.

Drugs are property. As the State cannot constitutionally take anyone's house, car, or other belongings without due process, neither should it be able to confiscate personally owned drugs. Drug laws also violate the property that is each person's self. The individual owns his or her body and its contents and thus has the sole right to say what goes into a body (food, drink, drugs, sexual preferences, etc.) or what comes out of it (free speech, babies, blood, DNA, organs, etc.).

Since drug use does not violate common law or any valid rules of organization, and is a personal matter, use in one's home is also protected by the right to privacy (under the umbrella of liberty). During Prohibition, government put alcohol suppliers out of business, but there were no random tests of individuals for alcohol use, no searches of private homes for alcohol, and no jailing of citizens for possessing it. To incarcerate people for private drug use is an egregious wrong, far more invasive than rights violations during Prohibition.

Sentencing for drug-related crimes can also violate the right to liberty. Courts sometimes order people to attend Alcoholics Anonymous or a similar program, which legally constitutes a religion in that the individual is supposed to turn himself over to a "higher power" and make a spiritual awakening. State-mandated attendance forces a religion on people, a violation of the Establishment Clause of the First Amendment.[481] An argument can also be made that drug law sentencing violates the Eighth Amendment: if a person places a marijuana seed in soil, he can lose his house and savings, be imprisoned for years, and lose his ability to earn a living. This seems cruel and unusual punishment of the sort usually associated with regimes considered evil.

Legalization

Drug use can have adverse effects on the family of an addict, but so can a bad marriage, promiscuity, alcoholism, or gambling, and none of these are illegal, nor should they be since they are personal affairs, as is drug use. Some argue that drugs must be prohibited because they're dangerous, but so is jogging or bathing, each of which kills hundreds of people in the United States each year. Potato chips, pecan pie, and tanning salons can harm health. Statistically, a drive to the store to buy vitamins is more dangerous than staying home and smoking marijuana. Fewer than 1 in 1,000 users of cocaine die from it, while 1 of every 34 people who have tried to climb Mount Everest have died, yet only the first is illegal for being dangerous.[482]

Others have argued that drugs must be prohibited because drug use is an illness in which the addict loses his capacity for rational choice and so the decision must be made for him. But drug use is a choice. Though sometimes called a sickness, drug use is not a disease in the sense that cancer is. No drug invades your body of its own accord, as cancer does. Nor do drugs enslave people any more than love or obsession do. Enslavement by drugs is a self-serving claim used to try to mitigate responsibility. Recreational drug use provides a release. Heavy use is self-medication. An addict is someone who develops physical symptoms when use is discontinued or for whom acquisition of the drug is his greatest imperative. Addiction need not be permanent. People can go through withdrawal and stop using, find a substitute, or just tire of the drug's effect. People choose to smoke pot, do harder drugs, or quit altogether for the same reason: they seek happiness. At different stages of their lives, that means different things. People get bored and quit. After long drug use, the novelty of being clean can be attractive for the same reason drugs were many years before.

Using drugs is normal—smoking, drinking, taking aspirin or cold medicine, drinking coffee. People take drugs to relieve pain, anxiety, or depression, for escape or experimentation, for energy, or to enhance imagination. Why should a person be punished for ingesting something that makes him feel better temporarily? The desire to diminish awareness, to self-desensitize, is innate and occasionally pervasive. At least 300 million people worldwide choose marijuana as a means. For many of them, what caffeine does for wakefulness, pot does for peace of mind. Marijuana may be less harmful than alcohol or cigarettes and is probably easier to quit. Though habit-forming, like any drug, pot produces no physiological dependence. Smokers don't rob liquor stores to get money for weed. Relatively few people seek treatment for marijuana abuse. In one study, less than 1 percent of marijuana users considered their habit a problem for which they needed help, as opposed to 64 percent of heroin users.[483] If you divided all adult Americans into two groups—those who have smoked marijuana and those who haven't—the two would be equal in size, and health-wise, indistinguishable from one another. If it was really so bad, if more people found marijuana seriously damaging, more would quit. Churchill wrote, "I have taken more from alcohol than alcohol has taken from me." Millions today feel this way about marijuana: a net positive.

You can't name a less lethal drug than marijuana. There is virtually no such thing as a marijuana-related trip to the emergency room. Each year in the United States, cigarettes kill about 430,000 people. Alcohol kills about 150,000. Prescription drugs kill 33,000 people a year (some of which are suicides). Aspirin and other anti-inflammatories, 7,600. Cocaine, heroin, and all other hard recreational drugs combined kill about 6,000. Marijuana kills not one.[484] Marijuana law enforcement, however, usually kills a few.

Some have claimed that marijuana is a "gateway" drug to cocaine and heroin. Most people who try heroin have indeed smoked pot before. Most people drink milk before they drink bourbon. There is a difference between a chronological relationship and a causal one. Marijuana use does not *cause* harder drug use, and the numbers prove it. If marijuana truly led to heroin use, more than one smoker in one hundred would make the jump.

In Britain, during the first two-thirds of the twentieth century, heroin was legal. Licensed clinical psychiatrists prescribed it to addicts. US users of hard drugs faced long prison sentences, but an Englishman with an addiction to cocaine, morphine, or heroin could get a dose at the local drugstore. Most addicts led relatively normal lives, worked, had families. Drug-related crime was nonexistent. But under pressure from the United States, hard drugs were criminalized in England, creating the same problems as here. The point: if it's possible to have legal heroin, maybe legalizing marijuana is not such a far-fetched idea. Instead of arresting and charging people with marijuana crimes, the State could educate and advise. Cigarette smoking has fallen by two-thirds without government imprisoning anyone for it. Anti-cigarette dogma may grate (one ad likened second-hand smoke to death in a gas chamber), but in persuading rather than coercing, it doesn't violate rights.

There are so many advantages to legalizing drugs that it's hard to know where to begin. If drugs were legal, there would be no black market (or a much smaller one), no huge profits going to thugs, no violent crimes needed to protect drug enterprises, and less means for illicit empire building. Funding for gangs would become visible income for legal sellers, generating tax revenue that could fund education and treatment programs. Crime would fall by almost half overnight. Prison overcrowding would end. Police corruption would decrease. If drugs were legal, there would be less justification for sting operations, wiretaps, surveillance, paid informants, raids on residences, questionable searches, and property seizures. Millions of Americans could stop thinking of the police as the enemy. There would be less impetus for lawmakers to make end runs around the Constitution. Legalization might even become a first step in a renewal of respect for the Five Rights.

Economically, legalization is mouthwatering. Perhaps $30 billion would be saved each year.[485] Additionally, legalization would raise billions in tax revenues, since presumably marijuana sales would be heavily taxed, like cigarettes and alcohol. Federal taxes on each of those currently raise about $9 billion annually; marijuana tax revenues would likely be comparable. Then there is the revenue gained by taxing the incomes of marijuana workers. More than a million people earn at least $15 billion each year by growing, processing, or dealing in pot.[486] If legal, the money now earned by tax-evading producers would be earned by taxable businesses and tax-paying employees. The cultivation of cannabis hemp—which has no psychoactive effect at all—is outlawed despite its many economic uses. It too could be grown, processed, and exported, raising billions more. What is now a net cost of $40 billion annually could become a net gain of $15 billion or more. Money now spent to enforce drug laws and build prisons could be used to address real needs. Good things happen when you respect free choice rather than try to suppress it.

Legalization would permit marijuana's medical use. For some patients, it has greater therapeutic value than any other drug. It relieves the nausea, vomiting, and loss of appetite caused by AIDS or by the side effects of AIDS treatments like AZT. AIDS is no longer terminal, but victims must take handfuls of drugs daily, requiring an antiemetic. Marijuana is the best one.[487] It has been used to treat the side effects of chemotherapy, improving the lives of cancer patients. It can relieve the bronchial constriction of asthma. It can relieve intraocular pressure, alleviating the pain of glaucoma, which affects two million Americans and sixty-seven million worldwide. It can help relieve arthritis pain and possibly that of Crohn's disease. It can help prevent epileptic seizures and suppress the twitches and tremors symptomatic of multiple sclerosis and paraplegia. Marijuana has been used successfully to treat spasticity—uncontrollable jerking movements accompanied by pain—associated with brain damage, spinal cord injury, stroke, and cerebral palsy.[488] Hemp oil from the nonpsychoactive oil from marijuana seeds may have applications in fighting cancer or the AIDS virus—but being illegal, there has been scarcely any work done on it for the past half century.

If harder drugs were decriminalized, users would buy their supplies from registered sellers of accurately represented, FDA-approved drugs. Composition and purity would be insured. There would be fewer unsanitary procedures, fewer unintentional overdoses, and less avoidance of doctors. Some form of drug maintenance would be available for intravenous addicts to prevent the sharing of needles. In the Netherlands, addicts have been treated compassionately; in a program called *gedogen* (tolerance), they are given a fix when necessary or clean needles to reduce the chances of contracting AIDS. The Dutch government is not pro drug use; it is pro harm reduction. It would rather see its citizens live free even if on drugs than imprison them, so public funds are used to try to help addicts rather than punish them.

While people can possess drugs in the Ukraine, here in the land of the free, hundreds of thousands of Americans go to jail for it each year. Millions more could in the future. Bad laws hurt not-bad people. Jailing a person for taking drugs is like beating a child to get him to improve his grades: the goal is inconsequential relative to the destructiveness of the method used. More laws, arrests, and prisons—they're never the answer if the question is, how do we improve life for people?

Directives and Happiness

Though a democratic government represents the people, the two are often at cross-purposes where the pursuit of happiness is concerned. Individuals crave fun, camaraderie, excitement, escape, sex, love, and variety. The State's goal is order and efficiency. It wants to keep the individual healthy and employed because, from its point of view, if he doesn't work and pay taxes, he's a liability. If government had its way, every person would be conscientious, sober, chaste, hardworking, and compliant. Government representatives are thus given to moralize. Whatever the perceived travesty, they exaggerate the prevailing sentiment, add a helping of practiced indignation, and shape the grandstanding into directives of policy, the number and severity of which determine whether a nation feels free to the individuals who comprise it.

Because directives of policy appeal to that part of a person that likes having authority and citing rules, they sow officiousness. Tollbooth operators peer at each windshield for the proper stickers and into each car, looking for violations. Sanitation workers police neighborhoods for compliance with pick-up and recycling rules. School officials pass dress codes and search unlocked cars in the school lot. Regulations can effectively deputize carpenters, electricians, bartenders, nurses, doctors, morticians, landlords, bank tellers, airline employees, undertakers, and others who, in stipulating what their customers must do, become de facto officials of the State. Unlike a business relationship, in which either party can decline, a State representative and a customer are not individuals on equal footing, but one person offering terms fixed by law and another who can only accept them. Regulation reduces product differentiation, competition, and civility. The sentiment of the merchant changes from, if we can't get together, it harms us both, to, you have to comply and we both know it, and sometimes to, comply or I'll report you. When rules replace choices, abruptness replaces service.

Directives of policy are the wrong course altogether. When rules ban indulging in a pleasure, indulgence itself is sought. When opportunities are ever-present, the individual is forced to develop self-restraint. Whereas forced abstinence builds passion, voluntary abstinence builds character. The individual finds that enjoyment lies in the refinement of an act of pleasure, not in its repetition, and that excess deadens pleasure, but excess has to be experienced for the benefits of moderation to be appreciated. Freedom brings self-cultivation. Wrong choices teach humility and impart wisdom; a series of right ones create proficiency and self-assurance. The individual learns to abide by the rules out of a sense of responsibility and empathy rather than fear of penalty—an essential development if people are to trust one another enough for spontaneous order to function. Cicero asked, "How will a man behave in the dark if his only fear is a witness and a judge?"[489] The fruitful creation of values from within cannot occur if government acts like an overprotective parent.

Freedom of choice is utilitarian. Overruling people because they may make choices harmful to themselves assumes they are irrational, but if so, then government must be assumed irrational too, since government is made up of human beings. If, on the other hand, it is assumed that people generally act in their rational self-interest, those closest to a situation are in a better position to decide than government officials. Laws are rigid and can be applied out of context. Free will is specific to each case and flexible, allowing the individual to risk his health or safety if he chooses.

Some feel that if every individual lived for his happiness, it would be a hedonistic world, but as long as common law and rules of organization prevent people from harming one another, each can harm only himself. This is prevented by instinct; instruction from parents; information from friends, teachers, books, television, and the Internet; and firsthand experience and peer pressure, along with ever-present human examples of success and failure. The more good decisions a person makes, the better his life goes. If he is unable or unwilling to do what's best for him, if his choices are too far or too often wrong, life supplies penalties in the form of pain, illness, addiction, loneliness, accidents, and economic hardship. He pays for sloth, waste, drunkenness, drug dependence, lying, pettiness, or rage. A liar, for example, is not taken seriously by anyone. Frauds, users, and manipulators are exposed. Ill-mannered people are shunned. People who are overbearing or dismissive or treat people with irony find themselves isolated. And those with too many nonconformist views run into glass ceilings everywhere. Individuals unable or unwilling to contribute to the extended order on *its* terms are disassociated from it. For government to further penalize them achieves little and violates their rights.

In a free order, government gathers and reports truthful

information and issues warnings and recommendations, but it presumes the individual to be self-determining. It does not compel him to orthodoxy. If "correct" choice supersedes free choice, self-determination is ended—the State rules and individuals must obey or be punished, like pets. Perhaps in the future, government forces going into private homes and arresting people for something they are doing alone or with consenting adults will be recognized as the violation of the right to pursue happiness that it is.

CHAPTER 10
The Right to Equality before the Law

Equality before the law means that any law that applies to one must apply to all, including the lawmakers. Laws must be impartial, making no references to any particular group. There cannot be a stop sign that applies only to people with red hair. There can't be one rule for a rich person and another for a poor one. Laws must be written without knowledge of who the plaintiffs and defendants will be. They must be enforced, or unenforced, equally, and people who commit the same crime should receive the same punishment. The right of the individual to equality before the law prevents lawmakers from making rules favorable to themselves or their supporters. It precludes arbitrary laws or class legislation, taking from some groups to give to others. The right to equality also restrains government spending: when a privilege or payment granted to one group must be given to all, economic considerations often make the plan impracticable.

Equality has another meaning: individuals and the State are equal in that neither can act unilaterally; each must have the go-ahead of the other. As Paine observed, in an absolute monarchy the king is law, but in a free order the law is king, and no one, including the king, is above it.[490] This is the *rule of law,* and it subordinates actions to principles. Individuals violate the rule of law when they commit a crime. Government violates the rule of law when it oversteps its authority. If the people ignore the laws, there is anarchy. If the government ignores the Constitution, there is tyranny. Each answering to the other is government by consent of the governed.

Racial Equality

Regarding rights violations in United States history, nothing compares to slavery. From the time the first slaves arrived in 1619 in Jamestown until Lincoln's Emancipation Proclamation in 1863, tens of millions of individuals had no right to life or liberty, no property rights, no right to manage their own affairs or to move freely. Today, we decry rights violations, but we cannot conceive of having no rights at all: no privacy, no right to raise children or remain together as a family. For 244 years, over half of our history, human beings were bought, worked, and sold. They could legally be beaten.

In *Dred Scott,* the Supreme Court held that African American slaves were property and had no rights and no access to the federal court system for a redress of grievances. The Court further ruled that the federal government had no power to limit the expansion of slavery. Federal territories could become new slave states. The decision enraged abolitionists and ushered in the Civil War three years later and, finally in 1863, emancipation. After the war, the federal government passed the Thirteenth Amendment (abolishing slavery), Fourteenth Amendment (granting ex-slaves, and reaffirming for all others, the right to equality before the law), and Fifteenth Amendment (granting ex-slaves the right to vote), and two civil rights acts, all between 1866 and 1875.

In the South, most whites would not accept the new order and they mistreated ex-slaves, so under the policy of Reconstruction, the federal government intervened. Troops occupied the southern states to help guarantee the rights of freed slaves to vote and to participate in elections, which they did. Two African Americans were elected US senators, and twenty others were elected to the House of Representatives. Coalitions of blacks and whites established the first public school systems in the South. Reconstruction prevented the southern states from restoring slavery in all but name through anti-black state laws, but Reconstruction ended in 1876, when President Rutherford Hayes withdrew the troops, discontinuing enforcement of the laws passed to protect the freed slaves.

White hostility toward blacks permeated the South. Some historians claim that the traditions of racism were so deeply ingrained that segregation was inevitable and that the only question was whether it would happen with or without government sanction. The Fourteenth Amendment protected the civil rights of African Americans, but the protections were eviscerated in two subsequent Supreme Court decisions. In the *Slaughterhouse Cases* (1873), the Court ruled that "equal protection" applied only to rights directly associated with being a national citizen, like access to the courts, and not to general racial discrimination. Then in the *Civil Rights Cases* (1883), the Court backtracked further, ruling that the Fourteenth Amendment did not give the federal government the power to prohibit discrimination by privately owned businesses. The decisions reinterpreted the Fourteenth Amendment and invalidated the Civil Rights Act of 1875 that had guaranteed African Americans equal access to goods and services and had prohibited racial discrimination by railways, inns, and theaters. When these businesses chose to discriminate anyway, the Court let them. Justice John Harlan, the only dissenter, argued that Congress's power to regulate interstate commerce included the power to ban discrimination in privately owned businesses that were "quasi-public," like railroads and theaters,[491] but Harlan was outvoted. By 1890, every southern state had enacted laws that applied to blacks only. States employed poll taxes, literacy tests, white-only primaries, and extra-legal means to prevent blacks from voting. Slavery had ended a quarter-century before, but white supremacy was still entrenched.

On June 7, 1892, a thirty-year-old African American man named Homer Plessy was jailed for sitting in the "white" car of the East Louisiana Railroad. Plessy claimed that the state of Louisiana's Separate Car Act, in segregating blacks and whites on trains, violated his Fourteenth Amendment right to equality. The judge in the case, John Ferguson, had previously declared the same act unconstitutional on interstate trains, but in Plessy's case the train traveled only in Louisiana and therefore was subject to Louisiana state law. Plessy appealed to Louisiana's supreme court, but it upheld the decision.[492] Reasoned Plessy, if he was equal, why should he be separated from others? In 1896, the US Supreme Court heard Plessy's case, but it too ruled against him. Justice John Harlan, again the lone dissenter, agreed with Plessy. Harlan thought that separating people by skin color was wrong and feared that the decision would lead to widespread segregation, which would ultimately "stimulate aggressions ... upon the admitted rights of colored citizens." He wrote that such discrimination was precisely what the Fourteenth Amendment was invented to forestall and that the decision was "conceived in hostility" to humiliate African Americans, and he rightly predicted that the majority's decision would in time be regarded "as pernicious as the decision in the Dred Scott Case."[493]

Why did the Supreme Court uphold segregation? Justice Henry Brown wrote for the majority in *Plessy*, "The object of the Fourteenth Amendment was undoubtedly to enforce the absolute equality of the two races, but in the nature of things it could not have been intended to abolish distinctions based upon color, or to enforce social, as distinguished from political equality." The Court ruled that segregation was not wrong because separate did not necessarily mean unequal and so did not abridge rights. It noted that the same laws that prohibited blacks from white cars prohibited whites from black cars. The "separate but equal" doctrine quickly took hold in the South. Soon drinking fountains, restaurants, theaters, inns, and restrooms were segregated, with shoddy alternatives forced on blacks. Separate facilities pertained to swimming pools, telephone booths, and checker games. There were separate entrances and exits to buildings for blacks and whites, and separate buses, reform schools, prisons, public and private schools, churches, and cemeteries. State fairs had a "colored day," allowing blacks to attend on only that day.[494] Some states excluded blacks from parks and entertainment centers altogether. North Carolina segregated its state libraries. Louisiana had a law mandating the separation of blind black people from blind white people. Oklahoma banned teachers from taking a job at a school in which the two races were not segregated. In Georgia, it was illegal for a bartender to serve whites and blacks in the same room at the same time.[495]

During the period, "Jim Crow" was the name given to laws made to prohibit blacks from doing things a white could do. In an attempt to impose a caste system, black people were treated like and expected to act like second-class citizens. Jim Crow laws excluded blacks from juries, jobs, and neighborhoods. Under Jim Crow etiquette, blacks were to step aside for whites. White motorists had the right of way at intersections. A black man could not offer to shake hands with a white man because it implied equality. Blacks were introduced to whites, never whites to blacks. Blacks did not call whites by their first names. A black man was to remove his hat when talking to a white person. Blacks were not permitted to show affection toward one another in public because it offended whites. Blacks were not to eat with whites in public; a black person could buy food to take out, and wait at the counter while it was prepared, but he could not eat it there. Because restaurants would not provide plates, dishes, or boxes for black customers, they commonly had to bring their own tin pails or buckets to be filled. A black person could not accuse a white person of lying no matter what; he could not challenge, show up, curse at, or laugh at a white person; he could make no comment whatsoever on the appearance of a white female. A black man could not offer to light a woman's cigarette; it implied intimacy. Any sexual activity between a black man and a white woman constituted rape. Blacks were forced to sit in the rear of streetcars, and motormen were not to assist black women with bags. Blacks were to surrender their seats to whites during crowded times.[496] Stores would not allow blacks to try on clothing or shoes on before buying them.

President Woodrow Wilson formally segregated the federal civil service, and in 1913, on the fiftieth anniversary of the Battle of Gettysburg at the hallowed location where Lincoln had proclaimed "a new birth of freedom," Wilson spoke to an all-white audience because the War Department had barred African Americans from the ceremony.[497] The color line was strictly observed in public hospitals with separate wards for whites and blacks. If a black person needed an ambulance, a black-owned vehicle was required—even in emergencies. The same code applied in the US Army. Though there was a shortage of nurses during World War II, black nurses were not allowed to care for white soldiers until Eleanor Roosevelt intervened.[498]

Racial violence was routine. White mobs attacked black men, sometimes in the spirit of pogroms. It was terrorism, an attempt to instill fear in African American men by example. From 1877 to 1965, there were 4,730 known lynchings.[499] According to the social scientist W. E. B. DuBois, during 1919 alone, there were 77 black men lynched and more than 200 murdered by other means in racial incidents in twenty-six US cities.[500] Lynchings were most frequent in small to middle-sized towns, in which blacks competed economically with whites, to the whites' resentment. Black men were also beaten, shot, burned at the stake, castrated, and dismembered. Whites were rarely arrested or charged. Blacks had no legal recourse because the justice system was all white. Racial abuses led to riots in Wilmington, Atlanta, Springfield, St. Louis, Tulsa, Chicago, Knoxville, Nashville, Charleston, and Omaha.

Emmett Till was a fourteen-year-old boy from Chicago. He had an awkward sense of humor, and childhood polio had left him with a stutter. He lived with his great uncle in Mississippi, where race relations were poor. On August 21, 1955, Till and some friends went to Bryant's Grocery and Meat Market for candy and soda, run by Roy and Carolyn Bryant. Roy Bryant was not present. On a dare, Till flirted with the twenty-one-year-old Mrs. Bryant. He wolf-whistled at her and said, "Bye, baby," as he left the store. The story got around, and her husband heard it. Roy Bryant and his half brother, J. W. Milam, abducted Till and took him to an abandoned shed, where they beat him, broke his legs, gouged out his right eye, and then shot him. They tied a seventy-five-pound cotton gin fan around his neck with barbed wire and threw the body into the Tallahatchie River near Glendora, Mississippi.[501]

When the body was found, it was bizarrely swollen and too disfigured to be recognizable, but Till was identified by a ring he wore that had been his father's. At the funeral, Till's mother insisted on leaving the casket open and invited people to take photographs of the grotesque corpse, repeating, "I want the world to see what they did to my baby." Over fifty thousand Chicagoans saw the body firsthand; millions saw magazine photos of it. On the day Emmett Till was buried, Bryant and Milam were indicted by a grand jury, but at trial, an all-white, twelve-man jury acquitted both defendants after deliberating for just sixty-seven minutes. One juror reported that the verdict would have been faster, but the jury had taken some time "to drink a pop."[502] The case caused a national outrage and enflamed the Civil Rights Movement. Two months later, Rosa Parks refused to surrender her seat on a bus to a white man.

Earl Warren took a driving tour of southern Civil War monuments in Virginia. He told his chauffeur that he'd like to stay overnight at a local hotel. When Warren came downstairs the next day, he found that his chauffeur had spent the night in the car. The man, the personal assistant to the Chief Justice of the United States, could not find a hotel that would accept him because he was African American. Warren was ashamed by the incident and it influenced him for the rest of his life. Explaining why the Supreme Court overruled *Plessy* in *Brown v. Board of Education,* Warren said the issue boiled down to one question: "Does segregation of school children solely on the basis of color, even though the physical facilities may be equal, deprive the group of equal opportunities in the educational system? We believe that it does." Warren added, "To separate [African American children] from others of their age solely because of their color puts the mark of inferiority not only on their status in the community but upon their little hearts and minds in a fashion that is unlikely ever to be undone.[503] ... We conclude that in the field of public education the doctrine of separate but equal has no place. Separate educational facilities are inherently unequal."[504]

Real desegregation in the South did not come about until a decade later in 1964, when Congress passed the most important piece of civil rights legislation in American history, the Civil Rights Act, which President Johnson signed into law. The act prohibited racial discrimination in any place of public accommodation, defined as any restaurant, cafeteria, lunch counter, park, hotel or motel, store, movie theater, gas station, private school, or workplace. The act was challenged as unconstitutional by proprietors in Alabama and Georgia, but it was upheld by the Court under the federal government's power to regulate commerce.

Title Seven of the Civil Rights Act prohibited businesses and labor unions of more than twenty-five people from discriminating against an individual due to race, religion, national origin, or sex. If a discriminatory practice was found, Title Seven authorized the courts to take "affirmative action" in rectifying the situation through reinstatement, back pay, and possibly damages.[505] It required employers to adopt nondiscriminatory policies and to furnish workforce statistics. During the 1970s, the statistics were used to pressure companies that were "underrepresented." Working from demographics, activists accused firms employing few minority employees of discriminating, and affirmative action became a call to fix it. The Nixon administration required contractors in the construction industry in Cleveland and Philadelphia to adopt quotas and timetables for hiring more individuals from racial minorities. The Department of Labor extended the requirement to all contractors.[506] If a company wanted to do business with the US government, it had to hire more minority employees.

Then the Supreme Court transformed Title Seven in a series of decisions, ultimately ruling that after a finding of discrimination, courts could *force* employers to hire more members of minorities. Was it illegal discrimination for an employer to seek the most qualified candidate and hire on that basis alone? Perhaps it was, implied the Court in *Griggs v. Duke Power Co.* (1971) and *McDonnell Douglas v. Green* (1973). The Court sought to impose a racially proportional allocation of jobs by compelling employers to adopt preferential hiring practices. Fearing discrimination lawsuits, employers dropped tests and hiring criteria previously considered objective and started hiring "by the numbers," that is, trying to achieve a racially balanced labor force.[507]

In *Bakke v. Regents of the University of California* (1978), the Supreme Court ruled that a white male's rights had been violated by a medical school's plan that reserved spaces for members of minority races only. As a case of "reverse discrimination," it got a lot of attention, but the Supreme Court in its next two major decisions sustained the new interpretation of affirmative action. In *Weber v. United Steelworkers of America* (1979), it upheld the right of government to impose racial hiring quotas on private employers. And in *Fullilove v. Klutznick* (1980), it ruled that Congress could enact policies that were preferential to African Americans on the basis of the history of slavery, segregation, and discrimination. After *Weber* and *Fullilove*, rules could intentionally favor minorities. In 1987, the Court reiterated that employers may favor women and members of racial minorities over better-qualified applicants. Wrote Justice Antonin Scalia in a dissenting opinion, "The Court today completes the process of converting Title Seven of the Civil Rights Act of 1964 from a guarantee that race or sex will not be the basis for employment determinations, to a guarantee that it often will."[508]

Whereas the Civil Rights Act of 1964 protected rights by guaranteeing equality, affirmative action sought to undo past injustices by imposing unjust policies now—trying to make two wrongs into a right. Equal opportunity permits the individual to advance on merit alone, irrespective of any group affiliation. Age, sex, race, and religion are to be ignored. It's the opposite with affirmative action, which awards jobs, college enrollments, grants, loans, and tax advantages to individuals on the basis of their membership in a favored group.

Affirmative action violates equality before the law. One cannot say that individuals are equal *and* that some must be treated favorably by law. People are equal or unequal, and if equal, they must be treated the same. In *Bakke*, the Supreme Court noted that the "guarantee of equal protection cannot mean one thing when applied to a person of another color." The Court declared that any racial classification was thus "inherently suspect."[509] Hiring people *because* of their race is as wrongheaded as rejecting them because of it. Perhaps worst, politically favored groups cannot easily claim to be equal competitors, nor are they likely to be accepted and regarded as truly equal by nonfavored groups while receiving patronizing treatment. It makes accomplishments suspect. If individuals from different races are equal, why categorize them by race at all? Affirmative action should be seen for what it is: a distasteful condescension. Those who favor equality before the law are not making presumptions based on race; those who patronize are.

Granting privileges can also promote racial chauvinism. In 1996, anthropologists discovered a 9,300-year-old human skeleton, one of the oldest in North America, on the banks of the Columbia River in Washington State. It was that of a male, between forty and fifty-five years of age, and significantly, it exhibited a narrow skull, receding cheekbones, prominent chin, and square mandible: all traits associated with Asians, specifically Polynesians, rather than Native Americans. Chief anthropologist James Chatters felt it raised the possibility that Native Americans were not the first humans to people the New World, but before scientists could investigate, the

Department of the Interior seized the remains. Five local Native American tribes claimed the remains as their property under the Native American Graves Protection and Repatriation Act. The tribes claimed that they knew that the skeleton was one of their people because their oral histories said that their people had occupied the region "since the beginning of time." Interior Secretary Bruce Babbit honored their claim and turned the remains over to the tribes, who planned to bury them in a secret location.[510]

Other Violations of Equality

In some Asian and African countries, women today have no more rights than slaves in America did; it's the contemporary scourge of the planet. But in the United States, women have achieved, if not equality before the law, something approximating it. Elizabeth Cady Stanton and Lucretia Mott initiated the women's suffrage movement in Seneca Falls, New York, in the summer of 1848. Lucy Stone and Susan B. Anthony joined the effort soon after. Two decades passed, and African Americans won the right to vote with the passage of the Fifteenth Amendment, but it took another half century for women to get equal voting rights, which they won in 1920, two years after women in Kyrgyzstan. In the nineteenth century, women in the United States faced some serious sexism. An 1872 Supreme Court verdict upheld a law that forbid women to join the Illinois state bar because God created women "to fulfill the noble and benign offices of wife and mother."[511] A century later, things had changed. By the 1960s, the movement was called women's liberation, and the focus was on equal pay and reproductive rights.

The Supreme Court upheld women's rights to birth control and abortion. It overturned an Idaho law that preferred males to females for handling estates. It ruled that female military personnel were entitled to claim male spouses as dependents for medical benefits. In compliance with the Equal Pay Act, courts forced employers to raise the wages of female workers in a number of jobs. The Pregnancy Discrimination Act prevented an employer with fifteen or more employees from refusing to hire a woman because she is pregnant or may become pregnant, nor could an employer fire a pregnant woman or force her to take leave if she could still perform her job duties.

Women were guaranteed equal access to any education program receiving federal financial assistance, and gender discrimination was banned in all public schools and any private school receiving any federal funding.

The right of association permits private clubs to exclude women—but only truly private associations. Clubs that are large and not highly selective in awarding memberships are considered public accommodations. The Lions Club, for example, was forced to admit women, as was the Virginia Military Institute. In Minnesota, the Jaycees were found to be a public accommodation because they were nonselective, large, and impersonal, as were the Elks and Eagles: none could legally exclude women.[512]

The Equal Rights Amendment has been around since 1923, and at one point thirty-five of the necessary thirty-eight states ratified it, but to date it has not passed because it is superfluous to the Equal Protection Clause of the Fourteenth Amendment and to the Civil Rights Act of 1964, both of which prohibit gender discrimination. As individuals, women already have the same constitutional protections as men. It could indeed be argued that they have more (right to pregnancy leave, privileges in heavy industries or in a military draft, favorable treatment in divorce settlements) and the Equal Rights Amendment if passed could actually harm their position relative to men.

The War on Drugs has been especially hard on women because they are more likely than men to have been the primary caregiver for dependent children prior to an imprisonment for a drug conviction. Due mostly to harsh drug laws, more than a million women are now on probation, on parole, or in jail.[513] Over 200,000 children under the age of eighteen have a mother in prison, and the separation destroys families. The children typically live with two or more different caretakers during the incarceration. Because many states have only one prison for women, mothers are often unable to have much contact with their children due to geography. More than half of incarcerated mothers never see their children at all while in jail.[514]

Of any major group discriminated against in the United States, gays have made the greatest advances toward equal rights over the past half-century. In the 1960s, gays were treated like subhumans. Police commonly entrapped and arrested gay men in public restrooms and took any excuse to use billy clubs on them. In at least twenty states, an individual could be arrested and imprisoned simply for being gay. In some states, the "deviant" (even doctors used the term) could be imprisoned for life. In California, at the infamous Atascadero State Hospital, gays were treated nearly as atrociously as they had been by the Third Reich. Hundreds of gay individuals were committed there against their will and forced to endure tortuous electric shock therapy and chemical treatments, or were castrated or lobotomized. Trying to "cure" them, one man, Dr. Walter J. Freeman, lobotomized at least one thousand gay individuals, many by hammering an ice pick—from his own kitchen—through their eyes. (He later developed a machine—the orbitoclast—to increase capacity.) Government-sponsored harassment of gays did not begin to subside until June 28, 1969, when gays fought back for the first time in an uprising against police at the Stonewall Inn in New York City. To commemorate the event, one year later the first gay pride parade was held. It was the first time that a large group of individuals organized and openly, proudly admitted being gay and it marked the beginning of the end of their stigmatization.[515]

Gays are still discriminated against in the areas of child custody and adoption. Some state laws are archaic, criminalizing sodomy between consenting adults; some states exclude gays from employment as police officers or firefighters,[516] and same-sex marriage still faces ardent opposition. In 1993, a Hawaii court ruled that laws banning gay marriage constituted sex discrimination. Fearing that Hawaii might follow up by legalizing gay marriage, thirty-four states enacted legislation to avoid recognizing any out-of-state marriage in their state, and Congress passed the Defense of Marriage Act, which declared that the federal government did not recognize same-sex marriage. In 1999, the Vermont Supreme Court legalized gay marriage in all but name. Gays were granted rights to marital property, worker's compensation benefits, and family leave, and a gay union in Vermont required a legal divorce to terminate it, as with any other marriage. But Vermont's alternative and other civil unions or domestic partnerships were unrecognized by most states, so a couple could lose those rights if they relocated.

The right of every individual to equality before the law renders gay marriage a simple issue. If straights can marry, then gays can marry, and as with any marriage, it should be universally recognized. Because all arguments to the contrary are unpersuasive, change is happening. In 2003, the Massachusetts Supreme Court ruled that gays could marry and receive the same privileges as any other married couple. Since then, seven states and the District of Columbia have legalized same-sex marriage. Whether a gay person may adopt a child depends on the state in which he or she resides. Gay couples may not adopt in Florida, Mississippi, Oklahoma, or Utah. In many other states, local laws have the same effect. California, Massachusetts, New Jersey, Vermont, and the District of Columbia explicitly *do* permit adoption by gay and lesbian couples.

Don't-ask-don't-tell no longer exists in the military, but the Boy Scouts still maintain something similar to it. The Supreme Court ruled that the Boy Scouts were an expressive association and thus could legally exclude individuals who didn't share its beliefs, including gays. The Scouts' stated position is that homosexuality conflicts with Boy Scout values and to require the Scouts to admit openly gay members would undermine that position. (If the position is to change, it must happen by choice—not by mandate. Otherwise, there is no right to hold opposing views.)

The right to equality protects all minorities, including the wealthy. When factions differ, government is supposed to make sure every side allows every other side to be. Regarding religion, it's easy to see that this is right. When it comes to rich and poor, less easy. Nevertheless, as the State must prevent the rich from preying on the poor (monopolies, stock manipulation, corporate accounting fraud, price fixing, illegal discrimination in hiring, sweatshop conditions), it also must prevent the poor from preying on the rich (steeply progressive income taxes, other redistributions of wealth, excessive regulation of property). Rules that attempt to transfer wealth violate the right to property and the right to equality before the law.

Once adopted, a scale of progressive taxation tends to steepen because so many favor "taking from those who don't need it," but no majority has the right to impose a higher rate on any group. Optimally, there would be a single income tax rate, period, and no deductions for anyone or anything. No exemptions for colleges, churches, or charities. No deductions for homebuyers, business expenses, interest, or hospital bills. No exemptions for dividends or capital gains, and no tax tricks or finagling for the rich, most of whom would likely pay more in taxes than now. A flat tax would be a simple, more effective system from which everyone would benefit, except the accountants and lawyers who profit from the current muddle.

The best thing about a flat tax is that instead of pitting the majority against the rich, creating constant pressure to increase the top rate, it promotes unity. When the same percentage is taken from all taxpayers, any increase affects everyone, reducing for all earners the incentive to raise taxes and giving the people one voice in saying how much government can spend. As for it being "unfair" to tax rich and poor at the same rate, that comes from our conditioning. Equal treatment is the only just system. At a flat rate of 20 percent, a person earning $50,000 per year pays $10,000 in taxes, while a person earning $1 million pays $200,000 in taxes. The second person is doing more good for the nation than the first—twenty times more. He should not be penalized for it. Even a fairly high flat rate would be ethically preferable to the current system. Why care about the property rights of people with millions of dollars? Because you have the same rights, and however their money can be taken from them, yours can be taken from you.

CHAPTER 11
Liberty's Two Opponents

On Capitalism

Improvements in storage methods trigger leaps in human progress. Writing was a better way of storing information. Through the written word, a person could inform others living centuries later. Computers, able to store many times as much data, sparked another revolution. Money was a better way of storing value. Before money, individuals had no incentive to produce more than they could eat plus some nonperishables. Money's longevity—you can store what you don't use—created incentive to produce a surplus as a means to exercise liberty and pursue happiness. Money was fungible, portable, and convenient. Finance arose when people realized that money itself was a commodity that could be advanced to a person to be returned later with a bit more. The desire to profit by "renting" money made capital available and forced people to be trustworthy if they wanted to receive credit.

Work underlies property. An individual can trade his work for pay, accumulate earnings, and trade them for things he wants. He is motivated by need, but also by pride, by the quality of life he can provide for his family, and by the wish to serve a larger purpose both in his work and with his savings. Saving is crucial, but it requires an ability to restrict consumption, self-regulate, and delay gratification. If one is thrifty, a first job is the first rung on the ladder of ascent. If not, it's the start of a life of drudgery. Goes a Chinese proverb, the saving man becomes the free man. Whatever a person wants to accomplish, no matter how unselfish, money will help; the more, the better.

As for the idea that wealth-building is somehow wrong, consider Lincoln's views on the subject: "I take it that it is best for all to leave each man free to acquire property as fast as he can. Some will get wealthy. I don't believe in a law to prevent a man from getting rich; it would do more harm than good." "Let not him who is houseless pull down the house of another; but let him labor diligently and build one for himself, thus by example assuring that his own shall be safe from violence when built." "That some should be rich, shows that others may become rich, and hence is just encouragement to industry and enterprise." "There is no permanent class of hired laborers amongst us. Twenty-five years ago, I was a hired laborer. The hired laborer of yesterday, labors on his own today; and will hire others to labor for him tomorrow. Advancement—improvement in condition—is the order of things in a society of equals."[517] Man trying to improve his material position is not greed; it is ambition, without which, he achieves only enough to survive, not advance. Nor is the desire for comforts properly called greed. From the most basic need to the most wasteful indulgence, our wanting things creates opportunity and prosperity, which can broaden horizons because aspirations increase with greater means.

When people with money try to turn it into more, they must do something with it—make something, deliver something, or provide a needed service—which is impossible without creating jobs and choices: an individual can apply for employment wherever he likes; if offered a job, he can accept or decline. An investor can choose to buy a company's stock, or not. A consumer can choose to buy a company's products, or not. Or, if dissatisfied with the options available, he can make and sell a competing product, filling a niche and increasing the menu for all.

Specialization—also called the division of labor—multiplies efficiency and output. Adam Smith used the example of a company that made pins from wire. With each person doing every operation, ten people could produce a few hundred pins in a day, but with ten people each doing one operation—one person drawing out wire, another straightening it, another cutting, another forming the point, two more making and attaching the heads—the company could produce 48,000 pins in a day.[518] Specialization brings proficiency and innovation. People are more likely to find better methods and materials if their attention is completely focused on one task rather than divided among many. Wealth comes from making what you make best and trading for the rest.

Trade need not be a zero-sum game in which one person loses what the other gains. Because people have different needs and a trade requires mutual consent, it can be advantageous to both. It usually is, otherwise the "loser" would pass. If each trader can act self-interestedly and both can benefit, as well as third parties, then private interests can create public goods.[519] The self-interested businessman can often serve people better than the government employee trying to do so directly: to serve himself, the businessman *must* serve others. He must provide things people actually want to buy, as opposed to things he wants to sell them.

Businesses compete with one another to sell their products. Each customer weighs the cost of an item against its value to him, and collectively, customers determine prices without deliberate intent. When gas doubles in price, people don't delve into research about light sweet crude oil production. Having limited funds for the things they need, they drive less, reducing demand, putting downward pressure on gas prices. When a product is hot, people in that business profit, which draws more suppliers to the market. More product becomes available, creating a glut and lowering prices. When prices are down, companies lose money, forcing layoffs and factory closures, reducing the supply of product available to meet the lower demand. Buying affects prices, which affect buying decisions, which affect prices, ad infinitum, forming the self-adjusting system that is the free market.

It might be asked, why compete? Why not work together and share the world's resources equally? Families and friendships are maintained through shared information and altruism. Camaraderie serves small groups well; they coordinate themselves through like perspectives and aims. But those dynamics don't work for big, diverse groups like nations or the world's population, because the members' aims are too disparate. Different groups have different priorities. In the extended order, as Hayek noted, each person seeks his own goals, but all do so according to shared rules.[520] Personal views rarely interrupt the process, because markets are impersonal; decisions are based on price (what you pay) and value (what you get). The customer doesn't know the politics of the many people responsible for the English muffin he pops into his toaster, nor are they relevant. Due to free market forces, people who never meet provide goods for one another. People who don't speak the same language, who may disagree on much and seek different or irreconcilable ends, can have access to each other's talents and specialties.

To share, as with a pizza among eight friends, is a romantic ideal but unworkable. By nature's genetic design, people care more about self and family than about strangers, and the earth's population and natural assets are not evenly distributed, so goods must be processed and transported to where they are needed, requiring labor and wages, establishing trade, prices, and market forces. In physics, quantum mechanics deals with the actions of particles at atomic and subatomic levels. Newtonian physics describes how things work at scales humans can relate to: inches, feet, miles. And at the high end—millions or billions of miles, light-years—neither of these disciplines apply; relativity is the basis of how things work. What works at one scale doesn't necessarily work at another. The same is true for human beings. What works for a group of five to live in harmony is different than what works for a group of ten million.

Market forces are not subject to moral judgment, because a phenomenon that is not the result of a deliberate act of human will cannot be judged good or evil. The free market is analogous to a game of skill and chance. All must play by the rules, and still the results are not always satisfying. Sometimes people win by being lucky, and many with promise fail. Some of the latter seek to redress the "injustice" by making corrective laws, but it defeats the purpose of law (to protect individuals' rights) to violate individuals' rights in the name of "fairness" or "social justice." You don't sacrifice rights to improve the outcome of a system that arises from honoring rights.

Laws must prevent deception, breach of contract, insider trading, and market manipulation, but other than to insure fair play, economic laws hamper spontaneous order. When government sets price floors or ceilings, limits quantities, or chooses who may provide particular products or services, it restrains competition and inflates prices. When it tries to save failing companies, it inhibits what Schumpeter called "creative destruction," a useful by-product of market forces. If demand for snow blowers is flat and production methods improve, then fewer people are needed to produce the same number of machines. If workers in that field are to maintain their past incomes, their numbers must be reduced. Layoffs occur. Losses knock out the least efficient companies, strengthening the survivors. But when government props up marginal players with bailouts or supports, it can debilitate an industry for years by preventing the changes needed to make it profitable again.

Economic legislation has another problem: it is often based on faulty reasoning. Analysts combine bits of information, hypothesize, crunch numbers, make forecasts, and believe them. Though they multiply relative error and entirely miss some factors, the process, being well lubricated by whim, bias, and ego, creates a canvas that is so self-satisfying that the predicted outcome *has* to be credible. A horseplayer thinks he knows how a race is going to be run, is wrong, has a plausible reason why, and by the next race has invented a scenario for that one, certain again. What handicappers do with the past performances of Thoroughbreds, analysts do with their knowledge of history, politics, human nature, and trends. So much to consider and integrate, all of which means nothing to the horses on the track.

When people are permitted to spend as they choose, they buy what they want. Suppliers of wanted products make money. They reinvest their earnings, and capitalism sprouts. It's organic, the result of human self-interest. Socialism must be imposed. Capitalism is like an ecological system; it emanates naturally from human interaction but can be inhibited severely by man. Socialism is a system, like daylight savings time is one—purposefully invented by man and applied from without. Capitalism harnesses the desire to be secure and comfortable while respecting the right to liberty. One cannot support socialism *and* the right to liberty, because liberty requires the right to property, which socialism contravenes. Socialists use government to accomplish what requires a weapon if done firsthand—taking money from some and giving it to others. Some socialists don't understand that they advocate thievery; others know but disregard the rights of the rich. Disdain for the wealthy helps keep socialism alive.

Capitalism gives outlet to the me-first aspect of our nature, to our competitive and acquisitive juices, but peacefully. Running a business requires reason, effort, self-reliance, risk-taking, showing up every day, handling details, courting customers—it takes real bother because merit is judged by the *recipient* of goods or services. In socialism, the distributors—the State—determine which products and services are to be produced and who gets them. Like a religion, socialism requires individuals to believe in something other than themselves, external and nebulous—the weakness of both ideologies—and makes hollow promises in return. Capitalism permits the individual to be an end in himself.[521] That's what makes it different. Nationalism subordinates the Five Rights of the individual to the good of the State, socialism to the good of "the people" as determined by the State. In either case, government sets the priorities, imposes the rules, and allocates the dollars. Capitalism—allowing individuals to keep their earnings less their fair share of the required common expenses of the nation—is the only system compatible with the Five Rights, not coincidentally, since it arises from honoring them.

Anticapitalism

In a system based on initiative, great disparities in wealth are to be expected, a natural consequence of individuals having equal rights but being unequal in their gifts, acquired abilities, and efforts. One person earning or having a lot more money than another is not an injustice to be rectified. Through their free actions, some get rich and others don't. What matters is not the size of the gap between them but the condition of those worst off, to be addressed through legitimate, equitable programs.

When private capital has been used productively for a long time, it becomes a pool of wealth. The anticapitalist sees these pools as appallingly inequitable. Irritated by the gap between rich and poor, he employs hyperbole: "How can it be right that one person has a mansion with a staff of twenty while another is barely surviving?" He relates unrelated extremes, implying that the poor are poor *because* some people are rich. He argues from emotion in inflammatory language, like someone trying to ban the right of a woman to terminate a pregnancy, as disgusted by the gap between rich and poor as some are by abortion. But neither abortion nor the gap between rich and poor are the results of rights violations. Rather, both are unsatisfying outcomes of *respecting* individuals' rights: the right to privacy in the first case, property rights in the second.

Think of all the wealth in the world—all the money held by individuals, banks, and governments, the gold, stocks, bonds, office buildings, factories, airplanes, ships, cars, and houses. There once was a time when there was no wealth. That means it had to be created. Because wealth is created, one person's wealth does not generally come at the expense of another. On the contrary, one person's affluence benefits many, whether he intends it or not. Though often cast as predatory, capitalism is in the larger sense a symbiotic system. People need things, so making things is profitable, so businesses form to make things. Businesses need employees, so they must pay people, who need incomes so they can buy things. The rich can't play without spending, and they can't get richer without risking their wealth, which is the capital that finances new undertakings. They tend to allocate capital well, and in the end, death separates every dollar of wealth from its holder, and it accrues to the living population of the planet. Until that time, no one has the right to another's wealth.

But the anticapitalist (anticap, for short) finds it curative to take money from those who earned it and give it to people who did not earn it. He seeks to reward the idle at the expense of the industrious, occasionally referring to those who oppose him as "fascists." He feels that money is just out there, ignoring that each dollar belongs to someone. He sees commandeering other people's earnings as "having a social conscience." As for the intended recipient of the earnings, paucity does not automatically entitle him to more. There can be no right to a certain income or position because it would require compelling someone to provide it, violating that person's right to liberty. In practice, a second problem arises: when government tries to take from the rich and give to the poor, it quickly becomes taking from most and giving to whoever is best at getting.

The anticap is less interested in permitting people to spend their money as they choose than in forcing them to contribute to his causes.

Say Ted wants a bicycle and Bob wants everyone in the United States to have one. Ted's wish is based on self-interest, so he can't expect others to volunteer their assistance, but because Bob's wish is unselfish, he may feel that all should contribute. His inner voice says, how can everyone not see that this is *right*? Sometimes people willing to sacrifice self are willing to sacrifice others.

Rather than acknowledge and harness self-interest, as the capitalist does, the anticap takes exception to it. From his perspective, the businessman exploits workers, cheats customers, bribes authorities, and harms the environment. The anticap equates prosperity with selling out. Having money, he reasons, is evidence of unscrupulousness. Some anticaps claim that taking from the rich is restorative, since the rich stole to get rich. The anticap may be a wound collector or have a thirst for class warfare. He may take pleasure in the humiliation or misfortune of the wealthy such that given the choice, he would favor substantially worsening his own lot if the rich would also be harmed. And yet, because he feels that the rich *ought* to be penalized, he sees himself as an agent of positive change.

Lenin was the ultimate hater of capitalism. He advised each town to "hang (hang without fail, so the people see) no fewer than one hundred known kulaks, rich men, bloodsuckers ... do it in such a way that for hundreds of [kilometers] around, the people will see, tremble, know, shout ... death to the bloodsucker kulaks." According to historian Richard Pipes, a kulak was someone ambitious, what an American might call a self-starter. Lenin also called them "spiders," "insects," "scoundrel fleas," "bedbugs," "leeches," and "vampires."[522] Lenin hated self-reliant people so much that he advocated their genocide. Though not going quite that far, some of today's American anticaps are as spiteful toward earning. Political activist Angela Davis, speaking at Dartmouth College, declared that the "socioeconomic system of capitalism has to be abolished if we are to be serious about eradicating the evils of racism."[523] One anticap author claimed that the United States was less well-represented by the colors red, white, and blue, than by "puke green."[524]

More commonly, the anticap is a self-dramatist who sees his inability to offer a wanted product or service as moral superiority. He rationalizes, *I'm a good person and I'm not rich. Good people*

213

have less. Christ was poor. Like him, I care about people more than money. To be rich, you have to be devious, and that's just not me. The anticap doesn't like the well-to-do and doesn't want to emulate them, but his aversion to wealth creates a syllogism: *I need money. I hate money. I need to hate.* Anticapitalism is less a political view than a misanthropic set of mind. "For the rain it raineth every day," wrote Shakespeare. The anticap doesn't discover an injustice and resent it; he resents first and searches for issues. Millions of savers and capitalists succeed, if not in their first endeavor than in another, but there are many nonstarters, and in a competition, there is no one easier to defeat than somebody who thinks that it's pointless or wrong to try. In the United States, economic caste constraints are self-imposed, effectively. Anticapitalism debilitates by removing the best means of accomplishing one's ends. The anticap never gains enough wealth to make compounding work for him, so he must keep working while the saver frees himself and leaves behind the whole of his estate accumulated over a lifetime.

It's easy to impugn capitalism, to cast it as a monster that has to be controlled, with the attendant litany: cutthroat competition, dog-eat-dog, the almighty buck, crony capitalism, corporate raiders, corporate welfare, corporate espionage, corporate bailouts. One hears often of "greedy corporations," rarely of prosperity-generating ones. Businesses practice "economic imperialism" and build "planned obsolescence" into their products. "Unbridled capitalism" "exploits" the "have-nots" as companies "devour" one another in "hostile takeovers." The portrayal has had an effect.[525] Make a remark that reveals that you are pro-business or against some new tax or proposed economic regulation and people gasp to find that you, a seemingly nice, bright guy, could side with *them*. Knowing he is on the good side of good and evil—the culture has told him so—the anticap is flabbergasted.

Ronald Reagan, who got elected by promising tax cuts, deregulation, and less government, seemed to embody capitalism both to supporters and opponents and consequently was loved and hated more than any president since FDR. To anticaps, Reagan was a malevolent president whose reductions in domestic spending *caused* poverty. They labeled the 1980s a decade of greed, in which the rich got richer and the poor poorer, but this was untrue, or only half true, because the poor did not get poorer. According to the US Census Bureau, the poverty rate stood at 13.7 percent in the middle of the 1980s, about the same as ten years earlier, or ten years later.[526] As a percentage of the population, the number of individuals below the poverty line was the same under Reagan as under Nixon, Ford, Carter, Bush, and Clinton: the three presidents that preceded Reagan and the two after him.[527] But homelessness was spotlighted during the 1980s. According to the average of three government estimates, there were about 300,000 homeless people in America at the time, but CNN and NBC claimed that there were more than ten times as many, putting the number at three million and five million, respectively.[528] CBS predicted that there would be nineteen million homeless by the turn of the century, an estimate that turned out to be off by a factor of about 60.[529] In one year during the Reagan administration, 1988, *The New York Times* ran fifty stories on the plight of the homeless, with five of them on page one. A decade later, during the Clinton administration, with the number of homeless virtually unchanged, the *Times* ran only ten such stories during the year, with none on page one.[530] Homelessness did not disappear; coverage of it did. But the unmistakable implication was that Reagan's capitalist policies caused homelessness.

Lowering the top tax rate did benefit the rich, as critics charged. The massive tax cuts left more money in private hands, promoting investment and reducing interest rates, which fell from 17 percent to 7 percent.[531] As inflation and interest rates fell, consumer confidence returned. New investment stimulated business growth and created jobs; unemployment fell from 10 percent to 5.5 percent.[532] As the economy advanced despite big budget deficits, Reagan observed, "The best proof that our economic plan is working is that they don't call it Reaganomics anymore."[533] The Dow Jones Industrial Average *tripled*. Reagan's tax cuts and deregulation stimulated economic growth to such an extent that although the top marginal tax rate was lowered from 70 percent to 28 percent, the rich became so much richer that they paid more of the total tax burden in the 1980s than ever before.[534] In 1981, the top 1 percent of income earners paid 18 percent of all taxes.[535] In 1988, they paid 28 percent.[536] In 1981, the top 5 percent of all wage earners paid 35 percent of all taxes; in 1988, 46 percent.[537]

Commentators couldn't understand Reagan's appeal because he was different from them. He saw capitalism as a marvelous engine and the State as too big, invasive, and expensive, a perspective that is anathema to pontificators aching to guide the American people. Reagan's popularity is indisputable: after he had been in office for four years, the people had a chance to reject or continue with his policies. In the 1984 presidential election, with the campaign slogan, "It's morning again in America," Reagan carried forty-nine of fifty states and won 525 electoral votes, the biggest landslide of the twentieth century. Four years later, in the months preceding the 1988 election, though Reagan was ineligible for another term and despite the misdeeds and mistakes of his second term, chants of "four more years" greeted him wherever he spoke; George Bush rode to easy victory on Reagan's coattails, demonstrating for a third time Reagan's popularity. The reason was simple: people liked lower taxes and less regulation.

It's unlikely you would graduate from high school today with that impression of Reagan and capitalism, however, because your views would be influenced by textbooks written by people who cringe at the idea of earning as a motivator. For example, in the textbook *The Americans*, the section about the 1980s features a maudlin story about a boy shocked by how many people are homeless and how awful their lives are; he brings them blankets. The authors of the book speak of the Moral Majority, religious fundamentalism, racism, AIDS, abortion, drug abuse, environmental rape, the Iran-Contra scandal, soaring deficits, and the savings and loan debacle. The words "Gorbachev" and "Soviet Union" do not appear at all in the section about Reagan. The economic turnaround and boom of the 1980s gets just two sentences, one of which implies that it was coincidental. Earlier in the same textbook, the sections about the New Deal, comprising thirty pages, are selectively edited to produce an equally severe positive slant. Learning history from *The Americans*, high school students could reach no other conclusion than that the New Deal saved America from the Great Depression, which had been caused by capitalism, and that the 1980s were a period of despair except for the wealthy few who grew fatter off of others' misery. Because academicians are given to rewrite history as they would have preferred it, a student's later success and his capacity for larger undertakings in life depend in part on his ability to unlearn.

Anticapitalism is common in reference books too. In one CD version of the *Encyclopedia Britannica*, under the listing "Ronald Reagan," every sentence about Reagan's economic policies is negative but one, which is an intentional understatement: "A recession in 1982 was followed by several years of growth."[538] (In fact, deregulation and lower taxes ignited the biggest, longest economic boom in US history.) One edition of *Bartlett's Quotations* has thirty-five entries from Franklin Roosevelt, twenty-eight from John Kennedy, and from Reagan, three, taken out of context to make Reagan look foolish. When asked about it, the editor of *Bartlett's* said, "I'm not going to disguise the fact that I despise Ronald Reagan."[539] On the evening news, Dan Rather once likened the Iran-Contra hearings to the Nuremburg trials, apparently confusing the Reagan administration's misappropriation of funds with the killing of fifty million people.[540] On television, contempt for Reagan and practitioners of capitalism was routine, fashionable, and to this day remains the not-so-secret handshake that helps aspiring writers and producers advance.

If anticapitalism was a religion, which it nearly is, then public schools would be its churches. State-employed educators do not create citizens who think the State should employ fewer people. Teachers tend to see government as a provider, money as temptation, and private wealth as potential for great evil. Industry and profit seeking are often treated not as progenitors of progress, but with suspicion. In the classroom, business competition's ability to breed efficiency and innovation is mentioned, but the emphasis is on nineteenth-century robber barons, child labor, and the ills of industrialization. In most public schools, US history is about self-serving individuals, those they harmed, and how government stepped in to fix things. Every kid learns that a lot of people were better off after the New Deal than before it. Few are told that the top tax rate before the New Deal was 25 percent, after it, 79 percent.[541] When the tale is told by State-employed teachers and State-approved textbooks, the hero is no surprise.

Due to this conflict of interests, a number of useful truths are unlikely to be heard in a public school classroom: that property rights and the right to liberty are inseparable; that democracy does not supersede the Five Rights; that self-sufficiency is more important than voting; that tax cuts help more people than they hurt; that what some call greed, others call ambition; that capitalism can benefit people other than the capitalists. Earning is underappreciated in education and, in some environments, despised. As reported by George Will in *One Man's America*, the Goddard School, a child-care center in Seattle, banned Legos because the fiendish children were building houses with them that the teachers felt conveyed "assumptions that mirrored those of a class-based, capitalist society—a society that we teachers believe to be unjust and oppressive." The vile plastic bricks were removed. Several months later they were returned, but the kids were only allowed to build "public structures" of "standard size" in a village that prized "collectivity and consensus."[542] At Antioch College in Ohio, a student was assaulted for wearing Nike shoes because they were "symbols of globalization."[543] In a CNBC interview, one graduating student remarked, "Fewer females are going into computer science because they'd rather do something important. They want to see the effect of their work—they don't just want to make money."[544] It didn't occur to this student that she could do more good with money than without it. Most students don't see earning as a means to achieve their larger goals, because their teachers do not.

Some teachers perform a separate disservice to their students. The anticap teacher, who has spent his life complaining about greed and unfairness and hating people who worked to make themselves successful, passes on to students his own aggravations. Though usually unintentional, his cynicism debilitates; his asides alone do more damage than he knows. He imparts not self-sufficiency (how to make rational decisions) but who to blame for lack of it (what to think). His students dutifully criticize the rich and their cupidity. Some of them will still be doing it fifty years later, but by then, they will have assumed the mantle of "less fortunate," the unfairness of "the system" explaining why they didn't accomplish more.

Since there are always more poor people than rich ones, populism contributes to wealth bashing. Individuals whose livings depend on wide acceptance—entertainers, politicians, journalists, advertisers, filmmakers—pick their politics as one would a baseball cap. They craft content and language to appeal to the greatest number while turning away the least. Since the rich are always an unpopular minority and a politically acceptable target, on television, even guys who wear suits don't like "suits." On TV, wealth comes from cheating or unfair advantage. The bad guy is the one who says, "This hospital has to be run like a *business*." In a tall building, a corporate bigwig gazes out his gargantuan office window at the skyscrapers, strokes the inside of his suspenders with his beefy thumbs, and says expansive, inane things about the greatness of free enterprise. People with money perpetrate most evils, including the odd murder and cover-up. Small businessmen do the killing themselves; executives have it done for them while at the theater.

If you lived in the world of TV, you'd choose your physician by his income—the lower, the better. Caring doctors live in hovels. Rich ones are philanderers involved in something sinister—an insurance scam or stealing the real drugs to support their habit. Rich people are haughty and act like they're above the law. ("I warn you, the McNulty name carries a lot of weight in this town …") Some even *hunt*. They abuse their assistants and then attend stuffy benefits while continuing the abuse on a cell phone. When a rich person is occasionally portrayed as decent, it's for philanthropy. Earning and having are bad; giving and sacrifice are good. The needy are humble and wise. A street person is often a poet who got screwed by a guy who got rich off of his genius, leaving him with just his scruples and esteem from those who really know him.

One-hour television dramas are loaded with anticap stereotypes: the contaminating manufacturer, its indifferent parent company, the money-laundering banker, the insolent high tech mogul, the scheming grand-dame, the mendacious car salesman, the messianic surgeon, the ruthless tycoon, his shifty operatives and lackies, the harried restaurateur, his hair-trigger chef, the pathologically lying ad man, the cheating stockbroker—all of them willing to harm people for money. Television's landlords, developers, and executives are autocrats. A character complaining about high taxes or big government is usually an overwritten rube. On TV, principled politicians are the ones who fight for budget increases (never called "tax increases"). Then there are the shows' smart, honorable main characters—cosmopolitan lawyers, doctors, or public servants who deal with the lurid every day, laden with concern about doing the right thing, trying to bear the weight of all the selfishness with dignity, more world-weary with each episode. They dislike the rich; their friends are workaday, witty, and likable, and they don't care for the rich either.

Science fiction writers tend to depict the future as bleak (e.g., machines rule and it's always dark), or, if the future is benevolent, money has become obsolete. But the writers never answer the question, without money, how do you get things done? If you need help to accomplish a task, how do you enlist it without paying people? The helpers can volunteer, which is possible if they so strongly support your goals that they are willing to sacrifice theirs to yours. Or tasks can be accomplished through a command structure, which is how writers usually depict successful future societies: people are no longer self-interested individuals; they are components, but ones that love being part of the structure, following orders, getting promoted. They share healthy priorities and a philosophy of service. Conscientious outsiders long to be part of the organization. Seedier outsiders are still selfishly incentivized by money, still traders and cheats.

Science fiction writers can handle the challenges of interstellar distances and time travel, and yet, while pooh-poohing a monetary system as primitive, they can come up with nothing to replace it other than commands. To incentivize any agent outside the command structure, the writers usually resort to barter, an exchange of favors or spare parts. Buying and selling is an ancient vulgarity, but it's acceptable to trade a kekaton cell for a half znert of antimatter. The writers hope the audience won't notice that a barter system is a big step *backward*, since it preceded money, but they prefer this subterfuge to depicting a future in which good people still use money. Blithely dismissive of the link between money and liberty, their premise is that bad old capitalism, which permits individuals to act independently, will blossom into a hierarchy in which each person has many superiors and constraints, as if that's progress, but to anticaps, whatever gets rid of money constitutes advancement.

Influenced by television and movies, young people equate big money with corruption, which deserves its comeuppance. (Note how the viewer is invited to share in vicarious delight when the hero successfully steals from a casino, insurance company, or bank.) Given the prevalence of anticapitalist culture, the Occupy Wall Street movement was perhaps inevitable. It started with a handful of activists inspired by a Canadian anticonsumer magazine, *Adbusters*, which called for a protest in lower Manhattan on September 17, 2011.[545] People responded, pitching tents in New York's Zuccotti Park. More joined them. Similar actions followed in other US cities and then in cities all over the world. Reporters and producers, as is their wont, trumpeted the occupy movements as the first stirrings of an overdue revolution.

Members of the occupy movements were upset about an olio of things; they just couldn't say specifically what. They wanted their voices heard; they demanded a paradigm shift; they wanted to rein in world trade; they opposed greed and corruption; they hated the political power of corporations. Said one protester in a comment typical of many, "They're using the money we gave them for bailouts to steal our democracy." Said another, "It's time to change the corporate culture of predatory capitalism." Another added, "It's all corporate greed," as he waved an American flag.[546] According to *Bloomberg Businessweek*, they wanted "more and better jobs, more equal distribution of income, less profit (or no profit) for bankers," "a more populist set of government priorities," and "bailouts for student debtors and mortgage holders, not just for banks."[547] Other than the first of these goals—more and better jobs—none can be achieved without violating the Five Rights.

There have been at least seven severe recessions or depressions in US history, and during each, people protested. The most recent movement revealed not just a lack of focus but of understanding (e.g., they wanted to create jobs by raising taxes) and their mantra, "We are the 99 percent," was simply untrue. All of them were angry, though. According to *Time*, in an informal poll a representative of *New York* magazine found that 34 percent of the protesters believed that the US government was no better than al Qaeda.[548] Based on their mutual vexation, the protesters, many of whom never bothered to acquire any marketable skills, felt that they were *owed* "more and better jobs."[549]

Anticap sentiment has created over a trillion dollars in entitlement programs. Who is not subsidized wants to be. Who is subsidized wants more, and you can't blame them for trying when politicians respond. Walter Mondale, after losing the 1984 presidential election, in his concession speech bemoaned the plight of all those in need of caring government including, "the poor, the elderly, the handicapped, the helpless, and the sad." Yes, "the sad" deserved to receive the earnings of others.[550]

The Dominator

Tolerance is gracious because it implies humility. It acknowledges differing views and fallibility. Tolerance says, I think you're wrong, but go ahead. Intolerance says, I think you're wrong, so you should change, or you *must* change. When enough people are driven to dominate others, intolerance creates directives of policy.

The dominator honors liberties according to his assessment of their propriety. He sees productive or benevolent actions as valid exercises of liberty, others as license, detrimental to the actor and the order, and prefers them prohibited. He may be willing to subjugate individuals' liberties to the will of God, morality, the environment, family values, politeness, or national security. He may want to make people healthier in mind or body, to make children safer, or to achieve efficiency. He may seek to ban abortion, or to deny the option of assisted suicide, or to ban gay marriage. He may favor prohibitions on stem cell research. He may favor laws that increase surveillance, or expand drug testing, or permit warrantless searches. Guns, alcohol, cigarettes, marijuana, cheeseburgers, sugary treats, sexual proclivities, dangerous hobbies, big cars, offensive speech—whatever the choice, the dominator's position is, I don't like it so you can't do it.

The dominator is sure of himself. Seeing passivity as weakness, he shuts out any second-order misgivings, and what might have been an inner struggle before all doubt was erased becomes an external one against other people. Rather than live and let live, his motto is, bother and be bothered. He rolls his eyes at the word "rights." (In some circles, when you suggest that you are concerned with the protection of individuals' rights, people look at the floor, embarrassed for you, and presume that you're an arms-hoarding xenophobe in need of education and more rules. One of the most consistently negative stereotypes in American culture is that of rights advocates as dangerous extremists.)

The dominator's mind-set is, if I'm right, and I obviously am, why *shouldn't* others be forced to act as I recommend? He is given to manage adult strangers as if they were his children. He believes in "correct" behavior such that imposing it comes naturally; he doesn't bother to justify the use of coercion because he doesn't see anything wrong with it. He sees it as a tool to improve people. One particularly obdurate kind of dominator goes though life so incensed by the transgressions of others that he likes rules and their enforcement because he likes seeing people get *caught*.

Recognizing no values unlike his, the dominator can't relate and doesn't pity. He can't identify with the innocent man wrongly imprisoned, the wretched drug addict, or the hopeless depressive. He can't identify with alienation or crippling reticence, with someone who will sit in a car in the freezing cold for an hour waiting for a friend to exit a restaurant rather than go in because he doesn't want to be seen. He can't conceive of someone who fears government though they have never significantly broken the law, or of people for whom alcohol or drugs constitute a lesser of evils. Whatever activity comes under the dominator's purveyance, including inaction, receives judgment. To him, a person who wants to be left alone is not to be trusted. *Why* does he want to be left alone?

The dominator mentality underlies the Patriot Act, which permits government to label someone an "enemy combatant" and his right to habeas corpus disappears; he can be imprisoned indefinitely without being found guilty of any crime. Dominators use the war on terrorism to justify secret arrests and detentions. Fear of terrorism has also produced "partnerships" between law enforcement and private citizen groups, like Infragard, which has 34,000 civilian members who watch employees, customers, coworkers, and neighbors, snooping, assessing, and reporting suspicious activity. Every FBI field office has an Infragard coordinator.[551]

A more benevolent kind of dominator seeks to create one big happy family by taking no notice of the rights of individuals with untraditional priorities. In support of a government expenditure to be financed by general taxation, Hillary Clinton once told *Newsweek,* "There is no such thing as other people's children." But DNA says otherwise. Because an individual shares more alleles with family members than with others, he or she is programmed to favor immediate family, especially offspring. That passion, though, does not permit parents to ignore the wishes of childless adults. Not procreating does nothing to diminish one's rights.

The ascetic-minded dominator hates seeing people have too good a time. From him come smoking bans, restrictions on drinking, blue laws, trivial sexual harassment laws, harsh penalties for drug users, and bans on gambling, nude dancing, and prostitution. The ascetic feels that such laws are required to stave off dystopia.

Dominators tell us what foods we must avoid and what oils can't be used for frying. We are told that red meat and smoking are tantamount to murder, that secondhand smoke has killed millions, that marijuana leads to heroin, and that drug use always ruins lives. We are told what safety devices we must wear; what kind of toilets, furnaces, and air conditioners we must install, and which objects on our property must be fenced and which others we cannot alter. The disposal of cat litter has been regulated. A San Francisco ordinance stipulates that a dog's water must be changed once a day and that it must always be served in a non-tipping bowl.[552] Government supervises people not just in their dealings with one another, but with their pets too. In New York State, bureaucrats have sought to regulate or ban kids' games at summer camps including Red Rover, kick ball, wiffle ball, and dodge ball because they posed "significant risk of injury."[553] In Central Park, a man's two daughters, nine and eleven, climbed a tree. An officer of New York City's Parks Department issued the father a ticket for $1,000. When the dad responded that there was no sign prohibiting it, he was told, "If we listed every rule, we'd have more signs than trees."[554] A friend just back from his camp where he celebrated Independence Day with his family confided glumly, "No drinking, no campfire or firecrackers, no toys in the water, and

I got stopped and questioned by police on a fifty-mile trip. Some independence."[555]

Smoking is unhealthy. Some people do it anyway. For a time, bars and restaurants responded to this reality by offering smoking and nonsmoking areas. The compromise was fine with smokers and with people who didn't care one way or the other, but dominators petitioned government to ban smoking in public places altogether, successfully, since coercion is easy to employ under the banner of health. There are no restrictions on high-calorie meals—yet—but you can see the warnings, limits, surcharges, and prohibitions coming. Obese people have a higher incidence of heart disease, diabetes, joint problems, and cancer, not to mention that they hate being overweight, because in addition to feeling lousy, they know it makes them less attractive. Dominators want to help them by taking more of their money. (And from the anticap perspective, taxing an extra quarter on a bottle of all sugared soft drinks might help rein in the morbid excesses of Big Soda.) Such a tax has been proposed under the slogan, "Help make New York healthier." Citing public health, New York state legislators also proposed a bill limiting how much salt chefs can use.

Small liberties can be quietly lost to the machinations of a well-placed dominator in city or state government eager to impose tighter rules to build a record on safety or cost cutting. Say the bars in a small coastal city with a better-than-average nightlife close at two o'clock. A public official proposes that they be closed at midnight. He argues that if the bars are forced to close earlier, people will have less time to drink and be less intoxicated. Forcing them to go home earlier might cut down on drunk driving and possibly reduce after-hours vandalism and violence, which would save police man-hours and tax dollars. And all of this may be plausible. But the same reasoning could be used to advocate closing the bars at ten o'clock, or eight o'clock, or shutting them down altogether. It's entirely arbitrary. And though the proposal is rational, it's not what the people involved want. The bar owners don't want earlier closing times, nor do their patrons; it impedes their fun—their pursuit of happiness. City officials are the only direct beneficiaries, but wrapped in the garb of the public good, authority often gets its way.

Stereotypically, the dominator and the anticap differ. The

dominator is self-confident. Assertive, intractable, sometimes puritanical, he feels his judgment is for the good of all. The anticap is recalcitrant and pervaded by an anxiety he calls conscience. Dominators doubt nothing; anticaps, everything. The dominator argues from sanctity, the anticap from contempt. The dominator sees people in terms of the responsible and irresponsible, the anticap in terms of haves and have-nots. A person may live as he pleases; the dominator ignores this right. A person can spend his money as he chooses; the anticap ignores this right. Though our nation makes over 350 pages of new laws and regulations each day, dominators want more. Though we send $2 trillion a year to Washington—$8 billion each business *day*—anticaps want to increase it. Each feels that he is acting in the name of something larger than himself, which justifies coercing others. Each wants to make a better world and each is willing to tax, command, fine, and imprison people to do it.

CHAPTER 12
Bogus Rights

The protection of the Five Rights was the aim of classical liberalism as advanced by Montesquieu, John Locke, David Hume, William Blackstone, Adam Smith, and Bernard Mandeville, the seventeenth- and eighteenth-century philosophers who most influenced the American authors of the US Constitution: John Dickinson, Oliver Ellsworth, Elbridge Gerry, Alexander Hamilton, William Johnson, Rufus King, James Madison, George Mason, Gouverneur Morris, Charles Pinckney, Edmund Randolph, Roger Sherman, and James Wilson. Fearing that a future government would find ways to overstep its lawmaking authority, the founders used every tool they could think of, including federalism, multiple separations of power, and a bill of rights, to prevent it.

Despite their efforts, the growth of the State during the twentieth century created two conditions now so familiar they seem to have been with us forever. First, of each dollar earned, about forty cents is allocated by government rather than the person who earned it. (The median income tax is 31.7 percent, and taxation by all other means—there are twenty-seven other taxes—comes to about 8 percent of income, according to the Congressional Budget Office, for a total of 39.7 percent.)[556] And second, government's assumption of a multitude of responsibilities forces it to pass laws that violate the Five Rights. To maintain their jobs, representatives must sacrifice constitutional covenants to expediency and quiet reason to strong sentiments, producing a discrepancy in the American system of government in which rights are based on principles and legislation on passion, a contest in which principles are in the position of a wise but soft-spoken man on an anything-goes television talk show.

One consequence of despotic democracy is that government can't avoid making laws that breach the rights of hated people—pedophiles and terrorists, for example—though doing so invariably leads to the same violations perpetrated against others. Nor can it avoid passing legislation favorable to a wronged group, though each concession broadens into a bogus right because whenever one group gets a favorable law passed, every group demands matching treatment—to which equality entitles them—and in time gets it, so that what was intended as an exception becomes a general rule.

The rights expressed in the Constitution and amendments are specific provisions of the Five Rights or procedural rules regarding their implementation. Other so-called rights are not rights at all. For example, Congress occasionally passes something like a Patient's Bill of Rights or an Airline Passenger's Bill of Rights. There have been bills of rights passed or proposed for consumers, applicants, clients, homebuyers, caregivers, grandparents, and graduate students. They aren't really rights but triumphant declarations of how things ought to be. Some bills of rights guarantee things like prompt attention and full consideration, which is like granting people the right to receive clear directions when they ask. Outlawing rudeness and ineptness cannot guarantee courtesy or skillful assistance. There can be no such thing as a customer's *right* to geniality. There is only the free market, which over time closes mismanaged businesses. Congress has good reason to pass spurious bills of rights, though, because in proclaiming how things *should* be and labeling it a right, it seems to be accomplishing something. Since the rights granted are vague, the courts must interpret them. Litigation establishes new law, as Congress intended, giving substance to the right, often in contradiction to an existing right of another party. Congress takes credit for acting while avoiding responsibility for the resulting civil disputes and conflicting case law.

Some examples of false rights:

1. The right to a job. No right can exist that violates the rights of another. As a job applicant can decline any job offered, an employer can decline to hire any applicant.

The right to a job would require forcing an employer to provide one.

2. The right to happiness. Individuals have the right to *pursue* happiness but not to secure it. There can be no right to any degree of psychological well-being.

3. The right to an education. Education is a product of human effort, which must be remunerated. If it has the means, a nation may choose to provide public education and most wisely do, but it's not a birthright of the individual. A person has the right to learn (rights to liberty and to pursue happiness) but no right to make others teach him.

4. The right to housing, food, clothing, shoes, medical care, power steering, or any other product or service that requires man-hours to produce. These things are not found in nature. Like education, they must be paid for, and beyond security, nothing that must be paid for can be a right. Who is to pay? If not the people receiving the goods and services, then the money must be taken from others against their property rights.

5. There is no right to any particular or "reasonable" price for any product—not for sellers who want to receive more or buyers who want to pay less.

6. The right to a secure retirement. As with education, government may try to provide for it, but it cannot be a right because it has a cost. If your efforts don't pay for it, someone else's must.

7. The right to freedom *from* undesirable events. The right to life protects against the coercion of others, and government, but that's all. No one can have the right to freedom *from* insults, infidelity, or poverty, or freedom *from* fear or want, as FDR sought, any more than he can have the right to freedom from illness, hurricanes, or car accidents. What happens happens.

8. The right to fairness. When an individual's rights are violated, the legal system exists to redress the injustice, but only if it was human-caused. Other kinds of injustice are not that, but the results of poor decisions or misfortune.

9. The "people's right to know" news about other people is not a right. It is the right to freedom of the press presented from the publisher's side, a phrase invented to help justify the betraying of a subject to the audience in order to deliver what sells: titillating stories.

10. Rights associated with race, religion, nationality, gender, sexual preference, intelligence, or income. If government favors individuals due to one of these group affiliations, it violates the right of the rest to equality before the law.

There are only Five Rights:

1. The Right to Life
   The free interaction of individuals yields spontaneous order, which gives rise to common law. In banning aggression or violence among individuals, common law establishes the right to life, which is the source of the other four rights. The right to life also protects against encroachment by government. It precludes a military draft or any abuse of coercive power by prosecutors or police.

2. The Right to Liberty
   Individuals have the right to think, say, or do as they choose. Liberty includes the right to freedom of philosophy and religion. It includes the right to run one's affairs, to travel, to seek a mate or an occupation, and to bear arms. Free speech includes the right to use unfashionable or provocative language and to criticize government. Freedom of assembly permits individuals to gather, picket, or protest. Freedom of association allows them to befriend or reject one another as they choose, to join clubs, or to start organizations. Liberty includes the right to privacy, which allows people to keep secrets or to make personal choices regarding their bodies, time, and family, including those involving contraceptives, abortion, and physician-assisted suicide. Privacy protects against unreasonable searches or suspicionless drug testing.

   As with all of the Five Rights, the right to liberty is not subject to majority rule. The freedom to do something has nothing to do with how many people favor or oppose it. It is government's job to protect unpopular exercises of liberty.

3.   The Right to Property
Private property gives each person his due by letting him keep the fruits of his labor. The property line sets the outer boundary of the protected sphere, separates public from private, and gives liberty a place to exist. On his property, an owner may shape his surroundings according to his tastes without having to ask permission or answer to others. Ownership includes the right to use, alter, or sell something. It includes the right to exchange money for goods by mutual consent. The desire to live better begets trade, which generates contracts, which promote people to follow through on their obligations.

   Government violations of property rights include rent control, partial takings, abuse of forfeiture, historic preservation, and environmental laws, and bans on ownership and trade in human organs.

4.   The Right to Pursue Happiness
Liberty's upside is the right to pursue happiness, which permits fun and foolishness. It allows people to eat the wrong foods, drink, smoke, or use recreational drugs. The individual may define happiness for himself even if it means risking his health or safety. When government breaches this right, it usually does so through a directive of policy, which is a law that bans a personal choice in an attempt to achieve a presumed greater good. Drug prohibition laws constitute the greatest violation of the right to pursue happiness, causing the imprisonment of millions of Americans.

5.   The Right to Equality before the Law
All individuals have the same rights, are subject to the same laws, have the same guarantee of due process, and if convicted of a crime, are subject to the same punishment. Disputes must be decided impartially. Laws cannot favor or penalize any group. Equality preserves freedom by engaging

self-interest: the laws we wish to live by limit how much we can restrain or tax others.

Equality also refers to the equal partnership between the people and the State. The people are to abide by the laws, provided government abides by the Constitution, an arrangement known as "government by consent of the governed."

According to Adam Smith, in a free order, government has three duties: to protect the people and their property from invaders, to protect them from each other, and to establish required public works and rules of organization that market forces cannot supply.[557] The State has been ceded a fourth role since Smith's time, that of humanitarian, providing aid in emergencies and for people who lack basic necessities. It has never been the State's responsibility to mold individuals into model human beings, nor can it be, because seeking positive ends for a society does not justify coercing individuals. Law cannot be used to align individuals' behavior with planners' aspirations or to make individuals serve any particular purposes since, as Walter Lippman observed, "In a free society the state does not administer the affairs of men. It administers justice among men who conduct their own affairs."[558] But as government is asked to cure every ill and seeks to oblige, it overlays general, objective rules with directives of policy, morphing a spontaneous order of individuals acting as they choose into a managed order of individuals serving aims other than their own.

The founders sought to limit the impact of government regulation, leaving individuals to their own devices as much as possible, but with constitutionality a virtual non-issue, no legislation is off limits. Government can make any law for which a momentary majority can be cobbled together, and it has been doing so for eighty years. Because we are a nation of faultfinders, alarmists, and controllers, and our government represents us, it has passed countless laws against actions that directly harm no other person, the result being that almost anyone can wind up in jail.

Say you're a resident of Florida, retired and living alone. You've had serious back pain on and off for decades. Physical therapy helps, but the pain comes back a few hours later. A doctor prescribes oxycontin, which doesn't eliminate the pain, but it works better than anything else you've tried, and you notice that it also makes you feel psychologically better. Being alone is easier to bear, especially the long, empty afternoons. The doctor gives you a second prescription but warns you that the drug is strictly regulated and that he can give you no more. After it runs out, you miss it. Your life seemed better with it than without, so you go to different doctors for new prescriptions, saying nothing about any previous doctor. You're committing a crime known as "doctor shopping," for which you can be sent to prison for five years. If you are successful in getting and filling the new prescriptions and the police discover it and come to your home with a search warrant, you can be arrested and charged with possession of narcotics. Your life as you know it just ended because you wanted to feel better.

To the police, you're just another junkie handcuffed in the back of the squad car, one bust among hundreds. To prosecutors, you broke the law and must be punished. Though you hurt no one, you may go to prison. The State sacrifices hundreds of thousands of individuals to "the public interest" this way each year. The true public good is best served by protecting individuals' rights and otherwise letting them be. People respect a government that does not burden them with excessive rules because it gives them what they want: security with minimal loss of liberty. But as religions preach brotherhood and practice segregation, governments preach freedom and pass laws that violate the Five Rights. If lawmakers were bound by "First do no harm," there would not be almost a million individuals living in cages that did not injure, coerce, or defraud anyone. To try but fail at self-mastery is to live a life. To be punished for it is persecution, which is never justified.

ENDNOTES

1. David Hume, *A Treatise of Human Nature* (Penguin Books, Middlesex, England, 1969), 629–632.
2. Immanuel Kant, "Fundamental Principles of the Metaphysics of Morals," in Isaac Kramnick (ed.), *The Portable Enlightenment Reader* (Penguin Books, New York, 1995), 16, 299. See also Immanuel Kant, *Groundwork of the Metaphysics of Morals* (Cambridge University Press, 1996), viii, xv, xviii, 33.
3. http://quotationsbook.com/quote/23653
4. Kant, *Groundwork*, xxii.
5. Friedrich A. Hayek, *The Constitution of Liberty* (University of Chicago Press, 1960), 143–144.
6. Ken Burns, *Thomas Jefferson.* Videocassette. Florentine Films and WETA (Washington, 1996).
7. Plato quotations (http://thinkexist.com/quotes/plato/).
8. Matt Ridley, *The Origins of Virtue* (Penguin Books, New York, 1996), 65–66, 106, 124, 130.
9. Adam Smith, *The Theory of Moral Sentiments* (Regnery Publishing, Washington DC, 1996), 32.
10. John Wooden quotations (http://en.thinkexist.com/johnwooden).
11. Winston Churchill quotations (http://en.thinkexist.com/winstonchurchill).
12. Friedrich A. Hayek, *Law, Legislation, and Liberty, Volume 1* (University of Chicago Press, 1973), 51.
13. Forrest McDonald, *Novus Ordo Seclorum* (University Press of Kansas, Lawrence, 1985), 170–171.
14. Ibid., 2.
15. Christopher Collier and James Collier, *Decision in Philadelphia* (Ballentine Books, New York, 1986), 64–65.
16. Thomas Jefferson quotations (http://thinkexist.com/quotes/ThomasJefferson).
17. Hayek, *Constitution*, 179, 205.

18. Richard Brookhiser, *Alexander Hamilton, American* (Touchstone, New York, 1999), 142.
19. http://www.neuwww.google.com=n&source=hp&q
20. Lenora M. Lapidus, Emily J. Martin, and Namita Luthra, *The Rights of Women* (New York University Press, 2009), 69.
21. *Wickard v. Filburn* 317 U.S. 111 (1942).
22. *Gonzales v. Raich* 545 U.S. 1 (2005)
23. Collier, *Decision*, 339.
24. Alexander Hamilton, *Federalist*, No. LXXXIV, ed. Beloff, 439.
25. David J. Bodenhamer and James W. Ely, *The Bill of Rights in Modern America* (Indiana University Press, Bloomington, 1991), 26–27, 186.
26. David G. Savage, *The Supreme Court and Individual Rights* (CQ Press, Washington DC, 2004), 40.
27. Jay M. Feinman, *Law 101* (Oxford University Press, New York, 2000), 62, 63.
28. Ibid., 61, 66.
29. Ibid.
30. *Slaughterhouse Cases* 83 U.S. 36 (1873).
31. *Brown v. Board of Education* 163 U.S. 537 (1954). See also David L. Hudson, Jr., *The Fourteenth Amendment* (Enslow Publishers, Berkeley Heights, NJ, 2002), 42, 43, and Saul K. Padover, *The Living U.S. Constitution* (Penguin Books, London, 1983), 213, 214.
32. Ayn Rand, *Capitalism: The Ultimate Ideal* (Penguin Group, New York, 1966), 80.
33. Milton Friedman, *Free to Choose* (Harcourt Brace, Orlando, FL, 1980), 82–86.
34. Ibid.
35. Jim Powell, *FDR's Folly* (Crown Forum, New York, 2003), 43–45.
36. Ibid.
37. Ibid.
38. Ibid. See also David T. Beito, *Taxpayers in Revolt: Tax Resistance During the Great Depression* (Chapel Hill: University of North Carolina Press, 1989), 6.
39. William F. Leuchtenburg, *The FDR Years* (Columbia University Press, New York, 1995), 6, 283.
40. Ibid.
41. Hayek, *Constitution*, 191, 192, 246.
42. Thomas Jefferson, Draft of Kentucky Resolution of 1789, in E. D. Warfield, *The Kentucky Resolutions of 1799* (2nd ed., New York, 1894), 157–158.
43. Powell, *Folly*, 162.
44. Kathryn A. Flynn, *The New Deal: A Seventy-Fifth Anniversary Celebration* (Gibbs Smith, Layton, Utah 2008), cover flap, 8, 109, 119.
45. Research note #3: Details of Ida May Fuller's Payroll Tax Contribution, Social Security Administration.
46. Leuchtenburg, *FDR Years*, 245, 252, 253, 255, 259.

47. William E. Leuchtenburg, *The Supreme Court Reborn* (Oxford University Press, New York, 1995), 82, 89. See also Edward Keynes, *Liberty, Property, and Privacy* (Penn State University Press, 1996), 132, 140.
48. *Schechter Poultry Corporation v. United States* 295 U.S. 495 (1935). See also Powell, *Folly*, 163–167.
49. Lee J. Alston, "Farm Foreclosures in the United States During the Interwar Period," *Journal of Economic History*, December 1983, 889.
50. Powell, *Folly*, 169.
51. Franklin D. Roosevelt, "Speech before the 1936 Democratic National Convention," June 27, 1936," http://www.austincc.edu/lpatrick/his2341/fdr36acceptancespeech.html
52. Leuchtenburg, *Reborn*, 133-134.
53. Ibid., 124, 134, 136.
54. Hayek, *Constitution*, 190.
55. Reorganization of the Federal Judiciary: Adverse Report from the Senate Committee on the Judiciary Submitted to Accompany S. 1392 (75th Congress, 1st session, Senate Report no. 711, June 7, 1937).
56. Ibid.
57. Ibid.
58. Leuchtenburg, *Reborn*, 155, 227, 235.
59. Ibid.
60. Hayek, *Constitution*, 205.
61. *U.S. v. Carolene Products Company* 304 U.S. 144 (1938).
62. "The Economic Bill of Rights," Franklin D. Roosevelt, State of the Union Address, delivered January 11, 1944. American Heritage Center. http://www.fdrheritage.org/bill-of-rights.html
63. Ibid.
64. J. S. Mill, *On Liberty* (Cambridge University Press, Cambridge, England, 1997), 15–17.
65. U.S. Federal Individual Income Tax Rates History, 1913–2011, The Tax Foundation. http://www.taxfoundation.org/taxdata/show/151.html
66. http://www.taxfoundation.org/publications/show/151.html
67. Powell, *Folly*, 245–246.
68. William Simon, "A Time for Truth," as quoted by Rod L. Evans and Irwin M. Berent in *The Quotable Conservative* (Adams Media, Holbrook, MA, 1995), 209.
69. Richard Epstein, *Principles for a Free Society* (Perseus Books, Reading, Mass., 1998), 182, 183.
70. Powell, *Folly*, vii, xiii.
71. Friedrich A. Hayek, *Law, Legislation, and Liberty*, vol. 3 (Uni-versity of Chicago Press, 1979), 15–16, 129, 138–139.
72. Hayek, *Constitution*, 13–14.
73. Thomas Jefferson, "Notes on Virginia," as quoted by McDonald in *Novus Ordo Seclorum*, 160.

74. http://thinkexist.com/search/searchquotation.asp?search=cicero See also Cicero, *The Republic* (Oxford University Books, 1998), 73.
75. Cicero, *Republic*, 23.
76. Abraham Lincoln, Fragment of a speech reprinted in *Collected Works of Abraham Lincoln*, vol. 2 (Rutgers University Press, 1953), 252.
77. http://archives.gov/federal-register/
78. Ibid.
79. Milton Friedman, *Free to Choose* (Harcourt Brace and Co., Orlando, Florida, 1990), 190–191.
80. Bureau of Economic Analysis, Index. http://www.bea.gov/national/index.html
81. Public Law 97-280 (Senate Joint Resolution 165, 96 Stat. 1211) passed by Congress and approved October 4, 1982.
82. Hayek, *Law*, vol. 1, 139.
83. Dinesh D'Souza, "How Reagan Reelected Clinton," *Forbes*, November 3, 1997, 126.
84. Ken Burns, *Thomas Jefferson*. Second inaugural address. Videocassette. Florentine Films and WETA (Washington, 1996).
85. http://archives.gov/federal-register/
86. http://rules.house.gov/archives/jcoc2s.html
87. "Correctional Population in the United States, 2010," Bureau of Justice Statistics, http://bjs.ojp.usdoj.gov/
88. Ibid.
89. Ibid.
90. United States Department of Justice, Bureau of Justice Statistics. Summary findings, December 31, 1998. August 16, 1999, http://www.opj.usdoj.gov/bjs/prisons.htm. (The statistic of 1.9 million total prisoners includes 1,302,019 individuals under federal or state jurisdiction and 592,462 individuals in the nation's local jails.) See also "Behind Bars: Substance Abuse and America's Prison Population," *Spectrum: The Journal of State Government*, Winter 1999, 72, 8, and Timothy Egan, "Less Crime, More Criminals," *New York Times*, March 7, 1999, sec. 4, 1.
91. Ibid.
92. *The Progressive Review*, "American Indicators," last modified July 15, 1999, http://prorev.com/stats.htm. See also Eric Schlosser, "The Prison Industrial Complex," *Atlantic Monthly*, December, 1998, 52.
93. Hayek, *Law,* vol. 1, 10, 39, 51.
94. M. Mitchell Waldrop, *Complexity* (Touchstone, New York, 1992), 145. "But regardless of how you define them, each agent finds itself in an environment produced by its interactions with the other agents in the system. It is constantly acting and reacting to what other agents are doing. And because of that, essentially nothing in its environment is fixed."
95. Hayek, *Law,* vol. 1, 40, 51.
96. http://www.thinkexist.com/jo-ju/jonathan-swift/
97. Hayek, *Law,* vol. 1, 10. See also Hayek, *Law,* vol. 3, 163.

98. Hayek, *Law*, vol. 1, 37. "Although there was a time when men believed that even language and morals had been 'invented' by some genius of the past, everybody recognizes now that they are the outcome of a process of evolution whose results nobody foresaw or designed."

99. Adam Ferguson, *An Essay on the History of Civil Society* (London, 1767), 187.

100. Michael Polyani, *The Logic of Liberty* (University of Chicago Press, Chicago, 1951), 202–204.

101. Ibid., 42–44, 53.

102. Ibid.

103. Hayek, *Law*, vol. 1, 98, 101–102.

104. Ibid, 85–87. "The chief concern of a common law judge must be the expectations which the parties in a transaction would have reasonably formed on the basis of the general practices that the ongoing order of action rests on." (See also 75, 100, 115–116, 122–123.)

105. Ibid. "The law will consist of purpose-independent rules which govern the conduct of individuals toward each other, are intended to apply to an unknown number of future instances, and by defining a protected domain of each, enable an order of actions to form itself wherein the individuals can make feasible plans."

106. George Q. Flynn, *The Draft 1940–1973* (University Press of Kansas, Lawrence, 1993), 2, 166.

107. Philip Gold, *The Coming Draft,* (Random House, New York, 2006), 91

108. James Tracy (ed.), *The Military Draft Handbook* (Manic D Press, San Francisco, 2006), 31, 65–77.

109. Paula McMahon, "DNA-Cleared Broward Man Might Seek Money for Years He Spent in Prison," *Sun Sentinel*, March 27, 2010.

110. Susan Greene, "District Attorney Turns Blind Eye to DNA Evidence," *Denver Post*, February 21, 2010.

111. http://www.nytimes.com/2009/12/02/nyregion/02about.html

112. Mandy Locke and Anne Blythe, "SBI Told to Re-Examine Old Cases," *News Observer*, February 28, 2010.

113. http://truthinjustice.org/immunity-case.html

114. Jennifer Emily and Steve McGonigle, "Dallas County District Attorney Wants Unethical Prosecutors Punished," *Dallas Morning News*, May 4, 2008.

115. Ibid.

116. "Last Child-Sex Ring Defendant Released from Prison after Court Action," *Seattle Post-Intelligencer*, December 7, 2000. http://seattlepi.nwsource.com/local/wena27ww.html.

117. Garance Burke, "Crusading California D.A. Retires, Leaves Painful Wake," Associated Press, November 15, 2009.

118. Ibid.

119. Ibid.

120. Ibid.

121. Ibid.

122. Ibid.
123. http://www.nytimes.com/2010/01/17/us/17cncpulse.html
124. Ellen Alderman and Caroline Kennedy, *The Right to Privacy* (Vintage Books, New York, 1997), 3–6, 9–10.
125. Ibid.
126. http://bloombergwatch.com/index,php/09/the-overpolicing-of-new-york-schools.html
127. http://www.nytimes.com/2009/03/27/nyregion/conn-ecticut/27priest.html
128. http://www.nytimes.com/2009/07/05/us/05texas.html
129. http://michaelbluejay.com/police/
130. http://www.aclu.org/nationalsecurity/aclu-sues-department-homeland-security-end-repeat.html
131. "Tasers," *Sixty Minutes,* segment 2, November 13, 2011.
132. "Police Chief Shot with Taser," BBC News Player, May 18, 2007.
133. Steven DiJoseph, "Arizona Sheriff Announces Test of Alternative to Taser Stun Gun" (reprint), http://orlando.injuryboard.com/defective-products/an-alternative-to-the-defective-and-deadly-taser.php
134. "Officer Uses Taser During Struggle; Man Dies." CTV News, December 12, 2007.
135. http://www.cnn.com/2009/CRIME/05/28/michigan.taser.death/index.html?iref=allsear
136. Abby Simons, "Man Hit with Taser in Police Scuffle Dies," *Star Tribune,* September 8, 2010.
137. "Barrow Taser Arrest Man Dies," BBC News, August 17, 2011.
138. http://www.forbes.com/sites/erikkain/2011/07/05/the-killing-of-allen-kephart
139. Michael R. Smith, Robert J. Kaminski, Geoffrey P. Alpert, Lorie A. Fridell, John MacDonald, and Bruce Kubu. "A Multi-Method Evaluation of Police Use of Force Outcomes," National Institute of Justice, http://www.rkb.us/contentdetail.cfm?content-id=236251
140. "Continuing Concerns about Taser Use," Amnesty International, 2006.
141. "Tasers a Form of Torture, Says UN," AFP, November 24, 2007.
142. "Tasers," *Sixty Minutes,* segment 2, November 13, 2011.
143. Gene Healy, *Go Directly to Jail* (Cato Institute, Washington DC, 2004), viii, ix.
144. Harvey A. Silverglate, *Three Felonies a Day* (Encounter Books, New York, 2005) xli, xlii, 115, 264–265.
145. Paul Craig Roberts and Lawrence M. Stratton, *The Tyranny of Good Intentions* (Random House, New York, 2008), 92–93.
146. http://www.nytimes.com/1988/07/10/books/no-target-seemed-too-big.html?
147. Ibid., 94–95. See also Silverglate, *Three Felonies,* 94, 99, 101.
148. Roberts and Stratton, *Good Intentions,* 186–187.
149. "a.k.a. Tommy Chong," documentary film, Showtime, March 7, 2010. See also http://newsblaze.com/story/2008/topstory.html
150. Ibid.

151. Adam Smith, *The Theory of Moral Sentiments* (orig. published 1759, Regnery Publishing, Washington, DC, 1997), book 2, 179.

152. John Dickinson, "The Letters of Fabius," letter 3, as quoted by McDonald in *Novus Ordo Seclorum*, 160.

153. Hayek, *Law*, vol. 1, 141–142. "'Social legislation,' second, may refer to the provision by government of certain services which are of special importance to some unfortunate minorities, the weak or those unable to provide for themselves. Such service functions of government a wealthy community may decide to provide for a minority—either on moral grounds or as an insurance against contingencies which may affect anybody. Although the provision of such services increases the necessity of levying taxes, these can be raised according to uniform principles; and the duty to contribute to the costs of such agreed common aims could be brought under the conception of general rules of conduct. It would not make the private citizen in any way the object of administration; he would still be free to use his knowledge for his purposes and not have to serve the purposes of an organization."

154. Smith, *Moral Sentiments,* book 2, 145-147.

155. Hayek, *Law*, vol. 1, 37, 132.

156. *Planned Parenthood v. Casey* 505 U.S. 833, 112 S. Ct. 2791 (1992) (majority), 2805.

157. *Doe v. City of New York* 364 U.S. 122 (1992).

158. David Brin, *The Transparent Society* (Perseus Books, Reading, MA, 1998), 71.

159. Ibid.

160. Jeffrey Rosen, *The Unwanted Gaze* (Vintage Books, New York, 2001), 169.

161. Ibid.

162. The Privacy Act bars federal agencies from disclosing information for any purpose other than that for which it was collected. The Driver's Privacy Protection Act protects motor vehicle records; the Fair Credit Reporting Act protects financial information, as does the Right to Financial Privacy Act. The Video Privacy Protection Act prohibits retailers from disclosing a customer's video rental records, and the Telephone Consumer Protection Act regulates telemarketing. But all of these contain big built-in exceptions. For example, the Fair Credit Reporting Act allows disclosure of financial information to all persons with a "legitimate business need." Enforcement and penalties are lax too, leaving the acts ineffectual.

163. Alderman and Kennedy, *The Right to Privacy*, 155.

164. Rosen, *Unwanted Gaze*, 50.

165. Ralph Waldo Emerson, "Friendship," *The Complete Works of Ralph Waldo Emerson* (New York, 1903), 202.

166. Janna Malamud Smith, *Private Matters* (Addison-Wesley, Reading, MA, 1997), 40.

167. Ibid., 42.

168. Rosen, *Gaze*, 46–48.

169. Ibid.

170. *Talley v. California* 362 U.S. 60 1960, *NAACP v. Alabama* 379 U.S. 449 1958.

171. *NAACP v. Alabama ex rel. Patterson* 357 U.S. 449, 78 S. Ct. 1163, 2 L. Ed. 2d 1488 (1958) http://www.answers.com/topic/freedom-of-assocation

172. *Silverman v. United States* 365 U.S. 505, 511 (1961).

173. *Kyllo v. United States* 121 S. Ct., 99-8508, June 11, 2001.

174. Ibid. See also Infotrac, *The Atlantic Monthly*, October 1, 2000, mag. Coll. 104H1033, Article A66581314, and Infotrac, *The New Republic*, October 6, 2000, mag. Coll. 104H0497, Article A65952651.

175. *Whren v. U.S.* 517 U.S. 806 (1996).

176. M. Chris Fabricant, *Busted* (HarperCollins, New York, 2005), 141–144, 152.

177. Richard van Duizand et al., *The Search Warrant Process: Preconceptions, Perceptions, and Practices* (National Center for State Courts, 1984), 21.

178. *United States v. Lattimore* 87 F.3d 652 (Fourth Circuit, 1996).

179. Judge James P. Gray, *Why Our Drug Laws Have Failed and What We Can Do About It* (Temple University Press, Philadelphia, PA, 2001), 96, 112.

180. Fabricant, *Busted,*102. See also Randy E. Barnett, "Curing the Drug-Law Addiction: The Harmful Side Effects of Legal Prohibition," in Dwight B. Heath (ed.), *Drugs*, 164–165, 172.

181. Ibid., 105, 107.

182. Alderman and Kennedy, *Privacy*, 58.

183. Carole Joffe, "Abortion and Medicine: A Sociopolitical History," in M. Paul et al. (eds.), *The Management of Abnormal and Unintended Pregnancy* (2009; PDF).

184. David G. Savage, *The Supreme Court and Individual Rights* (CQ Press, Washington DC, 2004), 329. See also Alderman and Kennedy, *Privacy*, 59–63.

185. Ibid., 76.

186. *Stenberg v. Carhart* 530 U.S. 914 (2000). See also Alderman and Kennedy, *Privacy*, 61–63, 76. See also Savage, *Supreme Court*, 329.

187. Sandra Day O'Connor, as quoted by Alderman and Kennedy in *Privacy*, 63.

188. Katha Pollitt, "Abortion in American History," *The Atlantic Monthly*, May 1997, 111.

189. Ibid.

190. Sue Woodman, *Last Rights* (Perseus Publishing, New York, 2001), 29. See also Alderman and Kennedy, *Privacy*, 133–134, 136, 138, 340, 341.

191. William H. Colby, *Unplugged: Reclaiming Our Right to Die in America* (AMACOM books, New York, 2006), 186.

192. Ibid., 186.

193. Caroline Daniel, "Killing with Kindness," *New Statesman*, August 15, 1997, v. 126, n. 4347, 16.

194. Gina Kolata, *New York Times*, May 23, 1996.

195. Alderman and Kennedy, *Privacy*, 133–134, 136, 138, 340, 341.

196. Ibid., 128.
197. Ibid., 129, 131–132.
198. Ibid., 131.
199. Ibid., 131–132, 136.
200. Ibid., 339–341.
201. Joan Biskupic, "Unanimous Decision Points to Tradition of Valuing Life," *Washington Post*, June 27, 1997, A01.
202. Ibid. See also Alderman and Kennedy, *Privacy*, 339–341.
203. Colby, *Unplugged*, 129–133. See also Sidney Wanzer, MD, and Joseph Glenmullen, MD, *To Die Well* (Da Capo Press, Cambridge, Mass., 2007), 8.
204. Wanzer and Glenmullen, *To Die Well*, 15–17.
205. Woodman, *Last Rights*, 10, 160, 161.
206. Ezekiel Emanuel, "Euthanasia: Where the Netherlands Leads, Will the World Follow?" *British Medical Journal*, June 9, 1991.
207. Colby, *Unplugged*, 84.
208. Cicero, *Selected Works* (Penguin Books, London, 1971), "On Old Age," 241.
209. Matt Ridley, *Genome* (HarperCollins Publishers, New York, 1999), 7–9.
210. Ridley, *Genome*, 55.
211. Ibid., 64. See also Bernadine Healy, "Rogue Medical Records," *U.S. New and World Report*, December 2, 2001, 61.
212. The Innocence Project, press release, May 11, 2007.
213. Dinitia Smith and Nicholas Wade, "DNA Tests Offer Evidence That Jefferson Fathered a Child with His Slave," *New York Times*, November 1, 1998.
214. Ridley, *Genome*, 135.
215. Ibid., 135. See also Simson Garfinkel, *Database Nation* (O'Reilly and Associates, 2001), 52–53.
216. Mark A. Rothstein, *Genetic Secrets: Protecting Privacy and Confidentiality in the Genetic Era* (Yale University Press, New Haven, CT, 1997), 475.
217. Tom Miller, "Should Insurance Companies Fear Genetic Testing?" *Consumers' Research Magazine*, October 2002, 15.
218. Rothstein, *Genetic Secrets*, 372–374.
219. Clive Norris and Gary Armstrong, *The Maximum Surveillance Society, The Rise of CCTV* (Berg Publishing, Oxford, England, 1999), 224.
220. Ibid.
221. Ibid., 198.
222. Ibid., 187
223. Ibid., 51.
224. Erving Goffman, *Behavior in Public Places: Notes on the Social Organization of Gatherings* (New York, 1985), 91.
225. Ibid. See also Norris and Armstrong, *Maximum Surveillance*, 59, 197.
226. Ibid., 32.
227. "Privacy in an Age of Terror," *BusinessWeek*, November 5, 2001, 82.
228. "How Bin Laden Made One Industry Boom," *Time*, May 20, 2011, 12.

229. Dick Armey, as quoted by David Kopel and Michael Krause in "Face the Facts: Facial Recognition Technology's Troubled Past—and Troubling Future," *Reason*, October 2002, 34, 5, 26–27.

230. *Skinner v. Railway Labor Executives Association* 489 U.S. 602 (1989).

231. William Bennett, as quoted by Jacob Sullum in "Urine or You're Out: Drug Testing Is Invasive, Insulting, and Generally Irrelevant to Job Performance. Why Do so Many Companies Insist on It?" *Reason*, November 2002, 34, 37.

232. Corey Fine, T. Zane Reeves, and George P. Harney, "Employee Drug Testing: Are Cities Complying with the Courts?" *Public Administration Review*, January-February 1996, 31–37.

233. Sullum, "Urine or You're Out," 37.

234. Ibid.

235. Craig M. Bradley, "Court Gives School Drug Testing an A," *Trial*, December 2002, 56.

236. *Board of Education v. Earls* 536 U.S. 822 (2002).

237. Ibid.

238. Ibid.

239. Ibid.

240. Richard Glen Boire, "Dangerous Lessons (Civil Liberties Watch)," *The Humanist*, November-December 2002, 62, 6, 39.

241. Robert Ramsey, "The Snoopervision Debate: Employer interests v. employee privacy," *Supervision*, August 1999, 3. See also Doug Buchanon, "Privacy Lost, Business First," *Columbus*, November 24, 2000, A25; Joan Greco, "Privacy, Whose Right Is it Anyhow?" *Journal of Business Strategy*, January 2001, 32; James Bovard, *Lost Rights* (James Bovard, New York, 1995), 88; and Rosen, *Unwanted Gaze*, 73.

242. Geoffrey R. Stone, *Perilous Times: Free Speech in Wartime from the Sedition Act of 1798 to the War on Terrorism* (W. W. Norton, New York, 2004), 186, 190, 230.

243. Fred E. Foldvary, *The Soul of Liberty* (Fred E. Foldvary, 1980), 122–123.

244. http://www.xbiz.com/news/85242 http://en/wikipedia.org/wiki/obscenity.

245. http://news.bbc.co.uk/2/hi/africa/2519595.stm.

246. "Nigerian Government Rejects Fatwa," BBC News, November 26, 2002, http://news.bbc.co.uk/2/hi/africa/2519595.stm.

247. Bodenhamer and Ely, *Bill of Rights*, 43–44.

248. Ibid., 50.

249. Ibid., 51.

250. Ibid., 51.

251. Ibid.

252. Ibid.

253. http://www.onemillionmoms.com/

254. Ibid.

255. Ibid.

256. David E. Bernstein, *You Can't Say That* (Cato Institute, 2003), 2.

257. Ibid.
258. George F. Will, *With a Happy Eye, But...* (Simon and Schuster, New York, 2002), 124.
259. Ibid.
260. Tammy Bruce, *The New Thought Police* (Crown Publishing, New York, 2001), 6.
261. Ibid.
262. Bernstein, *You Can't Say*, 24, 31, 50, 138, 143–144.
263. William McGowan, *Coloring the News* (Encounter Books, San Francisco, CA, 2002), 27–32.
264. http://www.cbsnews.com/8301...162.../taser-an-officers-weapon-of-choice/
265. http://nypost.com/p/news/local/sanchezfiredover47gkl
266. http://www.huffingtonpost.com/2011/11/09/david-gregory-grand-wizard-gop-n-1083881...11/14/2011
267. [http://articles.nydaily news.com/2012-03-28/news/31251848-espn-anchor-headline-lunch/ 4/16/12]
268. William McGowan, *Coloring,* 27, 30–31.
269. Ibid.
270. Ibid.
271. Bernstein, *You Can't Say*, 59, 61–62.
272. David Thibodaux, *Beyond Political Correctness* (Huntington House Publishers, Lafayette, LA, 1994), 118.
273. William F. Buckley, *Happy Days Were Here Again* (Perseus Books, New York, 1993), 95.
274. Bernstein, *You Can't Say*, 61–62.
275. Diane Ravitch, *The Language Police* (Random House, New York, 2003), 171–182.
276. http://www.msnbc.msn.com/id/28629118/ns/technologyandscienceinternet/t/rules-curb...11/6/2011
277. http://www.opencongress.org
278. http://www.boston.com/news/education/k_12/articles/2010/05/04/antibully_law_may_face...11/6/2011
279. James B. Jacobs, *Can Gun Control Work?* (Oxford University Press, New York, 2002), 37.
280. Ibid., 42–43.
281. Ibid.
282. Ibid.
283. Ibid.
284. Ibid.
285. Andrew J. McClurg, David B. Kopel, and Brannon P. Danning, *Gun Control and Gun Rights* (New York University Press, New York, 2002), 4, 7. 67, 194. See also Jacobs, *Can Gun Control Work?,* 10.
286. Richard Poe, *The Seven Myths of Gun Control* (Three Rivers Press, New York, 2001) 155–156. See also John R. Lott, Jr., *The Bias Against Guns* (Regnery Publishing, Washington, DC, 2003), 3, 22.

287. http://en.thinkexist.com/georgewashingtonquotes/
288. http://www.disastercenter.com/crime/uscrime.html
289. Ibid.
290. Ibid.
291. Jacobs, *Can Gun Control Work?*, 29, 51, 56–57, 125, 136.
292. Bernhard Rehfeld, *Die Wurzeln des Rechts* (Berlin, 1951), 67.
293. James DeLong, *Property Matters* (Free Press, Simon and Schuster, New York, 1997), 41, 66–67.
294. John Locke, in *Two Treatises of Government*, as quoted by Friedrich A. Hayek in *The Fatal Conceit* (University of Chicago Press, 1988), 34.
295. "Western Civilization," transcripts, 28, Eugen Weber, 1998.
296. Magna Carta, Chapter 29; 2 Coke, *Institutes* 41, 45, 46, 47, 50, 51.
297. David Hume, *A Treatise of Human Nature* (orig. published 1740, Penguin Books, Middlesex England, 1969), 543.
298. Bernard H. Siegan, *Property Rights* (Transaction Publishing, London, 2001), p. 32.
299. Ibid.
300. Ibid., 101
301. James Wilson, *Lectures on Law* (1790–1791), *Two Works of James Wilson* (Robert G. McCloskey, ed., 1967), 718–719.
302. John Locke, *Two Treatises of Government* (orig. published 1690, Cambridge University Press, New York, 1988), 289.
303. James Madison, *The Complete Madison* by Padover, as quoted by Bernard Siegan in *Property Rights* (Transaction Publishing, London, 2001), 81.
304. Arthur Lee, as quoted by James Ely in *The Guardian of Every Other Right* (Oxford University Press, New York, 1998), 26.
305. John Adams, as quoted by Ely in *Guardian*, 43.
306. Alexander Hamilton, as quoted by Ely in *Guardian*, 57.
307. Ibid., 61.
308. Report of the English Poor Law Commissioners of 1834, as quoted by Pipes in *Property*, 226.
309. President Grover Cleveland, as quoted by Pipes in *Property*, 226.
310. *Munn v. Illinois* 94 U.S. 113, 130 (1877).
311. *Fertilizing Company v. Hyde Park* 97 U.S. 659 (1878).
312. Ely, *Guardian*, 93–94.
313. Ibid., 86–87, 93–94.
314. Journal of Commerce, as quoted by Daniel Seligman in "Keeping Up," *Fortune*, February 27, 1989.
315. Ely, *Guardian*, 114–115.
316. *Home Loan Association v. Blaisdell* 290 U.S. 398 (1934).
317. Ely, *Guardian*, 119–121.
318. *Nebbia v. New York* 291 U.S. 537 (1934).
319. Ely, *Guardian*, 132–134. See also Timothy Sandefur, *Property Rights in 21st Century America*, (Cato Institute, 2006), 112.
320. *Williamson v. Lee Optical* 348 U.S. 483, 487–88 (1955).

321. *Armstrong v. United States* 364 U.S. at 49, 80 S. Ct. (1896). See also James Ely, "The Enigmatic Place of Property Rights in Modern Constitutional Thought," in Bodenhamer and Ely (eds.), *The Bill of Rights in Modern America* (Indiana University Press, Indianapolis, 1993), 87–100.

322. *Loretto v. Teleprompter Manhattan CATV Corp.* 458 U.S. 419, 438 (1982).

323. *Pennsylvania Coal Co v. Mahon* 260 U.S. 393, 415 (1922).

324. *Spears v. Berle* 48 N.Y. 2d 254, 422 NYS.2d 636 (1979).

325. Ely, *Guardian*, 150.

326. James DeLong, *Property Matters* (Free Press, New York, 1997), 264.

327. Ibid., 124.

328. Ibid., 124–135.

329. Ibid.

330. Ibid., 123.

331. Ibid., 136.

332. Ibid., 17.

333. Ely, "The Enigmatic Place of Property Rights," 97. See also DeLong, *Property Matters*, 248–249, 288–296.

334. DeLong, *Property Matters*, 296.

335. Ibid., 100.

336. Ibid., 100–103.

337. Endangered Species Program, US Fish and Wildlife Service, http:www. endangered.fws. See also DeLong, *Property Matters*, 110.

338. 16 U.S.C. 1533(a)(1), 50 C.F.R. 424.11(b)

339. Ike Sugg, statement to US House of Representatives, Task Force on Endangered Species Act, Hearings on Endangered Species Act Reauthorization, May 18, 1995. (16 U.S.C. 1533 (a) (1), 50, C.F. R. 424.11(b). http: www.endangered. fws. See also DeLong, *Property Matters*, 208–209.

340. De Long, *Property Matters*, 13.

341. Richard Shelby, "ESA Pits Property Owners Against Rats, Bugs, and Bureaucracy," *AMC Journal*, June, 1994. http://www.coaleducation.org/ issues/esapits.html

342. Gene Healy, *Go Directly to Jail*, (Cato Institute, Washington, DC, 2004), 58.

343. John K. Carlisle, "ESA Sends Two Retirees to Poorhouse," The Heartland Institute, August 1999. http://www.heartland.org/environment/aug99/victim. html

344. Dave Foreman, as quoted by David Boaz in *The Politics of Freedom* (Cato Institute, Washington, DC, 2008), 4.

345. Timothy Sandefur, *Property Rights*, 113–116.

346. Ibid.

347. DeLong, *Property Matters*, 115.

348. Ibid., 275–276.

349. *Calero v. Toledo* 416 U.S. 663; 94 S. Ct. 2080; 1974.

350. "Background on Forfeiture," Legal Information Institute, http://www.law. cornell.edu/background/forfeiture

351. Kyla Dunn, *Reining in Forfeiture: Common Sense Reform in the War on Drugs*, PBS documentary, 2000, http://www.pbs.org/wgbh/pages/frontline
352. "Asset Forfeiture," U.S. Newswire, November, 1998.
353. Ibid.
354. Dunn, *Reining in Forfeiture.*
355. Ibid.
356. DeLong, *Property Matters*, 275.
357. "Vehicle Forfeiture," New York State Defenders Association, http://www.nysda.org/vehicles forfeiture.html
358. http://www.pbs.org/newshour/bb/transportation/jan-june10/dui_02-15.html
359. http://www.kidney.org/news/newsroom/fs new/25factsorgdon&trans.cfm. See also Trevor Harrison, "Globalization and the Trade in Human Body Parts," *The Canadian Review of Sociology and Anthropology*, February 1999, 21. See also James DeLong, "Organ Grinders," *Reason*, November 1998, vol. 30, no. 6, 57.
360. Bruce Gottlieb, "The Price Is Right: How Much Is that Kidney in the Window?" *The New Republic*, May 22, 2000, 16.
361. Karen Wright, *Discover*, "The Body Bazaar," October 1998, v. 19, no. 10, 114. See also "The Organ Trade: Should the Sale of Kidneys be Legalized?" *CBC This Morning*, June 8, 2001.
362. "Who Owns John Moore's Spleen?" J.E. Ferrell, Chicago Tribune, February 18, 1990.
363. DeLong, "Organ Grinders." See also David L. Kaserman and A.H. Barnett, *The U.S. Organ Procurement System*, 27, 31, 33–34, 38.
364. Stephen R. Munzer, "Property Rights in Body Parts," in Ellen Paul, Fred Miller, Jr., and Jeffrey Paul (eds.), *Property Rights* (Cambridge University Press, Cambridge, England, 1994), 266–267.
365. Ibid., 275.
366. Gottlieb, "The Price Is Right."
367. David J. Houston and Lilliard E. Richardson, Jr., "Safety Belt Use and the Switch to Primary Enforcement," *American Journal of Public Health*, November 2006, 96, 11, 1949.
368. Matthew L. Wald, "U.S. Presses States for Strict Seat Belt Laws," *New York Times*, March 5, 2004, A17.
369. New York state public service announcement, aired on WNYT, June 25, 2002.
370. http://www.chacha.com.question.how-many-people-die-per-year.html>
371. Richard Pipes, *Property and Freedom* (Random House, New York, 1999), 49.
372. Ibid., 160.
373. Ibid., 210.
374. http://en.thinkexist.com/quotes/epictetus/7.html
375. McDonald, *Novus Ordo Seclorum*, ix, x.
376. Nora Volkow as quoted by Fenella Saunders in "Is Overeating an Addiction?" *Discover*, May, 2001, 14.

377. Abraham Lincoln, "Temperance Address," February 22, 1842, as reprinted in *Collected Works of Abraham Lincoln* (Rutgers University Press, 1990), vol. 1, 273.
378. Ludwig von Mises, *Liberalism, The Classical Tradition* (Quality Books, New York, 1996 edition), 53.
379. Peter McWilliams, "Prohibition: A Lesson in the Danger and Futility of Prohibiting," 5, http://www.mcwilliams.com/books/aint/402.htm.
380. Mark Thornton, *The Economics of Prohibition* (University of Utah Press, Salt Lake City, 1991), 16.
381. Alexander, Michaels, and Manley, *A Social History of the United States*, 182–183.
382. Ibid., 7.
383. Billy Sunday, as quoted by Mike Gray in *Drug Crazy* (Routledge, New York, 2000), 66.
384. Ibid., 8.
385. Mike Gray, *Drug Crazy* (Routledge, New York, 2000), 18.
386. Robert Schoenberg, *Mr. Capone* (William Morrow, New York, 1992), 57.
387. Ibid.
388. Gray, *Drug Crazy*, 18, 19. See also Schoenberg, *Mr. Capone*, 57.
389. Andrew Sinclair, *Prohibition: The Era of Excess* (Little, Brown, and Co., Boston, 1962), 222, as quoted by Gray in *Drug Crazy*, 18.
390. Charles Hanson Towne, *The Rise and Fall of Prohibition* (Macmillan, New York, 1923), 61.
391. Sinclair, *Prohibition*, as quoted by Gray in *Drug Crazy*, 67.
392. Gray, *Drug Crazy*, 67.
393. McWilliams, "Prohibition," 8.
394. Gray, *Drug Crazy*, 67.
395. Wickersham Report. See US National Commission on Law Observance and Enforcement.
396. Alexander, Michaels, and Manley, *Social History*, 177.
397. John C. McWilliams, *The Protectors: Harry J. Anslinger and the Federal Bureau of Narcotics, 1930–1962* (University of Delaware Press, Newark, 1990), 34.
398. Kyvig, *Repealing National Prohibition*, 32, as quoted by Gray in *Drug Crazy*, 69.
399. Gray, *Drug Crazy*, 67.
400. Henry Joy, as quoted by Gray in *Drug Crazy*, 67.
401. Pauline Sabin, as quoted by Gray in *Drug Crazy*, 70.
402. Ibid.
403. Gray, *Drug Crazy*, 70.
404. Ibid.
405. Gray, *Drug Crazy*, 67–70.
406. Winston Churchill, *The Great Republic: A History of America* (orig. 1956, current edition, Winston S. Churchill, 1999), 270.
407. Ronald Weitzer, *Sex for Sale* (Routledge, New York, 2000), 11–12.

408. George F. Will, *One Man's America* (Random House, New York, 2008), 126.
409. Weitzer, *Sex for Sale*, 171.
410. Ibid., 178.
411. Gray, *Drug Crazy*, 76.
412. Ibid, 79–80.
413. United States Code: Title 21, 812, Schedule of controlled substances LII / Legal Information Institute. http://www.law.cornell.edu/uscode/21/812.html
414. Ryan Grim, *This Is Your Country on Drugs* (John Wiley and Sons, Hoboken, NJ, 2009), 57.
415. Gray, *Drug Crazy*, 97–98.
416. Ibid.
417. Mitch Earleywine, *Understanding Marijuana* (Oxford University Press, New York, 2002), 233.
418. Richard Lawrence Miller, *Drug Warriors and their Prey* (Praeger Publishers, Westport, CT, 1996), 81.
419. "After 40 Years, $1 Trillion, US War On Drugs Has Failed To Meet Any Of Its Goals," AP, Fox News. http://www.foxnews.com/world/2010/05/13/ap-impact-years-trillion-war-drugs-failed-meet
420. "History of drug laws and restrictions in US," History of Drug Laws. http://facultypages.morris.umn.edu/ratcliffj/psy1081/drug laws.html
421. Ibid.
422. M. Chris Fabricant, *Busted* (HarperCollins, New York, 2005), 8–9.
423. Thomas S. Szasz, "Drugs as Property: The Right We Rejected," in Heath, *Drugs*, 201.
424. http://www.druglibrary.org/olsen/norml//crazy/crazy/03.html
425. Grim, *Your Country*, 92–93.
426. Ibid.
427. Miller, *Drug Warriors,* 172.
428. Ibid., 7, 17.
429. Ibid.
430. Ibid., 23.
431. Judge James P. Gray, *Why Our Drug Laws Have Failed* (Temple University Press, Philadelphia, 2001), 125.
432. Rosenthal and Kubby, *Why Marijuana*, 54.
433. Grim, *This Is Your Country*, 85.
434. Gray, *Why Our Drug Laws Have Failed*, 212.
435. Ibid., 13.
436. "New US ads tie drug use to terrorism funding," CNN. http://articles.cnn.com/2002-02-04/us/ret.terrorism.drugs1illegaldrugs terrorism-funding.
437. Federal Justice Statistics, 2009. Bureau of Justice Statistics. http://bjs.ojp.usdoj.gov/
438. http://norml.org/news/2011/09/19/marijuana-prosecutions-for-2010-near-record-high

439. Federal Justice Statistics, 2009. Correctional Population in the United States, 2010. Bureau of Justice Statistics. http://bjs.ojp.usdoj.gov/
440. Ibid.
441. Ibid.
442. Ibid., Census of Jail Facilities, 2006.
443. Milton Friedman, "There's No Justice in the War on Drugs," in Heath, *Drugs*, 210.
444. Paul Craig Roberts and Lawrence M. Stratton, *The Tyranny of Good Intentions* (Random House, New York, 2008), 176.
445. "US prison population dwarfs that of other nations," Adam Liptak, *New York Times*, April 23, 2008. http://www.nytimes.com/2008/04/23/world/Americas/23iht-23prison.12253738.html?pagew
446. Ed Rosenthal and Steve Kubby, *Why Marijuana Should Be Legal* (Thunder's Mouth Press, New York, 2003), 30. See also Douglas Husak, *Legalize This! The Case for Decriminalizing Drugs* (Verso, London, 2002), 44–45, 47.
447. Federal Justice Statistics, 1970-2010. Bureau of Justice Statistics. http://bjs.ojp.usdoj.gov/
448. Miller, *Drug Warriors,* 81.
449. Ibid., 67.
450. Ibid.
451. Ibid., 68.
452. Ibid.
453. Rosenthal and Kubby, *Why Marijuana*, 19.
454. "War on Pain Control," Drug Reform Coordination Network. October, 1996. http://www.drcnet.org/guide10-96/pain.html
455. Mike Gray, *Drug Crazy*, 183–185. See also Judge James P. Gray, *Why Our Drug Laws Have Failed*, 135.
456. Article Collections, "Freed as Drug Suspects," *New York Times* http://www.nytimes.com/keyword/laboratory-tests
457. Gray, *Why Our Drug Laws Have Failed*, 103–107.
458. Miller, *Drug Warriors*, 75.
459. Ibid.
460. Ibid., 66.
461. Husak, *Legalize This!*, 5.
462. Ibid., 4.
463. Gray, *Drug Crazy*, 103–104. See also Fabricant, *Busted*, 314.
464. Husak, *Legalize This!*, 4.
465. Ibid.
466. Ibid.
467. Ibid.
468. Ibid.
469. Gray, *Why Our Drug Laws Have Failed*, 128–129.
470. http://www.washingtonpost.com/wp-srv/sports/longterm/memories/bias/launch/bias1.html
471. Ibid., 127. See also *Legalize This!*, 84, 86, 88.

472. Cynthia Kuhn, Scott Swartzwelder, and Wilkie Wilson, *Buzzed* (W.W. Norton and Co., New York, 2008), 292–293.
473. "Thirty Years Of America's Drug War," Frontline, PBS. http://www.pbs.org/wgbh/pages/frontline/shows/drugs/cron/
474. Husak, *Legalize This!,* 150.
475. Paul Ruschmann, J.D., *Legalizing Marijuana* (Chelsea House Publishers, USA, 2004), 85, 103–104. See also Miller, *Drug Warriors,* 9.
476. *Drugs, Inc.,* National Geographic Channel, July 13, 2010.
477. Miller, *Drug Warriors,* 27.
478. Marcia Angell, MD, *The Truth About the Drug Companies* (Random House, New York, 2005), 173–183.
479. Ibid., 26–27.
480. Grim, *This Is Your Country,* 211.
481. Ellen Leff, "The First Amendment and Drug Alcohol Treatment Programs: To What Extent May Coerced Treatment Programs Attempt to Alter Beliefs Relating to Ultimate Concerns and Self-Concept?" in Heath, *Drugs,* 341.
482. Douglas N. Husak, *Drugs and Rights* (Cambridge University Press, New York, 1992), 96.
483. Rosenthal and Kubby, *Why Marijuana,* 37.
484. Ibid., 39–41.
485. Randy E. Barnett, "Curing the Drug-Law Addiction: The Harmful Side Effects of Legal Prohibition," in Heath, *Drugs,* 162.
486. Rosenthal and Kubby, *Why Marijuana,* 25–26.
487. Ibid., 122–123.
488. Richard Glen Boire and Kevin Feeny, *Medical Marijuana Law* (Ronin Publishing, Oakland, CA, 53.) See also Rosenthal and Kubby, *Why Marijuana,* 50–51, 58.
489. Cicero, *The Laws* (Oxford University Press, New York, 1998), 111.
490. Jethro Lieberman, *A Practical Companion to the Constitution* (University of California Press, 2005), 436.
491. Jeffrey Rosen, *The Supreme Court* (Times Books, New York, 2006), 96.
492. *Plessy v. Ferguson,* http://www.watson.org/lisa/blackhistory/post-civilwar/plessy.html
493. Ibid. See also Rosen, *Supreme Court,* 99, and Hudson, *The Fourteenth Amendment,* 79, http://usinfo.state.gov/usa/infousa/facts/democrac/33.html
494. "Racial Etiquette: The Racial Customs and Rules of Racial Behavior in Jim Crow America," www.jimcrowhistory.org/resources/lessonplans/heesetiquette.htm
495. "What Was Jim Crow?" http://www.ferris.edu/news/jimcrow/what.htm. See also http://usinfo.state.gov/usa/infousa/facts/democrac/33.html.
496. "Racial Etiquette: The Racial Customs and Rules of Racial Behavior in Jim Crow America," www.jimcrowhistory.org/resources/lessonplans/heesetiquette.htm
497. Garrett Epps, *Democracy Reborn* (Henry Holt and Company, New York, 2006), 262–263, 267.

498. "Racial Etiquette: The Racial Customs and Rules of Racial Behavior in Jim Crow America," www.jimcrowhistory.org/resources/lessonplans/heesetiquette.htm)

499. "Jim Crow Laws," www.fact-index.com/j/ji/jimcrowlaw.html.

500. "What Was Jim Crow?", http://www.ferris.edu/news/jimcrow/what.htm

501. George F. Will, *One Man's America* (Random House, New York, 2008), 71–72.

502. Ibid.

503. Jim Newton, *Justice for All: Earl Warren and the Nation He Made* (Penguin Group, New York, 2006), 318.

504. Ibid., 324.

505. "Equal Protection and Affirmative Action, Herman Belz," in Bodenhamer and Ely, *The Bill of Rights*, 156.

506. Ibid., 158.

507. Ibid., 160.

508. Justice Antonin Scalia, as quoted by Rod L. Evans and Irwin M. Berent in *The Quotable Conservative* (Adams Media, 1995), 202.

509. Hudson, *The Fourteenth Amendment*, 86. See also Buckley, *Happy Days Were Here Again*, 48.

510. Tammy Bruce, *The New Thought Police* (Random House, New York, 2001), 155–157.

511. *Bradwell v. State of Illinois* 83 U.S. 130 (1873)

512. Lenora M. Lapidus, Emily J. Martin, and Namita Luthra, *The Rights of Women* (New York University Press, New York, 2009), 399–402.

513. Ibid., 283–285.

514. Ibid., 288–289.

515. "Stonewall Uprising," *American Experience*, PBS documentary, April 27, 2011.

516. Andrew Koppelman, *The Gay Rights Question in Contemporary American Law* (University of Chicago Press, Chicago, 2002), 1. See also US GAO, Defense of Marriage Act: Update to Prior Report 04-353r (January 4, 2004, http://www.gao.gov/new.itemsd04353r.pdf)

517. http://thinkexist.com/quotes/abrahamlincoln/

518. Adam Smith, *The Wealth of Nations*, 5–6, 9, 397.

519. Hayek, *Law, Legislation, and Liberty*, vol. 2, 109.

520. Hayek, *The Fatal Conceit*, 75–77.

521. F. A. Hayek, *The Road to Serfdom* (University of Chicago, Chicago, 1944), introduction, 35–36.

522. George F. Will, *The Woven Figure* (Touchstone, New York, 1997), 317.

523. Buckley, *Happy Days,* 97.

524. Alex Altman, "The Skimmer," Time, November 8, 2010, 32.

525. Hayek, *The Fatal Conceit*, 104–105.

526. Poverty Data, U.S. Census Bureau, Current Population Survey, Annual Social Economic Supplement. US Census Bureau. http://www.census.gov/hhes/www/poverty/data/index.html

527. Ibid.
528. Bernard Goldberg, *Bias* (Regnery, Washington DC, 2001), 66–67.
529. Ibid.
530. Ibid., 73.
531. Historical Charts of Interest Rates, 30 year bonds. http://www.sharelynx.com/chartsfixed/BondYield.gif
532. US Bureau of Labor Statistics, civilian employment status 1940 to date. ftp://ftp.bls.gov/pub/special.requests/1f/aat1.txt
533. D'Souza, "How Reagan Reelected Clinton," Forbes, November 3, 1997, 123. See also US Census Bureau.
534. Ibid.
535. Ibid.
536. Ibid.
537. Ibid.
538. Encyclopedia Brittanica, CD 2000 edition, "Ronald (Wilson) Reagan."
539. D'Souza, "How Reagan Reelected Clinton," 119.
540. Buckley, *Happy Days*, 30.
541. The Tax Foundation, *U.S. Federal Income Tax Rates History, 1913–2010.* http://www.taxfoundation.org/about/ http
542. Will, *One Man's America*, 127.
543. Ibid.
544. "After the Bell," CNBC, December 11, 2007.
545. Michael Scherer, "Taking It to the Streets," Time, October 24, 2011, 22.
546. http://timesunion.com/local/article/protest-big-banks-sold-us-out-2253938.php
547. Roger Lowenstein, "Occupy Wall Street: It's Not a Hippie Thing," *Bloomberg Businessweek*, October 27, 2011.
548. Joe Klein, "An Implausible Populist," Time, October 31, 2011, 24.
549. http://ferndale.patch.com/article/copy
550. Will, *Woven Figure*, 109.
551. Matthew Rothschild, "Exclusive! The FBI Deputizes Business," *The Progressive.* http://www.progressive.org/node/6052. See also "Infragard History," Infragard National Members Alliance. http://www.infragard.net/
552. Will, *One Man's America*, 191.
553. "Classic kids games like kickball deemed unsafe by state in effort to increase summer camp regulation," Glenn Blain, April 19, 2011. http://articles.nydailynews.com/2011-04-19/local/29467776_1_summer-camp-recreational
554. George F. Will, *With a Happy Eye, But...* (Simon and Schuster, New York, 2002), 61.
555. Steve Delorey, July 4, 2007.
556. "Effective Marginal Tax Rates on Labor Income, Distribution of Combined Federal and State Tax Rates," Edward Harris, Miami University Libraries http://www.muohio/multifacet/record/mu3ugb3492282

557. Smith, "Wealth of Nations," edited by Isaac Kramnick, *Enlightenment Reader* (Penguin Group, New York, 1995), 511–512.
558. Walter Lippman, *An Inquiry into the Principles of a Good Society* (Boston, 1937), 267.

INDEX

Pages numbers with *italic "n"* or *"nn"* indicate a reference to endnotes.

deaths
  from homemade liquor, 166–67
  involving drug law enforcement,
    179–80
  from overdosing on drugs, 180
  physician-assisted, 95–100
  related to cocaine, 179, 186
  related to heroin, 186
  using guns, 125–26
  worldwide from drug prohibition,
    180–81
decade of greed (1980s), 214–17
deception vs. coercion, 3
Declaration of Independence, 16
declarations of how things ought to be
    vs. rights, 228
decriminalizing
  harder drugs, 188
  marijuana, 172
Delaware (DE), lynchings in, 197
DeLong, James, *Property Matters*,
    140–43, 246n326
democracy
  associated with mob rule, 133
  consequences of despotic, 228
  despotic, 46–47, 49
  without principles, 46
Dent, Bob, 99–100
Department of Energy, under Carter
    administration, 51
Department of Health, Education, and
    Welfare, 41
Department of Interior, report on
    endangered species, 143
Department of Justice
  Bureau of Narcotics and Dangerous
    Drugs, 172
  Obscenity Enforcement Unit, 170
Department of Labor, adopting quotas
    and timetables for hiring for
    contractors, 199
depression of 1890s, 29
deregulation
  impact of, 217
  stimulating economic growth, 215

desegregation, in South, 198–99
despotic democracy
  allowing double standard of rights,
    49
  definition of, 46–47
devotion, reciprocity and, 10–11
Diana, Princess of Wales, 106
Dickinson, John, 76
directed vs. spontaneous systems, 59
directives of policy, 159
discrimination
  banning in public places, 43
  of gays, 203
  prohibiting laws in racial, 28
  reverse, 199
  through making choices, 117–18
diseases, linked to genetics, 101–4
District of Columbia
  gay couples adopting in, 204
  gay marriage in, 204
  rent control in, 137
diversion, as component of happiness,
    9–10
division of labor, 207–8
DNA databases, 102
DNA testing
  confidentiality of, 102–3
  for paternity, 102
  required of felons convicted of
    violent crimes, 102
  using to clear wrongful convictions,
    64, 102
domestic partnerships, 203–4
dominator, 222–26
do-not-resuscitate orders, 99
don't-ask-don't-tell, 204
dopamine receptors, 160–61
double standard of rights, 48–49
Douglas, Peter, 145–46
Douglas, William O., 89, 139
Douglas County (CO), police ignoring
    DNA evidence in, 64
draft, convictions during WWI for
    speaking against, 113
draft, military, 62–63

Hawaii (HI), gay marriage in, 203
Hayek, Friedrich
  on choosing government, 45
  on common law, 238n104
  on deceiving someone, 3, 234n5
  on government as impartial body, 54
  on government in directorial role, 54
  on individual seeking goals, 208–9
  on social legislation, 240n153
  on spontaneous order, 57–58
Hayes, Rutherford, 193
Healing, Kenneth, 146
health and safety, public officials
  defining, 52
Health Insurance Portability and
  Accountability Act, 104
Helvering v. Davis (1937), taxing both
  employees and employers for, 138
Hemings, Sally, 102
heroin users, 185
hiring
  employers giving preferential
    treatment in, 199
  refusing to hire women because of
    pregnancy, 201
historical sites, property designated
  as, 140
Hobbes, Thomas, 76
Holmes, Oliver Wendell, 139–40, 142
*Home Building and Loan Association
  v. Blaisdell* (1934), 137, 246n316
homelessness, in 1980s, 215
homosexuality. *See* gays
Hoover, Herbert, 31, 167, 168
hospice care, 100
hotels, racial discrimination by, 194,
  198
Houston (TX)
  drug law enforcement in, 179
  forfeiture of money at airport, 148
Hub Products, 166–67
Hughes, Charles Evans, 137
human nature, Madison on, 17
human organs, commerce in, 149–53

humanitarian efforts, using rules of
  organization for, 78
Hume, David, 133, 158
Huntington's chorea, 101–2
Hyde, Henry, 147

I

Idaho (ID), case of pesticide killing
  geese in, 145
ideas, spontaneous order and exchange
  of, 59
Identigene, 102
illegal enterprises, settling disputes of
  competitors in, 180
illegal searches, 25
Illinois (IL)
  lynchings in, 197
  Prohibition-related murders in
    Chicago, 165
  women joining state bar, 201
illnesses, linked to genetics, 103–4
Imclone, 72–73
immorality, life and, 2
Immunization and Naturalization
  Service's "watch list," 107
import duties, 31
incarceration, rate in US, 56,
  237nn87–92
incarceration rate, rate in US, 175–76,
  250n439
income tax, federal, history of rates
  for, 40–41
indecent speech, banning, 113
indispensability, reinforcing self-
  image, 9
individuals
  choice of, 48
  forcing views on physician-assisted
    deaths on, 98
  importance of, 2–3
  justifying regulation of, 161–63
  owning guns, 127–28
  purpose of, 159
  self-interested actions of, 59
  spending as they choose, 210–11

K

Kansas City (MO), television stations showing solicitation of prostitutes, 170

Kant, Immanuel
categorical imperative of, 1, 234*n*1
on prostitution, 170

Kennedy, Anthony, 90, 110, 115

Kennedy, Caroline
on arrest-and-strip-search policy of Chicago Police Department, 66–67
The Right to Privacy, 66, 96, 239*n*124

Kennedy, John F., 53–54

Kephart, Allen, 69

Kern County (CA), child molestation cases overturned in, 65

Kevorkian, Jack, 96

Kimberly-Clark, urine testing at, 109

kindness, definition of, 13

King, Rufus, 16

Klebold, Dylan, 129

Klimek, Jim, 178

Knickerbocker Trust Company, 29

Knoxville (TN), lynchings in, 197

Kronen, Cara, 67

Kronen, Quinn, 67

Kuala Lumpur (MY), automated facial recognition systems in, 106

Kyllo, Danny Lee, 85–86

Kyllo v. United States (2001), 242*n*173

L

labor, storing as asset, 6

labor unions, desegregation of, 198

LaGuardia, Fiorello, 171

Lake Arrowhead (CA), death of suspect from Taser in, 69

Lancet (medical journal), on legalizing organ sales, 153

landmarks, property designated as, 140

language terms

banned by publishers of educational materials, 121
taken as racist and sexist, 122
using to discriminate, 118, 120–21
using to offend, 119–20

Lattimore, Neel, 84

law enforcement, applying "special needs doctrine," 25

law of morality, 1–2

laws. *See also* Supreme Court
antibullying, 123
banning abortions, 89–93
banning contraceptives, 89
consisting of purpose-independent rules, 238*n*105
equality before law, 12
in free market, 209–10
Jim Crow, 195–97
known as black codes, 26
making at will, 21
managed order and, 59
on ownership of guns, 125
vs. personal liberties, 17
on physician-assisted deaths, 98, 99
on physician-assisted suicide, 99
power to create laws, 19
prohibiting racial segregation and discrimination, 28
prohibition, 161–69
to protect genetic privacy, 104
protecting privacy, 82
restricting individuals liberty, 75–80
violating right to liberty, 4

Lee, Arthur, 135

legalizing
drugs, 184–88
organ sales, 153

legislation, growth of, 51–56

legislative branch, creation of, 18

Legos, banning in Goddard School (Seattle), 218

Lenin, 213

LensCrafters, 39

lesbians. *See also* gays, equal rights for, 84

Mississippi (MI), American Family
    Association in Tupelo, 116–17
Missouri (MO)
  law banning abortions, 90–91
  right to die case in, 94
  television stations showing
      solicitation of prostitutes, 170
Mitchell, Robert, 69
Mondale, Walter, 221–22
money
  accomplishments and, 206–7
  equated with corruption, 220–21
  relationship to work, 6
  State management of individual's,
      159
  teachers view of, 217
monitoring, television programming,
    by watchdog groups, 116–17
monitoring of employees, 111–13
monopolies, splitting up, 29
Montesquieu, 76
Moore, John, 151
Moore, Sara Jane, 84
moral vs. natural, 1
moralism, 51–52
morality
  in decision making, 5
  definition of, 13–14
  law of, 1–2
  US imposing morality, 161–71
morphine, on pain relief using, 178
Morris, Gouverneur, 134–35
motor vehicles
  searching, 86
  seat belt laws with, 153–55
Mott, Lucretia, 201
movies, portrayal of wealthy in,
    220–21
Mugler v. Kansas (1887), 136
Munn v. Illinois (1877), 136, 245n310
Murray, Joseph, 149
Muslims, issuing a fatwa against
    writers, 114

mutual sympathy (empathy), affecting
    happiness, 12–13. *See also*
    empathy
My Own Country (Verghese), 83

N
NAACP v. Alabama (1958), 85,
    241n171
Napoleon, 62
Narcotics Control Act of 1956, 172
Nashville (TN), lynchings in, 197
national bank, creation of, 19
National Crime Prevention Council,
    definition of cyberbullying,
    122–23
National Firearms Act of 1934, 124
National Fish and Wildlife
    Foundation, 142
National Guard, arming, 126
National Industrial Recovery Act
    (NIRA), 34
National Labor Relations Act, 37
National Marine Fisheries Services,
    143–44
National Organ Transplant Act, 151
national parks, created by New Deal
    programs, 33–34
National Recovery Administration, 38
National Rifl e Association (NRA),
    128–29
National Youth Administration, 33
nationalism, 53–54, 210–11
Native American Graves Protection
    and Repatriation Act, 200
natural vs. moral, 1
Navarro, Pedro Oregon, 179
NBC (television network), on
    homelessness in 1980s, 215
Nebbia v. New York (1934), 138,
    246n319
Nebraska (NE), lynchings in, 197
"necessary," definition of, 19
Negroes. *See* African Americans
Netherlands
  euthanasia in, 99

racial quotas, and timetables for hiring
contractors, 199
racial violence, 196
racist, comments taken as, 122
racketeering laws (RICO), 169–70
Rahman, Akif, 68
railroad regulation, 29
railroads
laws regulating railroads, 136
racial discrimination by railways,
194
Rainbow Lounge (Forth Worth),
police using excessive force in
raid in, 67–68
Raleigh (NC), police posing in drug
undercover assignment in, 180–81
Ramirez, Rudy, 148
Rather, Dan, 217
Reagan, Nancy, 174
Reagan, Ronald
vs. FDR on business and economy,
52
free-market capitalism and, 51
on government bureaus, 53
presidency of, 214–17
resuming War on Drugs, 173
ushering in moralism, 51–52
reciprocity
begetting sense of justice, 10, 14
as component of happiness, 10
Reconstruction, policy of, 193
Reconstruction Finance Corporation,
33
recreational drug use, 185
Red Carpet Motel (Houston), police
seizure of, 148
reformers, rights of others and, 169
regulations, set by rules of
organization, 78
Rehfeld, Bernhard, 129
Rehnquist, William
on abortion, 90–91
on demotion of property rights, 138
on flag burning, 115
on right to die, 94

on taking private property, 140
religious beliefs, right to equality
protecting, 204
religious objections to commerce, in
organs, 152
Reno, Janet, 113
rent control, 137
representative democracy, protecting
individual rights, 45
reproductive rights, 201
The Republic (Cicero), 47, 237*n*74
Republican National Convention
(1984), burning of flag in Texas
at, 115
retirement, right to secure, 229
reverse discrimination, 199
Ridley, Matt, 101
right of peaceful assembly, in First
Amendment, 23
right to bear arms
about, 124–25
arguments about, 126–29
in Constitution, 23
interpretation of Second Amendment,
for, 126
right to die, 93–100
right to education, 229
right to equality, for all minorities,
204–5
right to equality before law
about, 7–8, 231–32
definition of, 193
for gays, 202–4
justice and, 12
racial equality and, 193–201
for women, 201–2
right to fairness, 229
Right to Financial Privacy Act,
240*n*162
right to freedom from undesirable
events, 229
right to happiness, 229
right to jobs, 228–29
right to liberty. *See also* liberty
about, 3–5, 230–31